TALES OF THE COCKTAIL® FROM A TO Z

TALES OF THE COCKTAIL® FROM A TO Z

by
Jared Brown & Anistatia Miller

with a foreword by
Paul Tuennerman

MIXELLANY

mixellany limited

Book design by Adrian Hodgkins.
Cover design by Dean Cavalier, Phillip Collier Designs.

First edition

Hardcover ISBN 13: 978-1-907434-26-6
Trade paper ISBN 13: 978-1-907434-27-3
eBook ISBN 13: 978-1-907434-28-0

British Library Cataloguing in Publication Data.
A catalogue record for this book is available from the British Library.

*To every person who loves to make
and experience a great drink and the tales that
each one has to tell.*

By the Same Authors

Shaken Not Stirred®: *A Celebration of the Martini Champagne Cocktails*

Spirituous Journey: *A History of Drink, Book One*

Spirituous Journey: *A History of Drink, Book Two*

Cuba: *The Legend of Rum*

The Soul of Brasil

The Mixellany Guide to Vermouth & Other Apéritifs

Contents

CHAPTER 3: A SPIRITED A TO Z OF COCKTAILS: The Tales of the Cocktail® Way

A SPIRITED A TO Z OF COCKTAILS: The Tales of the Cocktail® Way

A SPIRITED A TO Z OF COCKTAILS: The Tales of the Cocktail® Way

A SPIRITED A TO Z OF COCKTAILS: The Tales of the Cocktail® Way

A SPIRITED A TO Z OF COCKTAILS: The Tales of the Cocktail® Way

A SPIRITED A TO Z OF COCKTAILS: The Tales of the Cocktail® Way

Foreword

BY PAUL G. TUENNERMAN

In 2003 a then, unlikely group of drinks authors gathered around a small assortment of nondescript tables, off to the side, in the world-famous Carousel Bar at the historic Monteleone Hotel. Tales of the Cocktail® from A to Z is a tribute to what has unfolded since that first event.

There's been a lot. It begins with the story of what took place on that undoubtedly humid afternoon in the New Orleans French Quarter, as the eclectic group of authors gathered at the request of one tenacious, life-long resident of New Orleans, Ann Tuennerman, and how that grew to include bartenders, restaurateurs, spirits producers, and people who love what they do.

As I have often professed, the success of Tales of the Cocktail® is, in large part, due to the good fortunes of my wife Ann and I, and the generosity of the countless thousands of genuinely great people, which we have met along the way. Most of those who gathered on that Thursday afternoon in the middle of September, have weathered the journey of the past ten years including the unrivaled first couple of cocktail literature, Jared Brown and Anistatia Miller, who, like so many others, have lent to us their expertise in our never ending pursuit to promote the craft of the cocktail.

What began as a commemoration of the first anniversary of the Southern Comfort Cocktail Tour has evolved into what is often referred to as the "mecca" for bartenders, historians, authors, artisans, and enthusiasts from around the world, who share one commonality—an appropriate thirst and appreciate for the classic cocktail.

Tales of the Cocktail® from A to Z not only documents the resurrection of the craft of the cocktail over the past decade, but also recognizes the countless thousands who have come to pay homage to the cocktail, the third week of each July, and brought with them, their passion for the craft, and willingness to share their wealth of knowledge for the betterment of all man kind, and those who gather each evening to take a seat, at their local bar.

Like so many who have joined us on this journey, we have endued much over the past decade, the least of which was a hurricane. But like so many occurrences in our lives, the passage of time has shown that these events come bearing gifts. When we least expected it the great people who spend their days toiling over a still, seated behind a typewriter, or manning the rail at the local watering hole, stepped up, and for them Ann and I will forever be grateful; if it were not for them, neither this book nor Tales of the Cocktail®, would be possible.

As you would expect, Jared and Anistatia have done a masterful job with *Tales of the Cocktail® from A to Z*, getting the story right, setting the record, and preparing us for the next ten years.

To those who have lent an ear, I often share that Tales of the Cocktail® is their event; Ann and I are merely shepherds. We hope that you have benefited greatly from the collaboration of your peers and mentors over the past decade and that you continued to view our great city of New Orleans as your adopted home, one which you will return to each July, for years to come.

Like a perfectly balanced cocktail, Jared and Anistatia have done a masterful job in compiling this tribute to those who have joined us on this journey, one which is just beginning, and to them, I raise my glass. Cheers!

INTRODUCING THE TALES OF THE COCKTAIL® The Book

It ain't easy figuring out to put into a book that pays homage to an annual event that serves as the must-do gathering of cocktailians from across the US, from the UK, from Europe, from Central America, South America, Asia, and Australia. But that as the assignment Ann and Paul Tuennerman gave us.

Oh, the things we all have learnt and shared and tasted for the past ten years at Tales of the Cocktail® could fill a book twice this size, indeed!

We've kept this as tidy a tome as we could as we gear up to celebrate the craft of the cocktail and the Tales of the Cocktail®'s tenth anniversary. What will you find as you turn the pages?

Naturally, we begin with a history of the event itself and how it blossomed from a small gathering of drink book authors talking to guests about our books and sampling our recipes in the Hotel Monteleone's Carousel Bar on a single day. Today, it's a multi-day extravaganza of seminars, workshops, tastings, competitions, parties, tours, and awards ceremonies that celebrate the incredible growth of the bartender's craft over the same ten years.

If you didn't know, Tales of the Cocktail® began as an anniversary of the Southern Comfort Cocktail Tour conducted by the spritely, spirited Joe Gendusa and inspired by the 2001 book about New Orleans drinking establishments—Kerry McCaffety's Obituary Cocktail. For those of you who have never experienced the sights, sounds, aromas, and ambiance of New Orleans French Quarter, we've include a drinking tour of this historic district, highlighting some of the best places to visit when you're in town. There are even a few classic New Orleans drink recipes.

What's there to learn at Tales of the Cocktail® in between sips of libations crafted and presented by the world's finest mixologists? A lot! The A-to-Z chapter of this book provides even the freshest cocktail novice with historical facts, trivia, and anecdotes about the sorts of things presenters deliver at Tales sessions—from absinthe to Zombie. The A-to-Z doesn't stop there, it also presents the biographies of past session presenters, session recipes, and other tidbits that will have you talking like a cocktailian in no time.

Make yourself a cocktail, find a comfy spot, and join us as we explore the world of the cocktail through the eyes of Tales of the Cocktail®.

CHAPTER 1

A TALE ABOUT THE TALES OF THE COCKTAIL®

BY ANISTATIA MILLER

"We are proud to welcome authors from around the country to take part in what will become an annual literary and cultural event for New Orleans," Ann Rogers (now Tuennerman) said when she announced the first Tales of the Cocktail®.

Little did Ann realize that ten years later she would welcome not only authors but mixologists, spirits producers, columnists, bloggers, chefs, foodies, and cocktail enthusiasts from nearly every corner of the world.

She had put together a two-day salute to the culture of fine dining and drinking in New Orleans, the city's intimate association with the history of the cocktail, and the first anniversary of the Southern Comfort Cocktail Tour led by Joe Gendusa. It was our first year. And was it a doozy!

YEAR 1: 18-19 SEPTEMBER 2003

The inaugural Southern Comfort's Tales of the Cocktail® was a simple affair. Centralized in the city's historic French Quarter, the agenda included a two-hour walking tour of the romantic Quarter's bars and restaurants, a cocktail hour hosted by a handful of cocktail book authors in the Hotel Monteleone's Carousel Bar, dinner and cocktail pairings at famed New Orleans restaurants, and a tribute to the city's historic bars and restaurants hosted by Brennan's Restaurant.

The ultimate vintage barware collector Stephen Visakay had recommended us to be part of the show. We had just moved back to New York from a few years in Vancouver, Canada and Idaho, where we consulted on making a gin and a rum for the country's first microdistillery restaurant. My husband Jared had never been to New Orleans. I was more than excited to go back to a city with so much life and fabulous food! (Hadn't been there myself since the 1960s.)

Welcome reception at Brennan's.

New Orleans' thick, late summer air was inspiration enough to belly-up to the oyster bar and revel in shucked-on-the-spot oysters and ice-cold beer at Felix's Restaurant & Oyster Bar. That was only the first stop upon landing in Louis Armstrong International Airport. (Our friend Stephen Visakay insisted that we go for an early snack. Thanks, Steve for inviting us in the first place.) Dale DeGroff and his wife Jill were on a quest to sip a Vieux Carré in the Carousel Bar—where it was invented—and to see the remarkable Chris McMillian make his legendary Mint Julep at the Ritz-Carlton's The Library Lounge.

That was followed up by a midnight sojourn to listen to New Orleans jazz in its purest form at The Preservation Hall. A pilgrimage to Mother's Restaurant for a massive breakfast of crayfish Étoufée, grits, and biscuits quenched with a Bloody Mary got us ready to present. But that was after Beignets and café au lait at Café du Monde at dawn and a stroll along the river to clear the head.

Each of us had an agenda beyond the agenda. That's the kind of place New Orleans is to people who revere the city's food and drink heritage. It's a pilgrimage, not just a pit stop to the next speaking engagement.

The Cocktail Renaissance was still in its toddler stage but it was pretty evident from the turn out that celebrities existed in this revived industry and so did their fans.

Who were the first speakers at Tales?

Chefs Alexandra and Eliot Angle (authors of *Cocktail Parties with a Twist*), Barnaby Conrad III (author of *The Martini: An Illustrated History of an American Classic* and *Absinthe: History in a Bottle*), Stephen Visakay (author of *Vintage Bar Ware*), Dale DeGroff (author of *The Craft of the Cocktail*), Christopher O'Hara (author of *The Bloody*

Mary and *Hot Toddies*), Robert Plotkin (author of *Caribe Rum, Toma! Margarita!,* and a bunch of others), Jessica Strand (author of *Holiday Cocktails*), Gary Regan and Mardee Haidin Regan (authors of *The Book of Bourbon,*

New Classic Cocktails, The Martini Companion, The Bourbon Companion, plus, plus), yours truly and my husband Jared Brown (authors of *Shaken Not Stirred®: A Celebration of the Martini* and *Champagne Cocktails*), and the woman who inspired the Southern Comfort Cocktail Tour, Kerry McCaffety (author of *Obituary Cocktail*).

Author Kerry McCaffety signing books in the Hotel Monteleone's Carousel Bar.

As you can well imagine, none of us wanted those two days to end. We all knew what the hospitable people of New Orleans mean when they say *"Laissez les bons temps rouler!"* ["Let the good times roll!"] We all wanted to come back for more.

YEAR 2: 18-19 AUGUST 2004

Can you imagine how excited we were when we were asked to come back for another round of Southern Comfort's Tales of the Cocktail®? We plotted where we were going to eat, what we were going to see, where we were going to drink when we weren't in the heat of the action. We were better organized for clothes this time: A minimum three changes of the lightest weight clothing we had to deal with the thick, humid air that made you realize why Creole and Cajun cuisine is so spicy and the drinks are so cold. Flip flops were mandatory.

We learnt that the second we arrived, we needed to procure at least two litres each of bottled water to swig down before we went to sleep each night. (Hydration before you hit the sack is the key to survival even to this day at Tales, followed by Beignets and café au lait at dawn at Café du Monde.) There was a brilliant cure that I had learnt about in North Carolina over a decade earlier that is stocked at the Walgreen's Drug Store across from the Hotel Monteleone— BC Powder. Aspirin in its most convenient form. Pop one down with a ton of water before you go to bed. You wake up ready to face any and everything.

The proceedings didn't just concentrate on us authors signing our books that year. There were seminars. One in particular, called "What's an Idea Worth?", portended the future of Tales' professional series. Robert Plotkin was joined by Perry Luntz, Senior Editor at Beverage Media Group, author and *Cheers* magazine editor Jack Robertiello, plus "The Food & Wine Radio Network" talk show host Jennifer English reminded us all that we had more to think about than making and creating great drinks.

The world was our oyster, if we knew how to deal with it. Dale DeGroff teamed up with the "Libation Goddess" Audrey Saunders, and Chris McMillian to present a cocktail clinic: the concept of cocktail cuisine reached a few more hundred disciples on both sides of the stick.

The "old guard" of authors at what was now called "The Cocktail Hour" were joined by a few newcomers, who represented growing factions of interest. The American champion of absinthe knowledge Ted Breaux led the charge, accompanied by Bev Church (author of *The Joys of Entertaining*), Thomas Connors (author of *Meet Me at the Bar*), John DeMers (author of *The Food of New Orleans* and *Caribbean Cooking*), James Waller (author of *Drinkology: The Art and Science of the Cocktail*), plus Katherine Fausset and Rebecca Gerstung (authors of *The Cooking Club Cookbook* and *The Cooking Club Party Cookbook*).

Joe Gendusa was on hand to show the new attendees around the French Quarter, entertaining them with bits of history and gossip during his cocktail tour. And the Spirited Dinners® became a high point for both chefs and mixologists to show their stuff, pairing cocktails and courses at some of the city's most historic eateries: Antoine's, Arnaud's, Brennan's, Broussard's, Café Giovanni, French Quarter Bar Restaurant, Galatoire's, Girod's Bistro at Napoleon House, the Hunt Room at the Hotel Monteleone, Louis XVI Restaurant, Muriel's Jackson Square, and Tujaque's.

Just as some of us were packing up to head back north, a series of major thunderstorms cancelled our flights for a couple of days. Did any of us really care? No. It just gave us more time to savour a dip in the pool, discover another food spot, another bar, another bit of New Orleans history.

What we also didn't realize was that it was an omen of events to come.

YEAR 3: 18-20 AUGUST 2005

If an event survives its freshman and sophomore years, you can pretty much guarantee that everyone is going to up their game—not a little but a lot. Seminars and panel discussions were spread across the French Quarter in restaurants, bars, and the Hotel Monteleone, covering topics as diverse as the Americanization of whiskey; the history of bitters and the term "cocktail;" how to start, run and market a bartending consulting business; classic and contemporary cocktails to make at home; and a luncheon/ demonstration on at-home entertainment.

More new faces appeared on the presentation roster. Gothic/horror novelist and author of *Liquor* Poppy Z. Brite joined the ranks along with Ted Haigh (author of *Vintage Spirits and Forgotten Cocktails*), Mittie Helmich (author of *The Ultimate Bar Book*), Robert "Drinkboy" Hess, and Audrey Saunders.

A direct descendant of Antoine Amedée Peychaud and dedicated cocktailian Philip Greene added another dimension to the proceedings: an unpublished but passionate drink historian could find a platform at Tales. So could

Brenda Maitland holding Tim McNally's glass along with her own during our Sunday drive.

a filmmaker. San Franciscan Peter Moody screened his film *An Olive and Twist* and led a discussion about the relationship between Hollywood and cocktails.

The relationship between presenters and attendees became more like a family reunion that year. A young local who had attended all three Tales came up to us during "The Cocktail Hour" to give us a vintage copy of the 1938 *WPA Guide to New Orleans* in thanks for the knowledge he'd gained from our history seminars. (The book proudly presides in our drinks library to this day.)

The day after the event we stayed to have brunch with Tim McNally and Brenda Maitland, two local media folks who wanted to show the city outside of the French Quarter. After a morning broadcast on Tim's Sunday morning show, we loaded into his vintage convertible with a few bottles of champagne and appropriate glassware to take a tour, starting with the area around Lake Pontrachain where they lived. Tim gave us the low down about the levees and the fragility of New Orleans infrastructure if a major hurricane were to blast through.

A couple more bottles of champagne over brunch in the Fauborg-Marigny district and we had forgotten about the gravity of what Tim had shown us. We packed up the next morning and went fly before another tropical storm system threatened to delay our return to New York like it had the previous year.

Before we had even completely unpacked our bulging bags of swag, clothes, bar equipment, business cards, and presentation gear, the news hit the radio, the web, the TV. It was 29 August 2005. Hurricane Katrina—one of the five deadliest storms in US history—decimated our beloved Crescent City. In one news clip, we saw a cases of champagne and empty wine bottles floating all what was a street on the shores of Lake Pontrachain. We thought of Tim and Brenda.

It took another two days to get Tim and Brenda on the phone, who had escaped to their pocket-sized French Quarter studio: their city pied-à-terre where they holed up during Mardi Gras, Tales, and other libatious events. The highest point in the city, the French Quarter was still high and dry.

Our friends and cohorts in The Museum of the American Cocktail—Dale and Jill DeGroff—were still trying to contact New Orleans buddies Chris and Laura McMillian.

We could sit ideally while our friends needed help and money. The city's 80,827 hospitality workers were homeless and broke.

I had a day-job as the Creative Director for a Manhattan public relations and marketing firm at the time, so after a quick meeting with my office colleagues, we came up with the idea of organizing a "Save the New Orleans Cocktail Hour". Since we were vice-presidents of The Museum of the American Cocktail, we called Dale and Jill into action. We located Ann, who had made it out of the city after her house (also near the lake) went under, to see if we could get some support from Southern Comfort. Dick Brennan of the Commander's Palace restaurant family had set up a New Orleans Hospitality Workers Disaster Relief Fund, managed by the Greater Houston Community Foundation, and was mobilizing the restaurant industry. Survivors could apply for a nonrefundable loan of up to $2,000 to get back on their feet.

Assured that the greater majority of any contributions collected would be distributed to the unemployed workers, we put the plan into action to mobilize the drinks industry—

across the nation. The date was set for 12 September 2005. We had 12 days to pitch newspapers, TV and radio stations, bloggers, and magazines plus convince the public to shake and sip classic New Orleans cocktails at participating bars and restaurants for a $10 donation per drink during a 2-hour "happy hour" slot.

The response was fantastic with 148 venues from Boston and New York, DC to Baltimore, Seattle to San Francisco, and every place in between signing up to take part. Ann got Southern Comfort to donate Mardi Gras beads to distribute to participants. (Imagine Jared's and my shock when our local mailbox drop called to say a palette had been delivered that could fit in the shop let alone our tiny mailbox! Jill rallying a delivery team to get beads, counter cards, and all sorts of stuff to the venues.

Jared and I checked the last couple of participating bars in our neighbourhood as the "happy hour" commenced—just before we headed to JFK Airport and a business flight to London. Dale and Jill made the rounds through the rest of Manhattan. By the end of the shift, we collected $55,383.14 for the New Orleans family.

Dale had found Chris, Laura, and their kids. A job was secured for Chris and the museum provided him with an emergency grant. Then it was Ann's turn.

My office was busting at the seams with new accounts. We needed another event person to accounts like Maybelline, illy Coffee, and Hasbro. So we hired Ann on a freelance contract so she could get her edge back and make new contacts in Manhattan.

As 2005 thankfully came to a close, new chapter in Ann's, Tales', and our lives unfolded.

Official Cocktail at Tales of the Cocktail®

Since 2005, bartenders from across the nation have furiously crafted recipes in hopes of being selected as the official cocktail at each Tales of the Cocktail®. Glasses of the winning drink are raised high, saluting these young talents at the kick-off Taste of the Cocktail® that opens the annual proceedings.

BACARDI BAJA MARTINI (2006) by Michael Brewer
2 oz Bacardi Superior Rum, 1 oz lemon juice, 1 oz Lime Juice, 2 oz Pineapple Juice, 1 oz Orange Juice, 1 oz Malibu Rum, 4 sprigs Cilantro, and 2 slices Avocado. Mix juices and muddle with cilantro and avocado. Add Bacardi and Malibu. Chill with ice and strain in martini glass.

STARFISH COOLER (2007) by Stacy Smith

1 oz Moët & Chandon White Star, 1 oz Limoncello, 1 oz PAMA Pomegranate Liqueur, 1 oz/ unsweetened ice tea, ½ oz simple syrup. Muddled orange slice and mint leaf in a Collins glass. Combine all ingredients.

THE PUNCH AND JUDY (2008) by Charlotte Voisey

1 oz Martell VSOP, ¼ oz Old New Orleans Crystal Rum, ½ oz Hendrick's Gin, ½ oz Bols Orange Curacao, 2 oz Pineapple Juice, ½ oz Freshly squeezed lime juice, ½ oz orange juice, ½ oz Partida agave nectar, 2 dashes Angostura bitters, 4 mint leaves. Assemble ingredients in a mixing glass with as much love and interest that is healthy (that is to say not in a obsessive fashion but certain passionate and perhaps as if you were preparing the drink for someone you respect, admire and love in a plutonic fashion) – no need to muddle the mint, just throw it in- shake properly (hard) and strain over fresh ice in a highball glass. Cut a thinly sliced lime wheel and place on top of the Punch and Judy; add a hearty sprinkle of ground nutmeg directly on the lime wheel fresh from the "nut" with a small grater of using already ground nutmeg from a small shaker.

CREOLE JULEP (2009) by Maksym Pazuniak

2 ¼ oz Cruzan Single Barrel Estate Rum, ½ oz Clement Creole Shrubb, ¼ oz Captain Morgan 100, 2 dashes Fee Bros. Peach bitters, 2 dashes angostura bitters, 8-10 mint leaves, 1 Demerara Sugar Cube. Muddle sugar, Creole Shrubb and bitters until sugar is dissolved in a 10 oz tall glass. Add mint and press to express oils. Add cracked ice. Add Cruzan and Captain Morgan 100 and stir until frost appears on outside of glass. Garnish with mint sprig.

DEATH IN THE SOUTH PACIFIC (2010) by Evan Martin

¾ ounce aged rum, 3/4 ounce aged rhum agricole, ½ ounce Grand Marnier, 1/3 ounce orgeat syrup (see headnote). 1/3 ounce falernum, preferably John D. Taylor's Velvet Falernum, 3 dashes absinthe, ½ ounce freshly squeezed lime juice, ½ ounce freshly squeezed lemon juice, Crushed ice, ½ ounce grenadine, ½ ounce dark rum, preferably Cruzan Black Strap. Combine the rum, rhum agricole, Grand Marnier, orgeat syrup, falernum, absinthe and juices in a Collins or highball glass (or Tiki mug) and fill with crushed ice. Swizzle the drink well to mix and to frost the glass, then add the grenadine. Overfill the glass with crushed ice, then pour in the dark rum.

RANGOON FIZZ (2011) by Eric Simpkins

1 ½ oz Old Raj Gin Blue Label, ¾ lime juice, 1 oz simple syrup, 1 oz heavy cream, 7 drops absinthe, 5 drops simple cardamom tincture, 3 dashes fee brother Jasmine water, 1 egg white, 1 oz FeverTree Bitter Lemon Tonic soda. Ice a tall Collins glass. Combine ingredients excepting tonic and absinthe in small cocktail tin. Remove ice from glass, swirl with absinthe and discard excess. Add tonic to glass. Ice shaker. Shake vigorously to chill. Strain into Collins glass without ice through fine strainer. Slide tall thin straw through center of foam and serve.

YEAR 4: 19-23 2006

Ann went home to New Orleans on New Year's Day filled with determination to get Tales of the Cocktail® back on its feet as well as herself. I got an email in the spring that simply said: "Taking a page from your life. I think I've found my soulmate." She met Paul Tuennerman that February. Besides dating, Paul joined in the organizing of Tales as chief financial officer.

Paul Tuennerman.

No longer called Southern Comfort's Tales of the Cocktail® , Ann extended the event to four days and unveiled Tales of the Cocktail®.

It was rough for us old-timers to arrive at Louis Armstrong Airport and see the level of devastation that the Crescent City had experienced. Some folks took taxis to the Ninth Ward and other spots, trying to comprehend what really happened. But by the time we all assembled for a "Toast to Tales of the Cocktail®" and the welcome dinner at Café Giovanni, we were ready to bring life back to the French Quarter and let the good times roll, which they certainly did.

What were we all talking about that year? Here are some of the highlights:

Get the Hot Dish—*Lorin Gaudin with chef/owners Frank Stitt (Highlands Bar and Grill in Alabama), Marcus Samuelson (Aquavit in New York), Aaron Sanchez (Paladar in New York), and Dale DeGroff.*

Pairing Cocktails and Food—*Robert Hess, Audrey Saunders, Ryan Magarian, Andrew Dornenburg, and Karen Page.*

Hot Drinks, Cool Bars—*Jack Robertiello with Simon Difford, Lucy Brennan, Edward F. Nesta, and Debra C. Argen.*

Vodka Classics: All About Vodka—*Anistatia Miller and Jared Brown.*

South of the Border ... Down Mexico Way—*Dale DeGroff.*

Cake-tails and Pie-tinis—*Michael Waterhouse*

YEAR 5: 18-22 2007

Jared and I made a major personal move during Tales of the Cocktail® 's turquoise (read: fifth) anniversary year. We pulled up stakes in Manhattan and moved to both London and southern France, where we archived and reorganized a private wine and spirits museum with over 12,000 spirits and wine bottles, labels, menus, books, glassware, and beverage ephemera. I held down the fort in France, while Jared and our assistant Eric Fossard soaked in the atmosphere and the camaraderie that lay at the heart of Tales of the Cocktail®. (At least he sent me blow-by-blow texts and photos of the action.)

And there was plenty of action! Fifty events were scheduled from Ed Hamilton's Ministry of Rum Tasting Competition to the Spirited Awards®.

Just look at this lineup:

Revolution to Evolution: The Story of the American Cocktail!

The Napoleon House: New Orleans Greatest Saloon

On the Rocks: The Importance of Ice

Spirited Women Past and Present

Lost Ingredients: Obtaining (or making) rare ingredients for even rarer cocktails

The Cocktail's Family Tree

Drinks and Dishes Born in New Orleans

Rum's Punch: A Spirited View of Rum's Rise, Fall and Return

The Martini

Ask the Experts

Sake to Me!

Johnny Appleseed, Hard Cider and Applejack - The Spirit of Americana

Cocktails on the Curve: The Future of Mixology

Enter the Distologist

From Farm to Glass

How to Conduct a Home Tasting

From Glen to Glen, exploring the making, the magic and the myths of Scotch Whisky

South American Spirits Presented by Barsol Pisco and Cocktailtimes.com

Martini Gras

The History, Oddities and Eccentricities of Galatoire's

Prohibition's Shadow

Tales of the Cocktail® Bar Chef Competition

Aromatics and Their Uses in Cocktails

Movie Night at Tales of the Cocktail®

Sippin' with 7

Cocktails and the Blogosphere

Cocktail Culture Around the World

American Rye Whiskey

South of the Border, Down Mexico Way—Encore Presentation History of the Cocktail

Vermouth

Wine Based Cocktails

Spirits Glass Tasting with Georg Riedel

Party Like A Pro

Tiki Drinks-From A to Zombie

Margaritas and Makeovers

Cocktails and Film

Gin

Stirrings Thing Up Block Party

Bartenders Bash

The Mint Julep: Its' History and Celebration

Absinthe—Encore Presentation

Ann and Paul take a quite moment together after their wedding.

Even though Tales was over for the year, Ann and Paul kept the party going when they got married on 17 November at Arnaud's Restaurant—Mr. and Mrs. Cocktail made it official!

Spirited Awards®

Inaugurated in 2007, the Spirited Awards® are one of the highlight events at Tales of the Cocktail®. Each year, the best and the brightest in the international cocktail world are honoured for their achievements, ranging from best bar to best bartender, new product, book, and mentor.

Best American Cocktail Bar (Inaugurated in 2009)
2009: Pegu Club, New York
2010: Death & Co., New York
2011: Drink, Boston

World's Best Hotel Bar (Inaugurated in 2009)
2009: Merchant Hotel, Belfast
2010: The Connaught Bar, Connaught Hotel, London
2011: The American Bar, Savoy Hotel, London

Best Restaurant Bar (Inaugurated in 2011)
2011: Eleven Madison Park, New York

World's Best New Cocktail Bar (Inaugurated in 2007)
2007: Bourbon & Branch, San Francisco
2008: Le Lion, Bar de Paris, Hamburg
2009: Clover Club, Brooklyn
2010: Mayahuel, New York
2011: Eau de Vie, Kirketon Hotel, Prahan, Australia

World's Best Cocktail Bar (Inaugurated in 2007)
2007: Pegu Club, New York
2008: Milk & Honey, New York
2009: PDT, New York
2010: The Merchant Hotel, Belfast
2011: Employees Only, New York

World's Best Drinks Selection (Inaugurated in 2007)
2007: ZigZag Café, Seattle
2008: Salvatore at Fifty, London
2009: Merchant Hotel, Belfast
2010: Bar Lebensstren in Café Einstein, Berlin
2011: Employees Only, New York

World's Best Cocktail Menu (Inaugurated in 2007)
2007: Paparazzi, Bratislava
2008: 1806 Bar, Melbourne, Australia

2009: Merchant Hotel, Belfast
2010: Death & Co., New York
2011: Artesian Bar, Langham Hotel, London

Best Classic Cocktail Bar (Awarded in 2007 and 2008)
2007: Zig-Zag Café, Seattle
2008: Milk & Honey, New York

Best High-Volume Cocktail Bar (Inaugurated in 2011)
2011: Rickhouse, San Francisco

American Bartender of the Year (Inaugurated in 2009)
2009: Jim Meehan, PDT, New York
2010: Murray Stenson, Zig Zag, Seattle
2011: Kenta Goto, Pegu Club, New York and Sam Ross Milk & Honey, New York

International Bartender of the Year (Inaugurated in 2007)
2007: Audrey Saunders, New York (*previous award title Mixologist/Bartender of the Year)
2008: Nick Strangeway, London (*previous award title Mixologist/Bartender of the Year)
2009: Tony Conigliaro, London
2010: Agostino Perrone, London
2011: Erik Lorincz, London

Best Cocktail Writing (Inaugurated in 2008)
2008: Gary Regan, San Francisco Chronicle
2009: David Wondrich, Esquire
2010: CLASS Magazine
2011: Imbibe Magazine

Best Cocktail Writer (Inaugurated in 2011)
2011: Camper English

Best New Cocktail/Bartending Book (Inaugurated in 2007)
2007: The Art of the Bar: Cocktails Inspired by the Classics by Jeff Hollinger and Rob Schwartz
2008: Imbibe! by David Wondrich
2009: The Essential Cocktail by Dale DeGroff
2010: Vintage Spirits and Forgotten Cocktails by Ted Haigh
2011: Punch by David Wondrich

Best New Product (Inaugurated in 2007)
2007: St. Germaine Elderflower Liqueur
2008: Fever Tree Mixers
2009: Bols Genever
2010: The Bitter Truth Celery Bitters
2011: Banks 5 Island Rum

Best American Brand Ambassador (Inaugurated in 2009)
2009: Simon Ford, Plymouth Gin and Pernod-Ricard
2010: Charlotte Voisey, William Grant & Sons Portfolio
2011: Jacques Bezuidenhout, Partida Tequila

Best International Brand Ambassador (Inaugurated in 2007)
2007: Simon Ford, Plymouth Gin (*previous award title Best Drink Brand Representatives/Brand Ambassador)
2008: Xavier Padovani, Hendrick's Gin (*previous award title Best Drink Brand Representatives/Brand Ambassador)
2009: No recipient
2010: John Gakuru, Sagatiba
2011: Dan Warner, Beefeater Gin

Best Bar Mentor (Inaugurated in 2010)
2010: Dale DeGroff, New York
2011: Audrey Saunders, New York

Helen David Lifetime Achievement Award (Inaugurated in 2008)
2008: Dale DeGroff, New York
2009: Peter Dorelli, London
2010: Brian Rea, California
2011: Dick Bradsell, London

Golden Spirit Award
2007: Charlotte Voisey
2008: Jeff Berry
2009: Francesco Lafranconi and Charlotte Voisey
2010: Jacob Briars
2011: Claire Smith, Belvedere Vodka

YEAR 6: 16-20 JULY 2008

Could Tales of the Cocktail® get any larger? It sure could. Cocktails were on everyone's mind around the world and the ranks of professional mixers multiplied by leaps and bounds. It's no wonder that the Professional Series grew in size and content. So did the roster of events, competitions, activities, and scope of Tales of the Cocktail®.

With the number of drinks being presented and served to attendees a new "back of house" program was instigated: The Tales of the Cocktail® Apprentice Program, giving talented young bartenders the opportunity to apprentice with some of the world's most influential mixologists, and further develop their bartending skills.

Tales of the Cocktail®, Cointreau, and the New Orleans Culinary and Cultural Preservation Society sponsor and support the next generation of mixologists through the Cocktail Apprentice Program (CAP), providing scholarships to select cocktail apprentices who will study at a location where they will be able to get hands on experience with renowned bartenders and spirits professionals. Life for the presenters got easier thanks to this new feature, even though the activity schedule got even more overloaded than ever before.

COCKTAIL FUNERALS

The Appletini gets buried in style.

Since 2008, Tales of the Cocktail has sponsored an annual Cocktail Funeral that, in the words of its creator Simon Ford, has buried cocktails belonging to "the exclusive club of drinks that bartenders wish were gone forever". Since the inaugural jazz funeral procession made its way through New Orleans' French Quarter, the Appletini (2008), Redheaded Slut (2009), Sex on the Beach (2010), and the Long Island Iced Tea (2011) have been buried with hundreds of reveling mourners in gleeful attendance.

Sitting over in Europe, the buzz dialed up to maximum load on Facebook, email, and at the bar. There may have been 12,000 attendees in 2007, but I don't think anyone was expecting—the 2008 European invasion! Professionals came from the UK, Germany, the Netherlands, Russia, Italy,

Tales of the Cocktail® Apprentice Program Graduates

Class of 2008
CAP Team Leader: Phil Ward and Don Lee and John Deragon

Alexander Day	Jim Kearns	Marian Beke
Armando Archundia	Joaquin Simo	Maxwell Britten
Catherine Fellet	John Paul Deragon	Peter Vestinos
Chris Hannah	Josephine Packard	Rhiannon Enlil
Don Lee	Kimbery Patton-Bragg	Ryan Fitzgerald
Jacquelyn Leon	LaTanya White	Thomas Waugh

Class of 2009
CAP Team Leaders: Don Lee and John Deragon

Ashley Greene	David Shenut	Jim Kearns
Blair Garrett Reynolds	Dylan Regan	Kelley Slagel
Brian Matthys	Eric Alexander	Kimberly Patton-Bragg
Brooks Kimsey Reitz	Rodrigues	Kyle McHugh
Cassie Fellet	Eric Simpkins	LaTanya White
Chris Hannah	Eryn Kathleen Reece	Leo Robitschek
Chris Ojeda	Franky Marshall	Maksym Pazuniak
Ciaran Donal Wiese	Hillary Joy Choo	Maxwell Britten
Corey Bunnewith	Jacquelyn Leon	Mike Ryan
Damian Windsor	Janet Kim	Nicholas R. Jarret
Daniel Eun	Jason Littrell	Thomas Waugh
Darby Kelly	Jeff Grdnich	Yael Rebecca Vengroff

CAP grads from the Class of 2010 were saluted at the Spirited Awards® gala.

Class of 2010

CAP Team Leaders: Don Lee, John Deragon, Jeff Grdinich, Eric Simpkins, Leo Robitschek, and Mike Ryan

Adam Robinson	Eryn Reece	Neil Kopplin
Bradley Bolt	Evan Martin	Nicholas Jarrett
Bradley Farran	Frank Cisneros	Patrick O'Brien
Bryan Matthys	Franky Marshall	Rachel Kim
California Gold	Hal Wolin	Robert Leavey
Cassie Fellet	Jamie Kilgore	Sharon Floyd
Chad Doll	Jared Schubert	Sierra Zimei
Chris Hannah	Jonathan Armstrong	Summer Voelker
Christine Nielson	Kimberly Patton-Bragg	Sudeep Rangi
Christopher Churilla	Leo Robitschek	Sylvia Cosmopoulos
Corey Bunnewith	Luis Bustamante	Ted Kilgore
Cristiana DeLucca	Matthew Eggleston	Thomas Klus
Cristina Dehlavi	Meaghan Dorman	Thomas Speechley
Daniel de Oliveira	Michelle Peake	Tiffany Soles
Eamon Rockey	Naomi Schimek	William Dollard
Erica Pearce	Navarro Carr	

Class of 2011

Cocktail Apprentice Managers: John Deragon, Jeff Grdinich, Don Lee
Cocktail Apprentice Team Leaders: Leo Robitschek, Mike Ryan, Eric Simpkins
New Orleans Liaisons: Chris Hannah, Kimberly Patton Bragg

Senior Cocktail Apprentices:	Brent Falco	Joann Spiegel
	Bryn Tattan	Justin Lane Briggs
Jonathan Armstrong	Carie Fuller	Katie Emmerson
Corey Bunnewith	Charles Veitch III	Kyle Ford
Cris Dehlavi	Chris Amon	Logan Lavachek
Franky Marshall	Christina Kuypers	Maggie Meskey
Heather Yau	Christopher "Churchy" Cummings	Matt Lanning
Lou Bustamante		Melodie Buell
Neil Kopplin	Cynthia Turner	Michael Saccone
Nicholas Jarrett	Danielle Marchant	Mike Henderson
Sudeep Rangi	David Burnette	Nate Selsor
Ted Kilgore	David Delaney Jr	Patrick Brennan
Tommy Klus	Jade Brown-Godfrey	Sabrina Kershaw
Trevor Kallies	James Betz	Sean Frederick
First time Cocktail Apprentices:	James Goggin	Sean Thibodeaux
	Jason Kemp	Susie Hoyt
Alan Akwai	Jean-Sebastien Dupuis	Thomas 'Fable' Jeon
Ali Tahsini	Jesse Card	Tom Macy

France, Canada, Japan, and Spain to be part of this tribal gathering of the cocktail, including the first annual Cocktail Funeral, created by Simon Ford.

Diversity and depth are the only words I can use to describe the sessions that took place that year. Have a look:

Professional Series: Is the Customer Always Right?— *Doug Frost*

Professional Series: The 2008 Ministry of Rum Tasting Competition— *Ed Hamilton*

Professional Series: Research Drink Recipes and Collecting Drink Books— *Brian Rea and Jonathan Pogash*

Professional Series: How to Create the Right Cocktail Menu for your Bar or Restaurant— *Julie Reiner*

Professional Series: How to Get your City, Bar, Recipe or Bartender More Media Coverage— *Lauren Clark*

The First International Symposium of Cocktail Shaker Collectors— *Stephen Visakay*

Professional Series: Emerging Spirits: What's the Next Big Thing?— *Donna Hood Crecca*

Professional Series: Designing Smarter Bars— *Tobin Ellis*

Great Bars of the World and What Makes Them Great— *Simon Difford*

To Have and Have Another: The Hemingway Bartender's Companion— *Phil Greene*

How to Taste Like a Professional— *Paul Pacult*

Swinging Sangrias— *Kim Haasarud*

Bourbon, Blues and Bluegrass— *Allen Katz and Kris Comstock*

Molecular Mixology— *Jamie Boudreau*

Juniperlooza: A Journey Deep into the Heart of Mother's Ruin— *Ryan Magarian*

History of Bar Snacks and Current Crispy, Crunchy Trends— *Jennifer English*

Artisan Spirits— *Allison Evanov*

Artisan Still Design and Construction— *Mike McCaw*

Cognac and Armagnac, Understanding the Nuances of the Spirits—*Debra C. Argen and Edward F. Nesta*

The Scented Trail: Techniques on How to Develop Aroma in Your Cocktails—*Audrey Saunders and Tony Conigliaro*

Making Your Own Spirits: A Look into Modern Nano-Distilling—*Matthew Rowley*

Latino Libations—*Tony Abou-Ganim*

A British Invasion of the American Cocktail Hour—*Charlotte Voisey*

How to View Beer As An Ingredient Rather Than the Drink Unto Itself—*Stephen Beaumont*

Pantry Raid: Brunch Drinks from the Fridge—*Todd Thrasher*

Amore Amari: A Very Bitter History of Bitter Spirits in Apertif Service and Cocktails—*Eric Seed*

Jerry's Kids: The Life, Drinks and Legacy of Professor Jerry Thomas—*David Wondrich*

Branding the Bride—*Maria McBride, Marcy Blum, and Sylvia Weinstock*

Cocktails with a Kick: Absinthe Returns to America—*Gwydion Stone, Paul Clarke and Jim Meehan*

Rum, Ron, Rhum—*Wayne Curtis*

Whiskies You've Never Tasted Before—*Paul Pacult*

Shochu-The Other Japanese Alcohol—*Paul Tanguay*

Grape Expectations!—*Francesco LaFranconi*

The Three Amigos: The Three Most Important Drinks You Need to Know and Why—*Simon Ford, Wayne Collins, Jason Crawley, and Phil Ward*

The Storied History of Liqueurs and Cordials and Their Important Role in Classic Cocktails—*Rob Cooper*

A Brief, Irreverent History of the Tavern/ Bar Trade—*Brian Rea*

Rye Nation—*Allen Katz*

Sensory Perception in Mixology/What Your Taste Buds Are Telling You—*Darcy S. O'Neil*

Cocktails of Old Raj: East Meets West at India's Bar—*Babs Harrison and Robert McGarvey*

Essential Guide to American Whiskey—*Gary Regan and LeNell Smothers*

Bottoms Up: A Spirited History of Drink in Canada—*Christine Sismondo and Kevin Brauch*

Regional Trends in American Cocktails—*Jeffrey Lindemuth and Camper English*

Potions of the Caribbean: Lost Cocktails from America's Post War Playground—*Jeff Berry*

The Cafés of Paris—*Anistatia Miller and Jared Brown*

Morning Glory Cocktails—*Robert Hess*

Spice and Ice: The Art of Spicy Cocktails—*Kara Newman*

The Green Seasonal Bar—*Bridget Albert, H. Joseph Ehrmann, and Allen Katz*

J.M. Legendre and the History of Herbsaint—*Jay Brian Hendrickson*

Encore Spirits Glass Tasting with Georg Riedel—*Georg Riedel*

Cocktail Garnish From Functional to Fabulous—*Martin Cate*

Cracking the Egg: The Traditions, Challenges and Potential of Eggs in Cocktails—*LeNell Smothers and Eric Seed*

Cocktail Cinema—*Christine Sismondo*

Making Your Own Cocktail Ingredients—*Paul Clarke*

Rediscover the Traditions of Vodka—*Stevel Olson*

Gentleman's Companion: The Life and Times of Charles H. Baker, Jr—*St. John Frizell and Brian Rea*

Bartending Techniques 101 and Barware—*Robert Hess and David Wondrich*

New Orleans on Fire—*Lorin Gaudin*

History of the Margarita—*Jacques Bezuidenhout and Robert Hess*

Flowing Bowl—*Allen Katz and David Wondrich*

Famous New Orleans Drinks—*Chris McMillian and Phil Greene*

The frosting on this libatious cake was the celebration of Beefeater master distiller Desmon Payne's Ruby Anniversary, commemorating his role as the master distiller of Plymouth Gin and then Beefeater Gin over the past 40 years. A deputation from the mayor's office arrived during the festivities at Muriel's on jackson Square to present him with the keys to the city.

YEAR 7: 8-12 JULY 2009

Apologies in advance for the fact that we did not attend Tales in 2009. We had to put the finishing touches on the new exhibitions in the freshly refurbished Exposition Universelle des Vins et Spiritueux in time for the 100th anniversary of its founder Paul Ricard and be present for its grand opening on 9 July 2009.

Aside from reports that we gleaned from emails and Facebook about the Beefeater Gin Welcome Masquerade Ball, the William Grant & Sons Swinging '40s Shore Leave Ball, Simon Ford and Audrey Saunders latest episode of the Bartenders' Breakfast after the annual Cocktail Funeral, and announcement of the year's Spirited Awards® recipients, we only knew from the list of sessions that we had missed a lot that year.

Take a look:

Big Trends 2009

The Bittersweet Truth of Starting a Bar

Responsible Beverage Program Consulting

A Special Relationship: Running your Bar With the Help of Consultants, Sales Reps and Brand Ambassadors

Teaching Technique: Improving Cocktails by Uplifting your Staff's Skills

Stop Talking…Go FRESH

The Fine Art of Banging Out the Drinks Like a Maniac: Great Bars Around the World and Throughout History That Make Great Cocktails Fast

Managing Rising Cost of Goods

Vintage Bar Ware Collectors

The How's and Why's of Cocktails

How Good is Your Palate?

Vermouth & Aperitif Wine

Mixologists and their Toys

From Down-Home to Downtown: A Lunch Celebrating the Evolution of Southern Traditions Luncheon

Take a Right at Albuquerque: Comparing and Contrasting Bars and Cocktails in the US versus Europe

History of Saloons in America

Sugarcane Spirits from Around the World

The Molecular DNA of Classic Cocktails

Christmas in July

Port: Not just your Grandpa's Drink Anymore!

From Brewer to Distiller

Chemistry of Cocktails (How Alcohol Works and its Implications for Mixology)

Creative Mixology: Finding Inspiration in the Everyday

New Orleans Pharmacists

American Whiskey Legends

L'heure Verte / The Green Hour

Cocktails of the Tales

Jazz, Cocktails and Storyville

Building your Brand Through Word of Mouth Marketing

Cask Strength 1:1

Low Country Libations: Obscure Cocktails and Spirits from the Netherlands, Belgium and Luxembourg

Drinks from the 1600s

21st Century Gin

Using Blogs and Online Tools to Promote Your Bar, Brand or Career

Wedding Cakes and Cocktails Luncheon

The Great Whisk(e)y Debate

The World's Biggest Bar Crawl

Cocktails Born from the Seven Seas

The Long Legacy of Cuban Rum

Sugar: The Science of Sweet

The Cocktails that Made Gin Famous

The Fine Art of Tending Bar

Drink Italy

On the Fly Competition

USBG Leblon Caipirinha Competition

Cocktail Legends

A Brief History of Alcohol

Cocktail Book Fetish

Secrets to Successful Cocktail Photography

Carnivorous Cocktails

Historical Approach to Cocktails

Hollywood Cocktails Innovation

Hammer of the Gods

Citrus: In History and Application

Cognac, from Vines to Shaker

The Three Amigos, the Three Most Important 19th Century Bartenders, the Bars They Ran and the Books They Wrote

Virgin Mixology® 101

The Great Bourbon Street Burlesque Clubs

Agavepalooza-Spirit of Mexico: The Agave Elixirs

The Science of Shaking

Seven Deadly Sins

Vintage Book Auction and Sale

The Old Fashioned

Buddy, Are Your Bitters Better...? Competition

Paying the Piper: Your Hangover and You?

Asian Influenced Cocktails

Liquid Nudging: Using Psychology, Showmanship, Manipulation and Choice Architecture to Help Guests Choose Great Drinks—and Love Them

Tell It Like It Is

After we closed the doors and turned out the lights on our project in France, that November, we moved our belongings and our cat Kitten back to London, already thinking about what to present at next year's Tales.

YEAR 8: 21-25 JULY 2010

Yes. We did show up in 2010, and to be honest, the action was running so hard and fast, we hardly had time to breath. We won't even discuss the warming welcome by Dita Von Teese at the House of Blues—need we say more?

But I think it's time to give you a taste of the depth and breadth of the cocktail creativity and knowledge that is served up at Tales session. Here's a sampling of what was mixed and served that year:

How to Give Great Presentations—*Philip Duff and Angus Winchester*

Clubland presented by Philip Duff
2 oz Stolichnaya vodka, 2 oz Fonseca Siroco white port, dash of Angostura bitters. Stir all with ice, and strain into an empty pre-chilled glass. Garnish with a lemon zest sprayed, rimmed, and dropped in.

Green Goddess presented by Philip Duff
1 ½ oz Stolichnaya vodka, 2 oz lemon juice, ½ oz Green Chartreuse, 2 oz simple syrup, 6 peeled and sliced Zespri green kiwifruits. Puree the kiwifruits. Shake the vodka, Chartreuse, lemon juice, simple syrup and 1 oz of the kiwi puree with ice. Strain into an ice filled glass.

Liquid Disc Jockey: Controlling the Flow of Any Room—*Tobin Ellis, Philip Duff, John Hogan, and Angela Laino*

Five Dragon presented by Tobin Ellis
2 oz Banks 5 rum, ¾ oz lime juice, ½ oz Monin Coconut syrup, dash of Angostura bitters, mint sprig. Tear mint leaves*, combine all ingredients, shake with ice, love, and a little anger... fine strain into a cup heaping over with crushed ice. Garnish with a big, bright, lovely mint sprig. If you're feeling randy, drop a handful of mint leaves into the bottom of the cup prior to filling with ice for a swankier look.
* You can muddle if you want, but torn mint leaves vigorously shaken will get 'er done.

Strategic Management: Systems of the Industry's Best Operators Revealed—*Sean Finter*

How to be Interviewed for Print, Television and Radio—*Camper English with Jennifer English*

Perudriver presented by Camper English
3 ½ oz fresh squeezed orange juice, ½ oz Gran Gala orange liqueur, 1 oz Gran Sierpe Pisco. Build and serve over ice.

Margarita presented by Camper English
2 oz Corazon blanco, 1 oz Gran Gala orange liqueur, ¾ oz lime juice. Combine all, shake, and serve over fresh ice.

Rear Admiral's Grog 2.0 presented by Camper English
1 oz Smith & Cross rum, 1 oz Pampero Anniversario rum, 1 oz Gran Gala orange liqueur, ¼ oz Averna amaro, ¼ oz maple syrup, 3/4 oz lime juice, ¼ oz orange juice. Add all ingredients. Hard shake and strain into crushed ice filled DOF glass. Garnish with an orange twist.

Intellectual Property—*Eben Freeman, Riley Lagesen, and Sheila Morrison*

Martini presented by Eben Freeman
1 ½ oz ABSOLUT®, 1 ½ oz Dolin dry vermouth. Shake and serve straight up.

Martini presented by Eben Freeman
3 oz Plymouth gin, ½ oz Dolin dry vermouth. Combine and stir. Garnish with a lemon twist.

Martini presented by Eben Freeman
1 ½ oz Plymouth gin, 1 ½ oz ABSOLUT®, ½ oz Dolin dry vermouth. Stir and serve straight up.

Vesper presented by Eben Freeman
3 oz Plymouth gin, 1 oz ABSOLUT®, ½ oz Cocchi Americano. Shake and serve up with an orange twist garnish.

Creative Cocktails and the Power of Brainstorming—
Kathy Casey and Cameo McRoberts

Southern Persuasion presented by Kathy Casey
1 ½ oz Ri1, ¾ oz Catdaddy Moonshine, ½ oz Cherry Bounce, ¼ oz Peach Pit bitters, ¼ ripe fresh peach. Muddle peaches in a pint glass. Measure in remaining ingredients. Fill with ice. Cap and shake vigorously. Place an ice ball into a large cocktail glass. Double strain cocktail over ice. Garnish with a Bounce cherry.

Planters Punch 'Berry Cup' presented by Kathy Casey
1 oz Cruzan® Silver, ¾ oz Cruzan® Spiced, ½ Monin Almond syrup, ½ oz Pimm's Cup, dash Peychaud's bitters, 5 Dricoll's raspberries. Drop raspberries into a pint glass. Measure in ingredients. Fill with ice. Cap and shake vigorously. Line a collins glass with a long very thin slice of cucumber. Pour into glass and garnish with a cucumber sliced long and thin.

Bollywood presented by Kathy Casey
1 ½ oz Tanqueray Ten gin, 2 oz Bollywood pre-mix*, 2 large sprigs fresh mint, Coconut Rose Foam**, Edible gold flakes. Tear mint and drop mint into pint glass. Measure in gin and Bollywood Pre-Mix. Fill with ice. Cap and shake vigorously. Strain into large martini cocktail glass. Top with a pouf of Coconut Rose Foam and garnish with sprinkle of gold.
*Bollywood Pre Mix
2 cups sugar, 2 cups water, ½ tb good curry powder, 3 cups fresh squeezed lime juice, 2 cups fresh squeezed pineapple juice. Combine sugar, water and curry in a small saucepan and bring to a simmer. Remove from heat and let sit for 20 minutes. Then strain syrup and discard any solids. After syrup has cooled stir in lime and pineapple juices. Place premix into a clean bottle. Store refrigerated.
**Coconut Rose Foam
Makes enough to fill one canister
1 ½ sheets gelatin, 3 oz Monin Rose Syrup, 2 oz fresh squeezed lemon juice, 10 oz water, 3 oz rich simple syrup, 3 tb of coconut powder. Meanwhile, combine the rose syrup, lemon juice, water, coconut powder and simple syrup and gelatin sheets and let set for 10 minutes in a small saucepan. Then place over medium-high heat just until gelatin melts. Do not boil.

So, You Think You're Ready to Go It Alone!—
Noah Glass

The Fine Art of Negotiating a Deal—Christy Pope,
Chad Solomon, Riley Lagesen, and Audrey Saunders

Gin & Tonic presented by Christy Pope
2 oz Plymouth gin, 4 oz tonic water. Serve over ice in a Collins glass. Garnish with a lime wedge.

Vodka & Soda
2 oz ABSOLUT®, 4 oz club soda. Serve over ice in a Collins glass. Garnish with a lemon wedge.

Bitter Admiral presented by Chad Solomon
1 oz Beefeater gin, 2 oz Campari, 4 oz grapefruit. Combine ingredients, stir over fresh ice. Garnish with a lime wedge.

Raising the Bar: Spirited Media Skills for Cocktail & Beverage Industry Professionals—*Lisa Ekus-Saffer and Virginia Willis*

The History of Bar Tools & Barware from the 1800s to Today—*Jim Walker, Mark Bigler, Greg Boehm, Dale DeGroff, and Michael Silvers*

Bariana: The Golden Age of French Cocktails— *Jared Brown, Anistatia Miller, Charles Vexenat, Mike Ryan, and Eric Simpkins*

Angler's Cocktail by Louis Fouquet
3 dashes Angostura bitters, 6 dashes orange bitters, 1 barspoon raspberry syrup, 2 oz Beefeater Gin. In a mixing glass filled with ice, add 3 dashes Angostura bitters, 6 dashes orange bitters, raspberry syrup, gin. Stir. Strain into a cocktail glass. Garnish with a lemon zest and serve.

Louis' Quina Cocktail by Louis Fouquet
2 oz Lillet Blanc, 2 dashes Cointreau®. Pour ingredients into an ice-filed shaker, stir, and strain into a cocktail glass. Garnish with lemon zest and serve.

Louis' Special Cocktail by Louis Fouquet
3 dashes Cointreau®, 3 dashes Crème de Noyeau, 3 dashes Angostura bitters, 1 oz Beefeater gin, 1 oz Noilly-Prat Rouge vermouth, 1 oz fresh orange juice. Pour all ingredients into a shaker filled with ice. Double strain into a cocktail glass. Garnish with a lemon zest and serve.

Whisky Flash by Louis Fouquet
1 barspoon superfine sugar, 1/3 oz lemon juice, 1/3 oz pineapple juice, 1 oz blended scotch whisky, 1 oz still water. Place all ingredients in a shaker filled with ice. Shake hard and strain into a rocks glass.

Globe by Louis Fouquet
2 oz Chivas scotch, ½ oz Noilly Prat Rouge vermouth, ½ oz Noilly Prat blanc vermouth, ¼ oz Cordial Medoc, 2 dashes Angostura bitters. Pour all ingredients into an ice filled shaker. Shake and strain into a cocktail glass. Garnish with a Luxardo cherry.

Little Sister
½ oz Cointreau®, 1 ¾ oz Beefeater 24, ½ oz lemon juice, 1 oz grapefruit juice, ¾ oz egg white, dash grapefruit bitters. Shake over ice. Strain into a cocktail glass.

Bartending Fun-da-mentals—*Angus Winchester with Jacob Briars*

Cecil Baker presented by Angus Winchester
2 oz Tanqueray gin, 1/3 oz Green Chartreuse, 1/3 oz Pomme Verte liqueur, ¼ oz Monin passion fruit syrup, ½ oz passion fruit pulp. Stir like an old fashioned on ice in tumbler and garnish with a sprig of fresh rosemary.

Corpse Reviver No. Blue presented by Jacob Briars
1 oz Tanqueray gin, 1 oz Lillet Blanc, 1 oz Bols Blue Curacao, 1 oz fresh lemon juice, 1 dash La Fee absinthe. Blend all and shake hard. Strain and serve straight up with a lemon twist garnish.

WYBMADIITY presented by Jacob Briars
1 ¼ oz 42 BELOW vodka, 1/3 oz Martini Rossi Sweet Vermouth, ½ oz simple syrup, ½ oz fresh lime juice, strawberries, lime leaves. Muddle strawberries and lime leaves, then combine all, shake well and serve over crushed ice. Garnish with a strawberry.

Paul Pacult's Spirits Critic's Workshop—*Paul Pacult*

The Other Side of the World—*Eben Freeman, Robert McKeown, and Linden Pride*

Old Fashioned presented by Eben Freeman
2 ½ oz Ron Zacapa,¼ oz rich simple syrup, Dash of Bitter Truth Aromatic bitters. Build and stir. Serve on the rocks and garnish with a lemon and orange twist.

Galangal Caipirinha presented by Linden Pride
2 oz Sagatiba Pura cachaça, 1 oz lime juice, ½ oz simple syrup, fresh galangal. Muddle galangal in lime and simple, add cachaça and ice , shake and serve on the rocks. Garnish with a galangal slice.

Brasil Basil Smash presented by John Gakuru
2 oz Sagatiba Pura cachaça, 10 basil leaves, ½ lime diced, ½ oz simple syrup (2:1). Dry muddle the basil in a Boston glass. Add the lime and sugar and muddle well. Add the Sagatiba and shake hard with cubed ice. Double strain over fresh cubed ice in a tumbler. Garnish with a basil leaf.

Botanical Garden—*Charlotte Voisey*

Cubeb Berry Snapper presented by Jim Ryan
1 ½ oz Hendrick's gin, ½ oz Fonseca Ruby Port, 3 oz tomato juice, ½ oz fresh squeezed, strained lemon juice, 2 dashes hot sauce, 2 dashes Worcestershire sauce, 1 dash rice wine vinegar, pinch sea salt, pinch ground black pepper, horseradish. Combine ingredients except port and plus a pinch of celery salt and celery seed, in a mixing container, add ice and roll. Serve over fresh ice, add port float and garnish with basil leaf, cucumber spear rolled in ground cubeb.

Citrus Fizz presented by Charlotte Voisey
1 ½ oz Hendrick's gin, ½ oz Solerno blood orange liqueur, ½ oz fresh lemon juice,¼ oz fresh lime juice, ¼ oz fresh grapefruit juice, ¾ oz bergamot simple syrup, 1 oz egg whites, dash orange bitters. Combine all ingredients and shake very well. Finish with a splash of soda. Spritz and discard an orange zest.

Pell Mell Punch presented by Jim Ryan
3 oz Hendrick's Gin, 3 oz fresh squeezed pineapple juice, 3 oz strengthened chamomile tea, 1 oz Wildflower Honey syrup (2:1), 1 oz freshly squeezed and strained lemon juice, 6 dashes Peychaud's bitters. Combine ingredients in a punch bowl, add punch ice, add mixed fresh berries and mint tips for garnish.

Rosa Verde #3 presented by Charlotte Voisey
1 ½ oz Hendrick's gin, ½ oz fresh lime juice, ½ oz simple syrup, 1 oz watermelon juice, arugula, pink peppercorns. Combine all ingredients and shake well. Serve over ice in a Tales cup. Garnish with a nice sprig of arugula.

Prohibition & Gin—*Simon Ford and David Wondrich*

The Last Word Cocktail presented by Simon Ford
1 oz Plymouth gin, 1 oz Luxardo Maraschino, 1 oz Green Chartreuse, 1 oz lime juice. Shake with ice, strain and serve straight up.

Satan's Whiskers Cocktail presented by Simon Ford
½ oz Beefeater Dry, ½ oz Dolin dry vermouth, ½ oz Dolin sweet red vermouth, ½ oz orange juice, ¼ oz Grand Marnier®, dash Regan's orange bitters. Shake and strain. Garnish with an orange twist.

Pineapple Julep (adapted from Jerry Thomas 1862) presented by Simon Ford
4 oz Plymouth gin, 4 oz Luxardo Maraschino Liqueur, 4 oz fresh orange juice, 1 bottle Perrier Jouët, fresh raspberry syrup*. Build and stir. Garnish with a piece of pineapple.
*Use 2 baskets of Driscoll's raspberries for every liter of simple syrup. (You can just marinate some pureed raspberries in the syrup over night or blend them on the same day)

Word-of-Mouth Marketing: Attend This Seminar & Grow Your Brand—*Ted Wright and Carter Reum*

Order of the Amazon presented by Carter Reum
1 ½ oz VeeV® Acai Spirit, ½ oz BÉNÉDICTINE®, ¾ oz lemon juice, ½ oz simple syrup, dash Angostura bitters. Shake all ingredients well with ice and strain into a chilled cocktail glass. Garnish with the lemon peel.

Basil Gimlet presented by Carter Reum
2 oz VeeV® Acai Spirit, 1 oz lime juice, ¾ oz simple syrup, 3 basil leaves. Tear and slap basil leaves to release oils and drop into the shaker. Shake all ingredients well with ice and strain into a chilled Martini glass. Garnish with a floating basil leaf.

The Hurricane presented by Ted Wright
3 oz Batiste rhum agricole, 1 oz passion fruit syrup, 1 oz fresh lime juice, ½ oz Falernum. Shake all ingredients with ice then pour into an ice-filled glass. Garnish with a blood-orange wheel.

The Hemingway presented by Ted Wright
1 ½ oz Batiste rhum agricole, ¾ oz fresh lime juice, ½ oz sugar cane syrup, ½ oz fresh grapefruit juice, ¼ oz maraschino cherry. Combine Batiste Rhum Agricole and all other ingredients in a mixing cup , add ice and shake. Strain into chilled cocktail glass.

Big Fish, Small Pond: A Guide to Self-Publishing—
Darcy O'Neil

Filby presented by Darcy O'Neil
1 ¼ oz Plymouth gin, ½ oz Amaretto, ½ oz dry vermouth, ½ oz Campari. Combine all ingredients in a shaker glass with ice and stir until well chilled. Strain into a cocktail glass and garnish with an orange twist.

From Convicts to Cocktailians: The Release of
Australian Flavor—*Simon McGoram, David Spanton,*
Matthew Bax, and Jacob Briars

Mint Julep Nitro Sorbet presented by Matthew Bax
1/3 oz Makers Mark, 1/3 oz Cognac VSOP, 1/3 oz Gomme syrup, 1 barspoon peach brandy, 4 oz liquid nitrogen, 10 mint leaves. Stir spirits gomme and mint gently. Churn with a whisk adding nitro slowly and carefully until a fine sorbet is reached. Sorbet to be served in DerRaum branded ice cream cups. Garnish with a mint leaf.

The Killer Bee presented by Jacob Briars
1 oz 42BELOW Honey vodka, 1/3 oz Jagermeister, ½ oz St-Germain, 1/3 oz vanilla syrup, ½ oz fresh lime juice, lime leaves, chili pepper. Muddle chilli and lime leaves with vanilla syrup. Combine all other ingredients, shake and fine strain into Cocktail glass. Garnish with a slice of chili pepper

At Full Sail: The History and Application of Spirits at
Proof, Navy Strength, and Overproof—*Eric Seed,*
Britt Chavanne, Wayne Curtis, and Audrey Saunders

Gimlet presented by Eric Seed
2 oz Plymouth Navy Strength gin, 1 oz Lime Cordial (Employees Only bottled). Stir over ice, strain, serve straight up.

Newark presented by Eric Seed
1 ½ oz Laird's Bonded Apple brandy, ¾ oz Carpano Antica Formula, 1 barspoon Fernet Branca, 1 barspoon Luxardo Maraschino. Stir and serve straight up. Garnish with a lemon twist.

Royal Million presented by Eric Seed
¾ oz Lemon Hart 151 Demerara rum, ¾ oz Plantation Jamaica rum, ¾ oz fresh lemon juice, ¾ oz simple syrup, 1 barspoon Angostura bitters. Shake, strain, and serve straight up with a lemon twist.

The Smooth and Creamy History of the Fern Bar—
Martin Cate

The Lola Granola presented by Martin Cate
1 ½ oz amaretto liqueur, 3 oz orange juice, 1 oz half and half, half a banana. Combine all with ice in blender and blend until smooth. Garnish with a sprinkle of wheat germ.

Maude's Berry Bomb presented by Martin Cate
1 ½ oz vodka, ½ oz cranberry liqueur, ½ oz grenadine, ¼ oz granulated sugar, ¼ oz canned cranberry sauce, 1 oz half and half. Combine above with ice in blender and blend until smooth. Top with whipped cream and garnish with a whole cranberry.

California Root Beer Float presented by Martin Cate
1 oz Galliano, 1 oz Kahlua, 3 oz half and half, 1 oz club soda. Combine above (except club soda) with ice in blender and blend until smooth. Top with 1 oz club soda.

The Fine Art of Crafting Your Own Charm, Magic, and Flair Behind the Bar—*Cheryl Charming, Doc Eason, and Dean Serneels*

So You Want to Be A Consultant: What It Really Takes—*Tad Carducci, Willy Shine, Jacques Bezuidenhout, and Andy Seymour*

Tazza d'Eva presented by Willy Shine & Tad Carducci
1 oz Averna amaro, 1 oz G'Vine Nouaison, 4 mint leaves, 1 rosemary sprig, ¼ oz chopped green apple, 3 oz tonic water. Muddle apple and rosemary. Add mint and press lightly. Add Averna and gin and shake. Strain over ice in highball glass. Top with tonic. Garnish with additional spoon of chopped apple and rosemary sprig.

Blue Mountain Daiquiri presented by Willy Shine
2 oz Appleton Estate Reserve rum, 1 oz lime juice, demerara syrup. Shake and strain ingredients into chilled coupe. Garnish with an orange twist, grated nutmeg, and Jamaican coffee grounds.

A Shot of Black Stuff: Amazing Amaros and Brilliant Bitters—*Jacob Briars and Sebastian Reaburn*

Bax Beet Pinot presented by Jacob Briars
1/3 oz Fernet Branca bitters, ½ oz Martini Rossi Sweet vermouth, 1 oz gomme syrup, ½ oz fresh lime juice, Beetroot juice. Combine all, add ice, shake and strain—ideally into a wine glass but otherwise straight up

Averna Pineapple Shrub presented by Jacob Briars
1 ½ oz Averna bitters, 1 ¼ oz fresh pineapple purée, 1/3 oz simple syrup, dash Bitter Truth Aromatic, ¼ oz white vinegar. Shake all VERY hard with ice, double-strain into glass.

Kiwi Collins presented by Philip Duff
2 oz Stolichnaya vodka, 1 oz lemon juice, ½ oz rich simple syrup (2:1), 1 oz Fizzy water, Kiwi fruit, quartered. Muddle kiwi fruit in shaker. Add other ingredients (EXCEPT fizzy water) and ice and shake. Strain into ice-filled glass then top with fizzy water. Garnish with a kiwi slice.

Corzo Margarita Rocks presented by Daniel Victory
1 ½ oz Corzo Silver tequila, ¾ oz fresh lemon juice, ¼ oz Corzo agave nectar, ½ oz Cointreau, wedge orange, wedge lemon. Shake and serve on the rocks.

The Pacific Rim presented by Jacob Briars
2 oz 42BELOW vodka, 1 oz agave nectar, 1 lime cut into wedges, 1 jalapeño pepper, Cucumber, Maldon Sea Salt. Muddle 4 lime wedges with 6 chunks of peeled cucumber and 2 slices of jalapeño. Add vodka and agave, a pinch of salt, and shake well with ice. Fine strain into an ice-filled rocks glass. Garnish with a jalapeño slice.

Umami in Cocktails—*Darcy O'Neil*

Fifth Sense presented by Darcy O'Neil
1 ¼ oz bourbon, 1 oz Serendipitea green tea, 1 barspoon Maraschino, 1 barspoon Marmite syrup*. Add the ingredients to a shaker with ice, stir and strain into a cocktail glass. Garnish with a tea leaf.
*Take 1 heaping teaspoon Marmite and dissolve in 1 cup of water.

Caesar presented by Darcy O'Neil
1 ¼ oz vodka, 3¼ oz Mott's Clamato, 1 barspoon Worcestershire sauce, dash of Tabasco. Build in a highball glass, stir and serve on the rocks. Garnish with a pickle spear.

International Barman of Mystery: The Saga of Joe Scialom—*Jeff Berry and Colette Roy*

Suffering Bastard presented by Jeff Berry
1 oz Plymouth gin, 1 oz cognac, ½ oz Rose's lime cordial, 1 ½ oz Fever Tree ginger beer, 2 dashes Angostura aromatic bitters. Shake all but ginger beer with ice. Then stir in 1 ½ oz Fever Tree ginger beer. Pour unstrained (ice and all) into a double old-fashioned glass, adding more ice to fill. Garnish with a mint sprig and orange slice.

Plymouth Julietta presented by Jeff Berry
1 ¼ oz Plymouth gin, ¾ oz white vermouth, 1 oz Fee Brothers orgeat syrup, 2 oz white grapefruit juice, 2 oz orange juice. Shake all ingredients with ice. Strain into a tall glass filled with fresh ice. Garnish with a mint sprig, orange slice, brandied cherry.

The How's and Why's of Cocktails: An Exploration of Techniques, Ingredients, and Methodology— *Audrey Saunders, Tony Conigliaro, and Harold McGee*

French Pearl presented by Audrey Saunders
2 oz Plymouth gin, ¼ oz Pernod Pastis, ¾ oz lime juice, ¾ oz simple syrup, fresh mint sprig. Muddle / shake / fine strain / no garnish.

Social Media: Creating Cocktail Legends—*Nick Nemeth, Camper English, Jennifer English, and Brian Rea*

Improved Summer Sour presented by Nick Nemeth
1 ¼ oz Disaronno Amaretto, ½ oz Green Chartreuse, fresh watermelon, cubed, ½ oz fresh lime juice. Combine all ingredients in shaker, over ice. Shake vigorously, and fine strain into serving glass. Garnish with mint leaves.

Homeward Bound presented by Nick Nemeth
1 oz Sailor Jerry Spiced rum, 1 oz Disaronno Amaretto, ¼ oz Galliano, 1 barspoon Angostura Aromatic bitters. Combine ingredients over ice in Boston glass, still until very well chilled, and strain over one large chunk of ice in serving glass. Flame orange zest, and discard. Garnish with a Luxardo cherry.

Gin Cocktails: From The Lost and Forgotten Classics To The New Contemporary—*Tony Abou-Ganim and Charlotte Voisey*

Black Cherry Ramos presented by Tony Abou-Ganim
2 oz Bombay Sapphire® Gin, 1 oz lemon juice, ½ oz lime juice, 1 oz simple syrup, 1 ½ oz cream, 1 oz egg white, 1 ½ oz soda water, 1 oz black cherry purée, drop of orange flower water. Shake vigorously, strain into a chilled highball glass. Top with chilled club soda. No garnish.

Cucumber Surprise Fizz presented by Charlotte Voisey
1 ½ oz Hendrick's gin, 1 barspoon ginger purée, ¾ oz Sonoma Lavender syrup, ½ oz fresh lemon juice, ¼ oz fresh lime juice, ½ oz cucumber water, dash of lavender bitters, lavender foam. Combine all ingredients (except Lavender foam) and shake well. Serve over fresh ice. Finish with Lavender foam and garnish with a lemon twist.

Lady Marmalade presented by Charlotte Voisey
1 ½ oz Hendrick's gin, ½ oz Solerno Blood Orange liqueur, ½ oz fresh yuzu purée, ½ oz orange marmalade. ½ oz egg white, ¼ oz simple syrup. Combine ingredients and shake very well. Serve up in a Tales of the Cocktail® cup. Garnish with a dried/dehydrated blood orange wheel.

Tom Collins presented by Tony Abou-Ganim
1 ½ oz Hayman's Old Tom, 1 oz lemon juice, 1 oz simple syrup, 3 oz soda water. Stir and serve on the rocks. Garnish with an orange wheel.

White Lady presented by Tony Abou-Ganim
2 oz Bombay Sapphire® Gin, 1 oz lemon juice, 1 oz Cointreau®, egg white. Shake and serve straight up.

Armagnac, France's First Brandy—*Dale DeGroff, Doug Frost, Philippe Gironi, and Alain Royer*

D'Artagnan presented by Dale DeGroff
1 tsp Chateau Busca Hor D'Age Armagnac, 1 tsp Grand Marnier®, ½ oz orange juice, Dash simple syrup, 4 oz champagne. Mix Armagnac, Grand Marnier, orange juice and sugar into a champagne flute. Top with Champagne and add a spiral of orange peel to extend the length of the glass.

Gascon Redhead presented by Dale DeGroff
1 ½ oz White Armagnac, ½ oz orange curacao, 1 oz pineapple juice, ½ oz Fonseca ruby port. Shake the first three ingredients well with ice and strain into a chilled white wine glass over ice. Float ruby port. And garnish with pineapple.

The History, Science, and Creativity Behind Essential Oils and Extracts—*Andrew Nicholls, Darcy O'Neil and Misja Vorstermans*

Maiden Hair Punch presented by Andrew Nicholls

2 oz Hendrick's gin, 1 oz Solerno Blood Orange liqueur, 1 oz fresh lemon juice, ½ oz Maiden Hair syrup, 3 oz chilled ginger ale. Place all ingredients except ginger ale in a punch bowl (or other vessel) and stir until thoroughly mixed. Place in freezer until thoroughly chilled and then add the chilled ginger ale. Serve over ice and garnish with grated nutmeg.

Experimental Corpse Reviver presented by Andrew Nicholls

1 oz Beefeater gin, 1 oz Solerno Blood Orange liqueur, 1 oz Lillet Blanc, 1 barspoon acid phosphate, dash of Angostura bitters. Place all ingredients in a shaker, fill shaker with ice and shake hard for about 8 seconds. Double strain and serve over ice; garnish with a lemon twist.

The Science of Stirring—*Eben Klemm, Dave Arnold and Thomas Waugh*

Manhattan presented by Eben Klemm

2 oz Sazerac Rye, 1 oz sweet vermouth, dash of Angostura bitters. Combine, stir, and serve straight up.

Bax vs Clift: Progressive Cocktail/Cooking Techniques from Tippling Club & Der Raum—*Matthew Bax and Ryan Clift*

Japanese Michelada

1 can of Japanese beer, 1 cup soy sauce , 1 cup yuzu, 3 1/3oz (100 g) wasabi, Togarashi spice mix (rim). Blend yuzu, soy and wasabi. Rim glass with Togarashi (wipe lime juice then dip in dry spice mix). Pour 10 ml Michelada mix (soy/wasabi/yuzu) into rimmed glass, then top with Japanese beer.

Smokey Old Bastard

1 oz Ardbeg or other Islay whisky, 1/3oz Roast Banana Cigar Maple, 2 dashes Peychaud's bitters, orange zest smoke. Combine, stir and serve in an airtight container (to hold in the smoke).

Mb's Apple Pie

1/3 oz Roasted Apple Calvados, 1/3 oz agave nectar, ½ oz G E Massanez Pomme Verte (or a good apple liquor substitute), ½ oz Carpano Antica Formula vermouth, 1 barspoon lime juice, ½ oz egg white, pinch of cinnamon. Shake ingredients and serve.

Velvet Fog

1 oz Tanqueray TEN, 1/3oz Crème de Violette, 1 barspoon Gum Arabic, 1 barspoon Velvet Falernum, ½ oz champagne, 1 oz dry ice. Shake gin, gomme, velvet falernum. Double strain into champagne flutes. Top with splash of champagne. Finish with velvet fog.

How French Products Contribute to Cocktails—*Fernando Castellon, Ted Haigh, and Olivier Paultes*

Blue Moon presented by Fernando Castellon
2 oz Tanqueray gin, ½ oz Pagès crème de violette, ½ oz fresh lemon juice. Shake with ice and strain into a cocktail shaker. Garnish with lemon twist.

The Ford Cocktail presented by Fernando Castellon
1 oz Old Tom gin, 1 oz Noilly Prat dry vermouth, 3 dashes Bénédictine®, 3 dashes orange bitters. Stir well over ice and strain into a cocktail glass. Garnish with an orange twist.

Charlie Lindbergh Cocktail presented by Fernando Castellon
1 ½ oz Plymouth gin, 1 oz Lillet Blanc, 1 barspoon Apry or Apricot Brandy liqueur, dash orange bitters. Stir well with ice and strain into a cocktail glass.

Cat's Eye presented by Fernando Castellon
1 ½ oz Beefeater gin, ½ oz Noilly Prat dry vermouth, ¼ oz Kirsch, ¼ oz Cointreau®, dash of fresh lemon juice. Shake well with ice and strain into a cocktail glass.

I Hate Vodka, I Love Vodka—*Claire Smith, Henry Besant, Ian Burrell, John Gakuru, Anistatia Miller, Jeremy J.F. Thompson, and Angus Winchester*

Apple Martini presented by Claire Smith
2 oz Belvedere vodka, 1 oz Apple sourz liqueur, 1 barspoon simple syrup, 1 barspoon lemon juice. Shake and strain into a Martini glass.

Whisper Vesper presented by Claire Smith
2 ¼ oz Belvedere Pink Grapefruit vodka, ¼ oz Bols Genever, dash of lemon bitters. Stir and strain into a Martini glass. Garnish with a grapefruit twist.

Sex on the Beach presented by Jeremy Thompson
1 1/2 oz Russian Standard vodka, ½ oz peach schnapps, 2 oz Oceanspray cranberry juice, 2 oz Tropicana orange juice. Shake and serve on the rocks. Garnish with a cherry.

The Harvey presented by Jeremy Thompson
1 ½ oz Russian Standard vodka, ¾ oz Galliano liqueur, ¾ oz fresh orange juice, cucumber, sliced. Shake and serve straight up. Garnish with a thin cucumber wheel.

Civilization Begins with Distillation—*Jacob Briars and Sebastian Reaburn*

The Auld Alliance presented by Jacob Briars
1 oz Drambuie, 2 oz champagne. Combine in glass, stir, serve.

The Black Nail presented by Jacob Briars
1 oz Drambuie, 1 oz Johnnie Walker Black Label scotch, 1 oz 42BELOW Honey vodka. Combine all, stir and strain over ice. Garnish with a lemon twist.

The F Word: Flair of Mixology—*Tobin Ellis, Joe Brooke, Philip Duff, John Hogan, and Danny Valdez*

Zamboni presented by Tobin Ellis
1 oz LEBLON® cachaça, 1 oz Campari, 1 oz Carpano Antica vermouth. Build over ice, stir, garnish with gusto. Yes, gusto.

Hollywood Cocktails: Louisiana Style—*Cheryl Charming, William Garver, Ted Haigh, and Alan Leonhard*

Sazerac presented by Alan Leonard
2 oz Sazerac Rye, 1 barspoon Herbsaint, dash Peychaud's bitters, sugar cube, lemon peel. Crush the sugar cube in the bottom of a mixing glass then add the rye and bitters. Add ice then stir. Rinse a rocks glass with Herbsaint then strain the mixture in the mixing glass into the rocks glass. Twist a lemon peel, rub the oils on the rim then discard.

Absinthe Suissesse presented by Ted Haigh
1 ½ oz Nouvelle Orleans absinthe, ½ oz orgeat syrup, ½ oz eg white or 2 tablespoons pasteurized egg white, 1 oz half-and-half. Shake all ingredients and strain over crushed ice.

The Many Faces of Canadian Whisky— *Stephen Beaumont, Lew Bryson, and Drew Mayville*

Canadian Bacon presented by Stephen Beaumont
2 oz Caribou Crossing whisky, ½ oz Torani Bacon syrup, ½ oz maple syrup, rosemary sprig (leaves only), dash of Fee Old Fashioned Aromatic bitters, dash of Peychaud's bitters, orange peels. In a shaker, muddle together maple and bacon syrups, rosemary leaves, both bitters and 2 pieces of orange peel, Add whisky and stir. Strain into an ice filled Old Fashioned glass and garnish with orange twist.

Rye & Ginger Revisited Again presented by Stephen Beaumont
1 ½ oz Royal Canadian whisky, ½ oz lime juice, ½ oz Domaine de Canton, 3 ½ oz ginger beer. Build over ice, stir, serve on the rocks. Garnish with a lime wedge.

New Tales for Old Cocktails: Techniques and Problems of Historical Mixography—*David Wondrich and Jeff Berry*

Punch Royal presented by David Wondrich
3 oz Martell VS cognac, 1 oz Smith & Cross rum, 2 oz Sandeman ruby port, 4 oz still water, 1 oz juice, lemon, 1 oz fine Demerara or raw sugar, lemon peel, fresh-grated nutmeg. Muddle lemon peel in sugar and let sit for 60 minutes. Add lemon juice and stir to dissolve sugar. If necessary, add 1 oz (or proportional quantity) hot water to aid dissolution, subtracting same amount from water added at end. Add cognac, rum and port. Stir. Add water. Stir. Grate nutmeg over ice in serving cup then pour over top.

Queue de Chanticleer presented by David Wondrich
2 oz Martell VSOP cognac, 1 barspoon Demerara simple syrup, 3 Dashes Peychaud's bitters, dash Pernod absinthe. Shake well with cracked ice; strain into glass and twist lemon peel over the top.

Tropical Itch presented by Jeff Berry
1 ½ oz Cruzan 151, 1 oz Smith & Cross rum, 1 oz Buffalo Trace bourbon, ½ oz Bols Curaçao, 6 oz Funkin passion fruit purée, ½ oz simple syrup, 2 dashes Angostura aromatic bitters. Fill a large hurricane glass with crushed ice, then add all ingredients. Swizzle

until well chilled. Serve over crushed ice. Garnish with a pineapple stick and mint sprig.

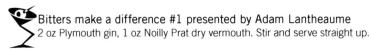

Western Sour presented by Jeff Berry
1 oz white grapefruit juice, ½ oz lime juice, ½ oz Fee Brothers Falernum, ¼ oz simple syrup, 2 oz Buffalo Trace. Shake all ingredients with ice cubes. Pour unstrained (ice and all) into glass.

Rolling Out the Red Carpet for Rookies—
Michael Dietsch, Robert Hess, and Adam Lantheaume

Bitters make a difference #1 presented by Adam Lantheaume
2 oz Plymouth gin, 1 oz Noilly Prat dry vermouth. Stir and serve straight up.

Bitters make a difference #2 presented by Adam Lantheaume
2 oz Plymouth gin, 1 oz Noilly Prat dry vermouth, 2 dashes Angostura orange bitters. Stir and serve straight up.

Bitters make a difference #3 presented by Adam Lantheaume
2 oz Plymouth gin, 1 oz Noilly Prat dry vermouth, 2 dashes Fee Brother's Grapefruit bitters. Stir and serve straight up.

Bitters make a difference #4 presented by Adam Lantheaume
2 oz Plymouth gin, 1 oz Noilly Prat dry vermouth, 2 dashes Peychaud's bitters. Stir and serve straight up.

Sidecar presented by Michael Dietsch
2 oz Courvoisier® VS, 1 oz Cointreau, ½ oz lemon juice. Shake with ice, strain into a cocktail glass, garnish with lemon twist.

The Pre-History and Evolution of Gin—*Philip Duff*

Jasmine presented by Philip Duff
1 ½ oz G'Vine Floraison gin, ½ oz Cointreau®, ½ oz lemon juice, ½ oz Campari. Shake all with ice and strain into pre-chilled cocktail glass. Garnish with a lemon twist.

Bartending in the 1940s, 1950s, and 1960s (The Dark Ages)—*Brian Rea*

Bombay Ruddy Mary presented by Brian Rea
1 oz Bombay Original gin, 3 oz Tabasco Bloody Mary mix. Pour gin, add Bloody Mary Mix, stir, add horseradish and pickle spear.

BBC presented by Brian Rea
1 ½ oz Bombay Original gin, 1 oz Cointreau, ½ oz Crème de Banana. Combine all ingredients, shake and pour over ice cubes.

Brandies of Jerez—*Francesco Lafranconi*

The Andalusian presented by Francesco Lafranconi
2 oz Lepanto Spanish brandy, 2 oz Fever Tree Bitter Lemon, 4 mint sprigs, dash peach bitters, lemon peel, 4 oz ice. Place the mint sprigs in a wine glass with 2 dashes of peach bitters and muddle briskly. Add half cup of ice, Lepanto and Fever tree bitter lemon soda. Stir and serve with a lemon twist.

El Sueno Prohibido presented by Francesco Lafranconi
1 ¾ oz Spanish Brandy Cardenal Mendoza, 1 oz Walnut Liqueur Nostalgia by Charbay, ¼ oz Briottet Crème de Framboise. Pour ingredients over ice in a short tumbler glass, stir and serve. Garnish with a twisted orange peel and dried fig on a spear.

Tiki Now! The New Breed of Tiki Bar—*Blair Reynolds*

Hilo Hala presented by Blair Reynolds
1 ½ oz Rhum JM Blanc, 1 oz pineapple juice, ½ oz St-Germain, ½ oz Falernum, dash Xocolatl Mole Bitters, lemon zest. Shake ingredients with cubed ice, strain into cocktail glass, serve with pineapple wedge garnish.

Swains Swill presented by Blair Reynolds
¾ oz Smith & Cross rum, ¾ oz Don Q Gold rum, ¾ oz Rhum JM VSOP, 1 oz Don's Mix, ¾ oz lime juice, ¼ oz Allspice Dram, dash Bitter Truth Aromatic Bitters, drop of Herbsaint Original, 1 oz Ting Grapefruit soda. Add all except Ting to 1 cup crushed ice. Mix for 5 seconds with top-down mixer (or stick blender). Serve in Double Old-Fashioned, top with 1 oz ting. Garnish with a sprig of mint and cinnamon stick.

Panah Manah presented by Blair Reynolds
1 ½ oz Ron Abuelo 7, ½ oz coffee syrup, ¾ oz lemon juice, 3 ¼ oz smoked banana soda, Dash of Amargo Bitters. Build all but soda in a chimney glass, stir, add soda, stir again gently. Garnish with a banana chip.

Ichigo/Ichie: One Chance/One Meeting - How to Synchronize the Bartender's Mind & Body— *Stanislav Vadrna*

Masataka Swizzle presented by Stanislav Vadrna
1 ½ oz Nikka Taketsuru 12 Year whisky, ½ oz Amaretto, ½ oz lemon juice, 1 barspoon simple syrup, 3 dashes Peychaud's bitters, 2 dashes Regan's orange bitters. Pour the ingredients into a 10 oz highball glass. Swizzle, then fill the glass to halfway with crushed ice, swizzle again, put more crushed ice, and swizzle again. Top it with the Peychauds bitters. Garnish 1 fresh mint sprig.

Japanese Boulevardier presented by Stanislav Vadrna
1 ½ oz Nikka Taketsuru 12 Year whisky, 1 oz Campari, 1 oz Dolin Rouge vermouth, dash of Bitter Truth Chocolate bitters, dash of Peychaud's bitters. Stir, strain, and serve straight up. Express the oils from an orange twist then discard.

Ladies Only: Hands-on with Tony Abou-Ganim— *Tony Abou-Ganim*

Moonshine Punch presented by Tony Abou-Ganim
1 ½ oz Catdaddy Carolina Moonshine, ½ oz Cherry Heering, lemon juice, sweet Luzianne tea, cold simple syrup. Stir and serve straight up. Garnish with a lemon and orange wheel.

Cosmo presented by Tony Abou-Ganim
1 ½ oz ABSOLUT® Citron, ¾ oz Cointreau®, ½ oz lime juice, ½ oz Oceanspray cranberry juice. Shake and serve straight up with a lemon twist.

Smash presented by Tony Abou-Ganim
2 oz Catdaddy Caroline Moonshine, 1 oz simple syrup, 4 pitted cherries, 12 mint leaves. Muddle, shake, and serve on the rocks. Garnish with mint.

Passion Punch presented by Tony Abou-Ganim
1 ½ oz Barsol Pisco, ½ oz Myer's rum, 1 oz passion fruit purée, 2 oz orange juice, 2 oz lemon juice, 2 dashes Angostura orange bitters, grated nutmeg. Stir and serve straight up; garnish with grated nutmeg.

Pisco Sour presented by Tony Abou-Ganim
2 oz Barsol Pisco, 1 oz lime juice, 1 oz simple syrup, egg white. Shake and serve straight up with a dash of Angostura bitters.

Blood & Sand presented by Tony Abou-Ganim
1 ½ oz DEWAR'S® scotch, ½ oz Cherry Heering, ½ oz sweet vermouth, 1 ½ oz orange juice. Shaken and served on the rocks. Garnish with a flamed orange twist.

The Mastery of Wisdom Behind the Bar—*Dushan Zaric and Aisha Sharpe*

Gimlet presented by Dushan Zaric
2 ½ oz Plymouth gin, 1 oz E.O. Lime Cordial. Pour all ingredients into a mixing glass. Add large, cold ice and shake briefly but with conviction. Strain into a rocks glass over ice and garnish with a lime wheel.

Negroni presented by Dushan Zaric
1 oz Plymouth gin, 1 oz Dolin sweet vermouth, 1 oz Campari. Pour all into a mixing glass, add ice, stir and strain into a rocks glass over ice. Garnish with an orange half-wheel.

Quiet Storm presented by Dushan Zaric
1 ½ oz Maker's Mark, 1 oz Silence Tea infused Red Bush vermouth, ¾ oz fresh lemon juice, ½ oz simple syrup, 3 oz Fever Tree ginger beer. In a tall Collins glass build the drink by combining all except ginger beer. Fill up with large, cold ice and cover the glass with a small shaker top. Shake briefly, remove the shaker top and top off with ginger beer. Garnish with lemon wheel and mint crown.

Soda's Influence Cocktails—*Darcy O'Neil*

Wet Grave presented by Darcy O'Neil
1 ¼ oz bourbon, ½ oz Claret syrup*, ¼ oz dry vermouth, 1 barspoon Acid Phosphate, 1 dash Peychaud's bitters. Combine the ingredients, stir and strain. Serve straight up with an orange twist.

*Equal parts 2:1 simple syrup and red wine (traditionally Bordeaux but any Cab-Merlot or similar variety will work).

Bite Cocktail presented by Darcy O'Neil
1 ¼ oz Brandy VS, 2 oz Barq's Rootbeer, ½ oz Gentian tea*, dash of Fee's Old Fashioned bitters. Build in a collins glass with ice. Serve with an orange twist.
*Steep 1 tablespoon of crushed gentian root in 1 cup of boiling water for 15 minutes.

Rum Running: Contraband, Customs & Taxes. How Alcohol Became Contraband from Past to Present— *Ed Hamilton, Jeff Berry, and Wayne Curtis*

Añejo Candido presented by Stephen Remsberg
2 oz Ron Abuelo 7 year old Panama rum, ½ oz fresh lime juice, 3 to 4 dashes Fee Brothers Whiskey Barrel bitters, ¼ oz Petite Cane Sugar Cane syrup. Stir the drink with ice cubes and serve in an Old Fashioned glass over crushed ice.

Rum Runner presented by Jeff Beach Bum Berry
½ oz blackberry brandy, ½ oz crème de banana, ¼ oz Funkin pomegranate syrup, ¾ oz Brugal Añejo rum, ¾ oz lime juice. Shake with ice cubes. Pour unstrained (ice and all) into glass.

Twelve Mile Limit presented by Jeff Beach BumBerry
1 oz Ron Viejo de Caldas Grand Reserve rum, ½ oz cognac, ½ oz Sazerac Rye, ½ oz Funkin pomegranate syrup, ½ oz fresh lemon juice. Shake ingredients with ice and strain into glass. Garnish with a lemon twist.

Subconscious Drinks—*Andrew Nicholls and Misja Vorstermans*

Sensory Analysis: A Deep Dive Into How We Experience Taste and Smell with Spirits— *Per Hermansson*

Rubiano Cocktail presented by Chris Patino
1 ½ oz ABSOLUT® Ruby Red, 1 oz Campari, ½ red grapefruit, dash of orange bitters. Shake all ingredients with ice and strain into a cocktail glass.

The Blue Reviver presented by Chris Patino
¾ oz ABSOLUT® Citron, ¾ oz blue curaçao, ¾ oz lemon juice, ¾ oz Lillet Blanc, 1 barspoon Pernod absinthe. Shake all ingredients with ice and strain into a cocktail glass.

The Julep Story: 1488 to Present—*Jared Brown, Anistatia Miller, and Charles Vexenat*

Julepum Stomachicum presented by Anistatia Miller
3 oz mint tincture, 1 oz cardamom water, ¼ oz simple syrup. Combine all ingredients, chilled but without ice. Stir and serve.

Infused Julep presented by Anistatia Miller

3 oz mint-infused whiskey, ½ oz simple syrup. Combine whiskey and simple syrup in a frosted silver julep cup over crushed ice. Add more ice to create a mounded top. Garnish with a small bunch of mint. Dust with confectioners sugar. Add short straws through the mint.

Mint Julep presented by Anistatia Miller

3 oz Buffalo Trace bourbon, 2 tsp superfine sugar, mint. Combine sugar, a little whiskey, and 5-6 mint leaves in a frosted julep cup. Muddle. Add a bit of crushed ice. Add the rest of the whiskey. Top with more crushed ice. Garnish with a small bunch of mint. Dust with superfine sugar.

Brandy Julep presented by Anistatia Miller

3 oz Hennessey brandy, 2 tsp superfine sugar, ½ oz orange juice, mint. Combine sugar, orange juice, and 5-6 mint leaves in a frosted julep cup. Muddle. Add a crushed ice and whiskey. Garnish with a small bunch of mint. Dust with superfine sugar.

Art of the Aperitif: Exploring Pre-Prandial Spirits, Wines, and Cocktails—*Paul Clarke and Neyah White*

Vermouth Shrub presented by Neyah White

½ oz strawberry shrub, 2 oz Noilly Prat dry vermouth. Stir with ice, strain and serve up. Garnish with a lemon twist.

Gavin presented by Paul Clarke

2 ¼ oz Noilly Prat dry vermouth, 1 oz Aperol, 1 barspoon Crème de Cassis, 2 oz club soda. Build vermouth, Aperol and crème de cassis in a highball glass filled with ice. Top with club soda, stir lightly to combine. Garnish with an orange wheel.

The Hotel Grunewald, Roosevelt, and Fairmont: Over 100 Years of Cocktail History—*Philip Greene and Chris McMillian*

Sazerac presented by Phil Greene

1 oz rye whiskey, 1 barspoon simple syrup, 1 tsp Herbsaint, 2 dashes of Peychaud's Bitters. Place ice into a rocks glass, set aside. Combine whisky, simple syrup, and Peychaud's in a glass, stir well, and set aside. Remove ice from rocks glass, add Herbsaint, then tilt glass sideways and rotate it around, to "rinse" interior of glass with Herbsaint. Discard excess. Strain whiskey mixture into rocks glass, garnish with lemon peel.

Ramos Gin Fizz presented by Phil Greene

¾ oz gin, ¼ oz freshly squeezed lemon juice, ¼ oz simple syrup, ½ oz half and half, 1 barspoon egg white, ¾ oz seltzer water, drop of orange flower water, fresh lime juice. Combine all ingredients, except for the seltzer water, in a shaker and shake well for 3 minutes. Strain into a Delmonico glass, top with seltzer.

The Flavor Trip—*Jim Ryan*

Alaskan Sour Surprise presented by Charlotte Voisey

1 ½ oz Hendrick's Gin, ¾ oz fresh lime juice, ½ oz simple syrup, ¾ oz Yellow Chartreuse, ½ egg white, 2 dashes Regan's bitters, 3 Szechuan buttons. Muddle buttons, add other ingredients and shake very well. Strain up into a Tales cup. Spritz an atomizer spray of orange

bitters. Garnish with a cucumber slice and whole Szechuan button.

Miracle Cucumber Gimlet presented by Jim Ryan
2 oz Hendrick's Gin, 1 oz fresh strained lime juice, 2 wheels English cucumber. Muddle juice and cucumber. Add beautiful gin, ice shake and double strain into a Tales glass. Garnish with cucumber wheel.

Cucumber Gimlet presented by Jim Ryan
1 ½ oz Hendrick's gin, 1/3 oz fresh strained lime juice, ¾ oz simple syrup, cucumber wheel. Muddle cucumber simple syrup and juice. Add Hendrick's Gin, ice and shake well. Double strain into a Tales glass. Garnish with a julienned English cucumber hair.

Scotland's Whisky Legends and Pacult—*Paul Pacult, Richard Paterson, and Colin Scott*

Religious Spirits—*Garrett Oliver and Allen Katz*

The Last Word presented by Allen Katz
¾ oz Plymouth gin, ¾ oz Green Chartreuse, ¾ oz Luxardo or Maraska Maraschino, ¾ oz lime juice. Shake ingredients vigorously over ice and fine strain into a tasting cup. Garnish with a lime wheel.

Vieux Carré presented by Allen Katz
1 oz Bourbon, Buffalo Trace, 1 oz Cognac, Pierre Ferrand Ambre, 1 oz Sweet Vermouth, ¼ oz BÉNÉDICTINE®, dash of Angostura bitters, dash of Peychaud's bitters. Stir ingredients over ice and strain into an ice-filled glass. Garnish with a broad lemon twist.

The Mysteries and Secrets of Distilling in Cognac: The Cellar Master's Essential Work and Classic Cognac—*Dale DeGroff, Salvatore Calabrese, Olivier Paultes, and Alain Royer*

Garlic Affair presented by Salvatore Calabrese
1 ¼ oz cognac, ¼ oz apricot brandy, ¼ oz lemon juice, fresh garlic, ginger beer. Add all ingredients into the shaker, except for the ginger beer. Shake sharply to break down the garlic and release the flavour. Strain into the glass. Garnish with a lime wedge.

French 75 presented by Dale DeGroff
1 oz Cadenhead Old Raj gin, ¾ oz simple syrup, ½ oz lemon juice, 3 oz champagne. Shake the brandy, lemon juice and simple syrup well with ice and strain into an ice filled wine glass and top with Champagne. Garnish with lemon peel.

Between the Sheets presented by Dale DeGroff
1 ½ oz Frapin cognac, ½ oz Verveine du Velay Extra, ½ oz Cointreau®, ¾ oz lemon juice. Shake all ingredients with ice and strain into chilled cocktail glass. Garnish with a burnt orange peel.

Godfrey presented by Salvatore Calabrese
1 ½ oz cognac, 2 dashes of Grand Marnier®, ¼ oz crème de mûre liqueur, lemon juice, 4 blackberries. Shake all ingredients with ice very sharply to break down the berries and release flavour. Strain into the glass filled with ice. Garnish with a blackberry and a small mint leaf on a cocktail stick.

The Eggpire Strikes Back—*Timo Janse, Henrik Hammer, and Andrew Nicholls*

G & Me presented by Timo Janse
1 oz Geranium gin, ½ oz lemon grass and ginger syrup, 1 barspoon absinthe, ½ oz egg white, ¾ oz fresh carrot juice. Add all ingredients in base of shaker. Dry shake first, then shake and fine strain. Grate pepper on top.

Coffee cocktail presented by Timo Janse
1 oz Martell brandy, 2 ½ oz Fonseca ruby port, 1 oz egg, 1 barspoon simple syrup. Shake and fine strain in egg cup. Garnish with cock's feather and grated nutmeg.

Clover Club presented by Timo Janse
2 oz Geranium gin, ½ oz raspberry syrup*, ½ oz egg white, ½ oz fresh lemon juice. Add all ingredients to the shaker, dry shake, shake, strain in glass.
*Warm 2 parts sugar with 1 part water and ½ a part fresh raspberries.

The Sprezzatura Bartender: The Way of the Charismatic Bartenders—*Stanislav Vadrna*

Keeping Ahead in an Online World—*Paul Clarke and Lindsey Johnson*

Mackenzie Cocktail presented by Paul Clarke
2 oz The Dalmore 12 year old, ¼ oz honey syrup, 1 barspoon Grand Marnier®, 1 barspoon Drambuie® liqueur, dash of Bitter Truth Jerry Thomas Decanter bitters. Stir with ice, strain into chilled glass. Twist orange peel over drink and use as garnish.

Sands of Life presented by Paul Clarke
2 oz The Dalmore 12 year old, ¾ oz Aperol amaro, 1 barspoon Grand Marnier®. Stir Dalmore and Aperol with ice and strain into rocks glass rinsed with Grand Marnier.

Plate & Glass, Finding Harmony—*Gina Chersevani and Peter Smith*

A Stone's Throw presented by Gina Chersevani
1 ½ oz Balvenie 12, 1 oz apricot poaching liquid. In a glass with 2 cubes, pour Balvenie 12 and the apricot poaching liquid, stir until chilled, and serve on the rocks. Garnish with apricot half and pine nut powder.

Smokin' Tutu presented by Gina Chersevani
1 ½ oz Plymouth gin, ¾ oz fresh strawberry purée, ¾ oz fresh lemon juice. Fill shaker with ice, combine all ingredients, shake, strain into glass. Garnish with smoked strawberry cotton candy.

S'more Rum presented by Gina Chersevani
1 ½ oz Zacapa 23, 1 oz bitter chocolate liquid, marshmallow whip. In a shaker tin filled with ice combine the Zacapa and the bitter chocolate liquid. Shake until cold, double strain into a glass, then garnish with marshmallow whip.

1100 BC presented by Gina Chersevani
1 ¼ oz Apostoles Palo Cortado Sherry, ¾ oz Plymouth gin, ¼ oz lime juice, 1 oz white fig purée. In a shaker, ¾ filled with ice combine ingredients. Shake, strain into a glass, and garnish with salt foam.

La Verdad (The Truth) About Mezcal: Its Past and Future—*Phil Ward, Richard Betts, Ron Cooper, Guillermo Olguin, and John Rexner*

Red Ant River Swizzle presented by Philip Ward
1 ½ oz Sombra Mezcal, ¾ oz lime juice, ½ oz Ed Hamiltons Cane Sugar Syrup, dash of absinthe, mint sprig. Build and swizzle in glass with pellet ice. Garnish with a mint sprig.

Gumptions #2 Cocktail presented by Philip Ward
2 oz Los Amantes Reposado Mezcal, ½ oz Luxardo Maraschino, dash of Regan's Orange bitters, dash of Angostura bitters. Stir and strain. Serve on the rocks and garnish with a grapefruit twist.

Oaxaca Old Fashioned presented by Philip Ward
1 ½ oz El Tesoro Reposado tequila, ¾ oz Illegal Joven Mezcal, dash of Angostura bitters, 1 barspoon agave nectar. Stir and serve on the rocks. Garnish with a flamed orange twist.

Now you can probably understand why it took 27,000 limes, nearly 300 pounds of fresh ginger, and thousands of sample cups to serve everything to the 17,000 attendees that year.

YEAR 9:25-29 JULY 2011

This particular Tales holds a very dear place my heart because our closest friends Audrey Saunders and Robert Hess tied the knot in true New Orleans style at the New Orleans Board of Trade—the surprise event at the annual Bartenders' Breakfast.

The invitation for the Bartenders' Breakfast.

With a cast of two dozen drinks luminaries in the wedding party led by a rockin' New Orleans funeral band into a crowd of nearly a thousand revellers, the surprise nuptials were presided by Plymouth Gin master distiller Sean Harrison and Beefeater Gin master distiller Desmond Payne and witnessed maid of honor Shawn Kelley and best man Ryan Magarian.

As a surprise wedding gift, lead guitarist for The Orchestra (Electric Light Orchestra, that is) Parthenon Huxley and I sang to the newlyweds The Beatles' song "All I Gotta Do" and Leon Russell's "A Song for You" while wedding cupcakes were distributed along with a bevy of cocktails. Once Space Capone kicked in with the jams and the cocktails continued flowing long after 3 AM, it was time to head to a regular after-hours hideout, Alibi, for a bit of bonding, pizza, and beers until the sun rose high in the sky.

Audrey Saunders and Robert Hess tie the know at the Bartenders' Breakfast.

Okay, okay. Of course, there were sessions on the days leading up to the blessed event and the standard bartenders' nightcap. Here's the rundown for the year:

Michel Roux: The 5-Million Case Man—*Philip Duff, Gable Erenzo, Alexandre Gabriel, and Michel Roux*

How to Build a Cutting Edge Ice Program—*Christy Pope, Chad Solomon, Richie Boccato, and Joseph Schwartz*

Brand Ambassadors—*Claire Smith, Nuri Djavit, Simon Ford, Allen Katz, John Lermayer, Dan Warner, and Angus Winchester*

Let's Not Sugar Coat It—*Gina Chersevani, David Guas, and Peter Smith*

Crooning to the newlyweds.

Your Own In-House Soda Program—*Andrew Nicholls and Darcy O'Neil*

Intellectual Property 2—*Eben Freeman, Riley Lagesen, and Sheila Morrison*

Occupational Hazards—*Charlotte Voisey, Kirsten Amman, and Ryan Magarian*

The Menu—*Angus Winchester and Sean Finter*

How the Global Drink Business Works—*Philip Duff*

Cool Bar Tools: Past, Present, and Future—*Dale DeGroff, Greg Boehm, Michael Silvers, and Jim Walker*

Beyond Punch: Colonial American Drinks—*Wayne Curtis*

Mysteries of Wood Maturation—*Dale DeGroff, Chauvet, Doug Frost, Francesco Lafranconi, and Alain Royer*

What the V.O.C. did for the Modern Bar— *Misja Vorstermans and Andrew Nicholls*

SavourEASE—*Gina Chersevani and Peter Smith*

Six Rums You'll Probably Never Taste Again— *Edward Hamilton*

The Negroni: An Iconic Cocktail—*Paul Clarke, Jacques Bezuidenhout, and Livio Lauro*

A History of Cocktail Glassware—*Angus Winchester*

Shhhhh! It's A Secret—*Charlotte Voisey, Jackie Patterson, Peter Schaf, and John Troia*

Ladies' Choice: Women Behind Bars— *Lynnette Marrero, Audrey Saunders, Kirsten Amann, Meaghan Dorman, and Misty Kalkofen*

Emperor's New Bitters—*Jacob Briars with Sebastian Reaburn*

The Bad, Bad Boys of Saloons—*Christine Sismondo and James Waller*

Swizzling Around The World, Here and Now— *Stanislav Vadrna*

What Would Aristotle Drink?—*Derek Brown and Charles "Kirby" Arinder*

The European Bartending Perspective— *Jonathan Pogash, Simon Difford, and Nicolas de Soto*

Around the World by (Brass) Rail—*David Wondrich*

Classic Hotel Bars—*Simon Ford, John Lermayer, Eric Lorenz, Ago Perrone, and Dan Warner*

The Chainsaw Shift—*Andrew Bohrer and Anu Apte*

Irish Whisky Legends—*Paul Pacult, John Cashman, John Ross, and Liam Donegan*

America's New Distilleries—*Matthew Rowley and Max Watman*

Timber! In History & Sensory Analysis—*Eric Seed, Derek Brown, Doug Frost and Wayne Curtis*

Below the Equator—*Jacob Briars and Sebastian Reaburn*

Eastern Eden—*Dave Broom and Takayuki Suzuki*

From Grain to Bottle—*Raj Nagra*

Cocktail Culture: Music—*Angus Winchester and Brother Cleve*

Who's Your Daddy? A Mai Tai Paternity Test—*Jeff Berry, Ian Burrell, and Steve Remsberg*

Making Love to His Tonic and Gin—*Jim Ryan and Charlotte Voisey*

Welcome to the Whiskey Business—*Christy Pope, Chad Solomon, Eric Castro, and Simon Ford*

David Embury and The Fine Art of Mixing Drinks—*Robert Hess*

Vanilla, Vanilla Baby—*Philip Duff*

The Sporting Life and Other Anecdotes—*Allen Katz, Patton-Bragg, Jeff Grdinich, Kimberly and Lynnette Marrero, Chris McMillian, Gary Regan, and David Wondrich*

The Chicken or the Egg?—*Tony Conigliaro, Dave Arnold, and Harold McGee*

Vinegar: The Other Acid—*Kelley Slagle, Karl duHoffmann, and Ashley Greene*

Ultra-Advanced Spirits Critics Workshop—*Paul Pacult*

Persia to Ponies: Julep Journey—*Jared Plummer, Jason Crawley, and Dylan Howarth*

Tequila's Rise and Redemption—*Frank Coleman, Ruben Aceves, Francisco Alcaraz, Junior Merino, and Armando Zapata*

Hotel Monteleone: 125 Years of History—*Philip Green, Jenny Adams, and Chris McMillian*

Sodatender or Barjerk—*Darcy O'Neil*

The Journey of Artemisia Absinthium—*Giuseppe Gallo, Jared Brown, Anistatia Miller, and Ago Perrone*

As American as Apple Brandy—*Paul Clarke and Misty Kalkofen*

H20 Cocktails—*Kathy Casey and Tony Abou-Ganim*

Born to Mix: Spirits "Made" for Cocktails—
Dushan Zaric, Jason Kosmas, and Marko Karakasevic

Barrel-Aged Cocktails—*Jeffrey Morgenthaler with*
Gable Erenzo and Naren Young

Before Man, the Plant—*Steve Olsen, Ron Cooper,*
Tomas Estes, David Grapshi, Misty Kalkofen,
Dr Ivan Salda–a Oyarzabal, David Suro, and Phil Ward

Drinking On Deadline—*Paul Clarke, Wayne Curtis, and*
David Wondrich

Hand-Crafted Cocktail: How Far is Too Far—
Cameron Bogue, Joe Fee, Craig James, and Ryan Magarian

Now do you get it? Now do you see why we who love cocktails and the people who make them plan our calendars each and every year for the past ten years to find ourselves in New Orleans and at Tales of the Cocktail®? I don't think any one of the great legends of our business—Jerry "The Professor" Thomas, Harry "The Dean" Johnson, The Only William, Harry Craddock of the Savoy, Harry MacElhone, Vic Bergeron, keep going—would ever have conceived that so many people from the around the world would gather year by year in one place to pay homage to the passion and the pride that is the cocktail. They do. And we hope they always will.

CHAPTER 2

A SPIRITED TOUR OF NEW ORLEANS

One thing you can say about the Crescent City, it is a cocktailian paradise and has been for as long as the city has served drinks, which is a pretty long time.

Joe Gendusa, author of *History with a Twist*, knows this better than anyone. Since 2001, he's been conducting New Orleans' Original Cocktail Tour through the French Quarter, narrating fascinating stories and secrets of the city's watering holes.

If you've never explored New Orleans' historic bars—and even if you think you know them all—take this armchair trip with Joe through some of the highlights. Better yet, head to the French Quarter to stroll and sip with Joe!

The 1938 *WPA Guide to New Orleans* sums up the city's relationship to its nightlife: "Traditionally, the 'city that care forgot', offers lovers of night life an unusual and varied number of nightclubs and bars, ranging from the more expensive ones in the better hotels, to the 'Harlem' clubs and honky-tonks of the less select sections of the city."

It's hard to find another place that so fully celebrates the history of its nightlife. Some of the places that the WPA recommended are sadly no longer with us, but we've noted them in this tour so at least you can stand before a memorable stop to breathe in the atmosphere of times past. Happily, many of the others are still there, so you can stop in for a glass or two of these living tributes to a grand history.

1 Jax Brewery, 600 Decatur Street

Built in 1890 on property worth $32,000 USD at the time, the Jackson Brewing Company produced Jax and Fabacher beers, employing 500 workers at its peak and producing

The Jackson Brewing Company as it looked when it was in full operation.

between 350,000 to 450,000 barrels per year. It was the largest independent brewery in the South before Prohibition, filling the French Quarter with a bready brewing aroma. Sadly it went out of business during the late 1970s.

Sold in 1982 to local investors for $10 million USD, the 65,000-square-foot property now houses more than 60 shopping and dining establishments as well as the Jax Collection—part museum, part shrine to the rich and colorful history that few beers experience. The panoramic views of the Mississippi River from the Promenade Balcony make a visit here worthwhile.

2 Pharmacy Museum, 514 Chartres Street

Some folks have claimed that this building was once the home of Mayor Girod, the man who masterminded a plot for Napoleon Bonaparte's escape from St Helena to New Orleans. And today, this museum tells the story of how

One of the impressive ground floor displays at the Pharmacy Museum.

the city's citizens were treated for numerous ailments back in the 1800s. (Peychaud's Bitters and a *coquetier* [egg cup] are displayed in window to remind visitors of a New Orleans' pharmacist's contribution to the legend of the cocktail.) But as the 1938 *WPA Guide to New Orleans* noted: "Examination of old records has disclosed what is probably an authentic account of the building. Six months after funeral services and mass were held at the St. Louis Cathedral for Napoleon, and almost a year after his death apothecary Dufilho purchased the site and erected his pharmacy there. The druggist opened his business on the ground floor and used the upper apartments for living quarters."

Just before Hurricane Katrina struck the city, in 2005, the second floor of this building was the first, temporary home to the Museum of American Cocktail.

3 Napoleon House, 500 Chartres Street

When Napoleon Bonaparte was exiled for a second time, in 1815, he was shipped to the island of St. Helena off the west coast of Africa. Three years later, a false rumour was reported in the *London Times* that the former emperor had escaped. Rumors also spread that he would flee to the New

World. Many people hatched plots to aid his flight including former New Orleans Mayor Nicholas Girod and Jean Lafitte's lieutenant, Dominic You, who planned, in 1821, to take the ship Seraphine to liberate Napoleon. According to the 1938 *WPA Guide to New Orleans*: "The boat was to be commanded by a certain Captain Bossier, and was to carry a daredevil crew of Baratarians under the

Not much has changed to Napoleon House's exterior since it was converted into a restaurant and bar.

leadership of the ex-pirate Dominique You. 'His [Dominique You's] intention was to effect a landing on St. Helena by night, abduct the imperial prisoner, and rely upon the fleetness of his vessel to outstrip pursuit.' It was claimed further that the plot had the knowledge and approval of Napoleon and his bodyguards, and that they had entered into the scheme."

Mayor Girod of New Orleans offered this—his home at the time—to the exiled emperor, should he arrive in the city. An apartment was prepared in this building to house Napoleon upon his liberation. But three days before their departure, word came that Napoleon was dead. (Dr Francesco Antommarchi, Napoleon's personal physician, brought the former emperor's death mask to New Orleans, where it is now on display at the Cabildo.) In 1834, Dr Antommarchi relocated one of his offices to this same building, "at which the poor of the city were given medical attention without charge."

The Impastato family, in 1914, took over the building. They ran the Napoleon Café and Grocery, but wasn't until 1940 that they opened a bar/restaurant called Napoleon House, which is famed for its Muffuletta, Pimm's Cup, and patio dining.

Did you know that laws in Louisiana differ from the rest of the United States, where laws are based on English Common Law? In Louisiana, the Napoleonic Code is still enforced.

PIMM'S CUP

2 oz Pimm's No. 1, 6 oz British-style lemonade (Sprite or 7-up). Pour ingredients into a collins glass filled with ice. Add an orange slice, lemon slice, apple slice, cucumber slice, sprig of mint, and serve.

4 Old Sazerac House, 13 Exchange Alley (116 Royal Street)

From the 1938 *WPA Guide to New Orleans*: "Before turning down Royal St from Canal, the visitor passes 'Monkey Wrench Corner' (downtown river corner), known to seamen all over the world as a meeting-place. Every major port has a corner so named. There yarns are swapped, and 'monkeys' (unemployed sailors) put the 'wrench' (borrow) to their more affluent fellow workers. Then one may pause for a glance at the birthplace of a drink New Orleans made famous the Sazerac Cocktail.

"When John B Schiller opened his place, in 1859, at 13 Exchange Alley, the rear of 116 Royal St, he called his establishment the 'Sazerac Coffee House' after the brand of cognac he used, which was manufactured by Messrs Sazerac-de-Forge et fils of Limoges, France. The old bar is now occupied by a barber shop, but the word 'Sazerac' may still be seen on the sidewalk."

Originally called the Merchants Exchange Coffee House when it was opened by Sewell Taylor, this saloon became better known as the Sazerac Coffee House when it was purchased, in 1850, by Aaron Bird. This spot was so popular that in 1872, the saloon had 18 bartenders presiding over a 125-foot bar. The signature drink was a toddy made with Sazerac-de-Forge et Fils brandy and Peychaud's Bitters that eventually became known as the Sazerac, America's first branded cocktail. (See also A Sidetrip Below Canal Street)

SAZERAC

Pack an old-fashioned or rocks glass with ice and water to chill the glass. In a second old fashioned glass, muddle a sugar cube or 1 tsp simple syrup with 3 dashes Peychaud's bitters. Add 2 oz rye whiskey. Stir to combine. Empty the ice from the first glass. Pour a splash of absinthe or Herbsaint into the glass and swirl to coat the sides of the glass. Discard any excess absinthe or Herbsaint. Pour the whiskey mixture into the coated glass. Twist a lemon peel over the glass and rub the rim of the glass with the peel. The peel can be discarded or placed into the cocktail.

Carousel Bar at the Hotel Monteleone, 214 Royal Street

Back in 1886, a Sicilian cobbler named Antoine Monteleone bought the 14-room Commercial Hotel that stood on this spot, which has now expanded to the 600-room Hotel

One of the Carousel Bar's finely detailed Mardi Gras faces.

Monteleone. Author Truman Capote loved the hotel. He that claimed that he was born there. But the truth is the hotel arranged his mother's transport to Touro Hospital where the future author was actually born, before returning to the hotel. But Capote was not the only literary great to spend time here.

Eudora Welty featured the Carousel Bar in her short story "The Purple Hat". Ernest Hemingway mentioned the bar in his short story "The Night before Battle". Tennessee Williams used the hotel as the setting for his play *The Rose Tattoo* and stayed there until he purchased a French Quarter manse. William Faulkner was also a frequent guest. The city's first revolving bar was installed here, in 1940, and makes a complete rotation once every 15 minutes. Before the Carousel Bar was opened, head bartender Walter Bergeron crafted the Vieux Carré Cocktail, in 1938, in the hotel's bar.

VIEUX CARRE COCKTAIL
½ teaspoon Benedictine, dash Peychaud bitters, dash Angostura bitters, 1/3 jigger each of rye whiskey, cognac, Italian vermouth, served over ice with a lemon twist.

Former site of Sloppy Jim's, 236 Royal Street

In the 1938 *WPA Guide to New Orleans,* Sloppy Jim's was mentioned as a popular night spot where the speciality drink was the Sloppy Jim Cocktail, a drink which appears to be lost.

Galatoire's, 209 Bourbon Street

This fourth-generation, family-operated establishment was founded in 1905 by Jean Galatoire. This site was formerly called Victor's Restaurant. Galatoire's nephews Leon, Justin and Gabriel purchased it from their uncle, in 1919, and became well known for their trout fillet served with maguery sauce as well as their crab dishes. The restaurant's bar had the city's largest "sit-down" space for sippers and had a status equal to none other than New York's Algonquin Hotel, home to the Algonquin Roundtable. In fact, Tennessee Williams had a favourite table at the back of the main dining room.

Original Absinthe House, 240 Bourbon Street

The original Absinthe House building was erected, in 1798, by Catalan importers Pedro Font and Francisco Juncadella, and operated as a combination residence and commission house for various foodstuffs until 1820, when it was converted into a grocery and later a boot shop. (There is a legend that General Andrew Jackson and Jean Lafitte, the Baratarian smuggler, planned the defense of New Orleans here in the entresol, a secret storage chamber situated on the second floor.)

The ground floor corner, in 1846, was converted into Aleix's Coffee House—owned by Jacinto Aleix and

his brother, who were Juncadella's nephews. Caeytano Ferrer—a Barcelona native who made his name tending bar at the old French Opera House—was hired in 1869 as chief bartender and eventually took over the establishment, in 1874, calling it the Absinthe Room. It wasn't long before, the spot was renamed again,

Absinthe House as it appeared circa 1920s.

in 1890, to Old Absinthe House. There it remained until US Marshals closed it down, in 1920, with the enactment of Prohibition in the United States. Pierre Casebonne purchased and moved the elaborate fountains, marble bar, and wall paintings to The Old Absinthe House Bar at 400 Bourbon Street, which was purchased by Owen Edward Brennan, in 1943, just before he opened Owen Brennan's French and Creole Restaurant across the street. Everything was returned to its original location in early 2004.

Arnaud's, 813 Bienville Street

Established in 1918 by "Count" Arnaud Cazenave, the original building dates to 1833, although now the entire restaurant complex is comprised of 12 buildings, some dating back to the late 1700s and reputedly operated as an opium den (the Richelieu Bar) and brothels before they were taken over. More than one waiter has been startled by a gentleman dressed in a turn-of-the-century tuxedo standing in the far left corner of the main dining room at windows. He seems to appear whenever the restaurant is at its busiest and most exuberant, smiling with a proprietary air. Another waiter saw a behatted woman leave the ladies room and stroll across the corridor to disappear through the wall. Inspection proved that the wall had been added in this decade and on the other side is a staircase at the spot she disappeared.

During Prohibition, a few chosen men had their own "skeleton" key to an unmarked entrance on Bienville Street. Once inside, they poured their own drinks and kept their own accounts. Count Arnaud—who reputedly drank champagne followed by 20 cups of bourbon and coffee (half-and-half) every day—went to jail for violating Prohibition laws.

The restaurant has 17 private dining rooms—most with call buttons to summon waiters—that can still be booked for intimate gatherings of 12 to 225 guests. Originally a "gentlemen's only area", the French 75 Bar was opened to the public in 2003, sporting a late-1800s bar and bar back that was custom built for a former Gulf Coast restaurant.

10 Brennan's, 417 Royal Street

Originally opened, in 1946, as Owen Brennan's French and Creole Restaurant on Bourbon Street, across from Brennan's Old Absinthe House Bar, Brennan's moved, in 1954, to its present location. The legendary building was erected, in 1794, by French artist Edgar Degas' great-grandfather, the engineer and inventor Vincent Rillieux. At various times in its history it was the home of the Bank of Louisiana (1805 – 1820) and of America's first chess champion, Paul Morphy, who won his title at the age of 15 in 1856. But as Brennan's Restaurant, it gained worldwide notoriety for its amiable owner, its "Breakfast at Brennan's" brunch menu, Eggs Hussarde, and Banana's Foster—a wonderful desert made with bananas, cinnamon and flamed with kirsch! Where's the kitchen of this landmark eatery? Chef Lazone Randolph's top-floor kitchen has a commanding view that overlooks the restaurant's secluded patio, with a glimpse of the French Quarter rooftops.

BRANDY MILK PUNCH
2 oz brandy, 8 oz whole milk, 1 tsp superfine sugar, freshly grated nutmeg. Shake over ice. Strain into a double old-fashioned, that is filled with cracked ice. Garnish with nutmeg.

CREOLE BLOODY MARY
4 oz vodka, 12 oz tomato juice, 2 ½ oz undiluted canned bouillon, 1 tb fresh lime juice, 2 tsp Pickapeppa Sauce, 2 tsp Worcestershire sauce, 2 dashes Pickapeppa hot red pepper sauce, 1/4 tsp salt (optional), lemon pepper seasoning, celery rib (optional). Shake all ingredients with ice in a shaker, just until chilled. Strain over fresh ice in 2 ½ oz. glasses. Sprinkle lemon pepper lightly over both drinks. Add celery stick if desired.

11 Antoine Amedée Peychaud's Apothecary, 437 Royal Street

Now housing Cohen's Antiques, Guns & Coins, this is the site where the young Creole pharmacist, Antoine Amedée Peychaud, opened his apothecary and in 1830 developed and began dispensing his aromatic digestive remedy Peychaud's Bitters. Legend has it that he offered his patrons a sample of his creation in a *coquetier* [egg cup] with brandy and sugar, which led to the legend that he created the original cocktail. His mixed drink was adopted in the late 1850s by the Sazerac Coffee House as its signature drink. Four years after Thomas Handy took over the business, in 1869, he altered the Sazerac, using American rye whiskey instead of brandy and adding a splash of absinthe to mix. But Peychaud's Bitters remained a key ingredient.

12 Antoine's, 713 St Louis Street

New Orleans' oldest restaurant—and reputedly the oldest in the south and the oldest in America still owned and operated by the same family—was founded, in 1840, by Antoine Alciatore, who opened Pension Alicatore on St Louis Street, a boarding house and restaurant that quickly earned its reputation for fine food. After his fiancée joined him from New York, in 1868, the couple moved down the block to the present location because the restaurant had outgrown its small quarters. Under his son Jules' direction as head chef, starting in 1887, the restaurant became famous for his Oysters Rockefeller, Pompano en Papiolette, and Baked Alaska. During Prohibition, the Mystery Room was accessed through a door within the ladies' room. Patrons would disappear to drink in this small secret parlor and return inebriated. The sumptuous Rex Room—named after the Mardi Gras Krewe of Rex—houses the family's fantastic collection of Mardi Gras memorabilia.

13 Pirate's Alley Café, 624 Pirate's Alley

Pirates Alley Café stands on the site of the former Spanish Colonial Prison of 1769. Called the "calabozo" it was demolished, in 1837, and the land sold to make way for the existing house. The famous pirate and American revolutionary hero, Jean Lafitte and his men were jailed in the "calabozo" by Governor Claiborne of New Orleans. Jean's brother Pierre Lafitte also served several months sentence here but eventually escaped.

14 Pat O'Brien's, 718 St Peter Street

During Prohibition, Benson Harrison (aka: Pat) O'Brien opened a speakeasy on the 600 block of St Peter Street called Mr O'Brien's Club Tipperary. The password to get in was "storm's brewin'". After repeal, in 1933, O'Brien moved his bar across street. The place became so popular, by 1942, it was forced to moved to its present location with O'Brien and partner Charlie Cantrell at the helm. Legend has it that the signature drink, the Hurricane, was invented when the owners were forced to buy fifty cases of rum just to buy one case of whiskey for the bar, while war-time grain shortages forced a short supply of any grain spirit. The bartenders teamed up to create the drink—its name inspired by the old speakeasy's password and served in a hurricane-lamp-shaped glass.

HURRICANE

2 oz light rum, 2 oz dark rum, 2 oz passion fruit juice, 1 oz orange juice, juice of a half a lime, 1 tb simple syrup, 1 tb grenadine. Squeeze juice from half a lime into shaker over ice. Pour the remaining ingredients into the cocktail shaker. Shake and strain into a hurricane glass. Garnish with a cherry and an orange slice.

15 Cat's Meow, 701 Bourbon Street

Opened in 1989, when American karaoke was still in its infancy, this bar was a pioneer of a concept that dreams can come true, if you've always dreamt of singing your heart out in public to your favourite tune.

16 Tropical Isle, 721 Bourbon Street

The strongest mixed drink that can be found on Bourbon Street—and in all of New Orleans—the Hand Grenade made its first appearance at the 1984 Louisiana World's Fair. But the Hand Grenade's secret recipe is closely guarded by the originators of this powerful brew, Tropical Isle, which has 5 additional locations in the French Quarter.

17 OZ, 800 Bourbon Street

Formerly the home of jazz great Pete Fountain's French Quarter during the 1960s and 1970s, the site is now home to one of the city's hottest gay dance clubs, which also sports a spectacular light show. This is a major gathering spot during Mardi Gras and Southern Decadence.

18 Bourbon Pub & Parade, 801 Bourbon Street

Featuring a downstairs video bar and an upstairs dance floor, this is the brother hot spot of the city's hottest gay dance clubs and party centrals for Southern Decadence and Mardi Gras.

19 Café Lafitte in Exile, 901 Bourbon Street

Reputedly the nations oldest gay bar, Café Lafitte in Exile's origins date back to 1933, when three partners leased Lafitte's Blacksmith Shop and opened it as a drinking establishment after repeal, welcoming their gay clientele with open arms whether they had money or not. However, the partners did not own the building and when the owner died, in 1953, the building went up for auction. The partners could not afford to buy and were forced to close. Years later, a box filled with unpaid bar tabs was discovered: The amount of those tabs would have bought the building many times over.

The partners were determined to reopen and acquired a lease down the street. For Café Lafitte in Exile's the grand opening, a costume party and mock funeral were held. Famed sculptor and regular, Enrique Alferez, designed the bar and the fountain of "the eternal flame". Tennessee Williams was a regular at the bar as were numerous other closeted celebrities.

Tom Wood of Wood Enterprises bought the building, in 1995, ensuring the bar would never be lost again and held a "lost our lease" party, burning the lease in the "eternal flame". The ashes are kept in a 20-ounce go-cup in the main office.

Café Lafitte in Exile has only closed once in its history, in 1998, when Hurricane George bore down on the city. Wood tearfully blew out the "eternal flame" for the first time in history. Less than 24 hours later the bar was back open.

20 Jean Lafitte's Blacksmith's Shop, 941 Bourbon Street

This is one of the oldest buildings in the entire city. Only the staircase in the Ursuline Convent, built in 1741, predates this structure in the French Quarter. Lafitte's is also one of the oldest bars in the US. It is a traditional Creole cottage: a briquette enter poteau [brick between post construction] that is commonly found here. Piracy was an accepted way of life

Lafitte's Blackmsith Shop, circa 1930s.

in the colonies and members of the Lafitte family were some of the best. The Lafitte brothers were privateers, holding a letter of marque allowing them to pillage ships that sailed under the flags of their enemies. Their booty provided the citizens of New Orleans with essential goods needed to support life in the colony. The most valuable cargo, by far, was African slaves.

Jean and Pierre Lafitte came to New Orleans, in the late 1700s, from San Domingue, Haiti. They set up this blacksmith shop as a front for their smuggling operation. Here, they arranged dealings with the city's wealthy citizens, providing them with goods they could obtain nowhere else! When the Americans took over—after the 1803 Louisiana Purchase—things changed. The French and Spanish laissez faire attitude did not mix well with puritan American attitudes. The Lafitte brothers were soon to become victims of that change.

William CC Claiborne, the first Governor of Louisiana, knew all about the Lafitte brothers' antics and put a price of $500 USD on the head of Jean Lafitte. Not to be outdone, Lafitte put a price of $1,500 USD on the Governor's head! In turn, Claiborne ordered an attack on Lafitte and his men in Grand Terre. It was the War of 1812, pitting the US and Britain in a trade dispute. British ships, in 1814, approached the city. A British admiral tried to cut a deal with Lafitte, offering him $30,000 USD and a naval commission. The ever-loyal Lafitte stalled and informed General Andrew Jackson, who consequently launched a successful Christmas Eve attack. A few days later, he also supplied the Americans with addition guns, ammunition, and men at the Battle of New Orleans. Lafitte and his men were all pardoned for their previous misbehavior and became American citizens.

General Andrew Jackson became New Orleans' hero and later President of the United States. Place de Armes was renamed Jackson Square, 37 years later. The Clark Mills statue of Jackson adorns the city's public square.

Now the Lafitte brothers' blacksmith shop is a landmark bar.

21 Tujaque's, 833 Decatur Street

Built, in 1827, on site of the old Spanish Armory this location became the site of Guillame and Marie Abadie Tujague's restaurant when they emigrated from France and, in 1856, established a breakfast and lunch spot in the French Market that served the local dock workers. The lunches were seven course affairs, but tradition says that Tujague's reputation was built on two dishes – a piquant remoulade sauce flavoring spicy cold shrimp and succulent chunks of beef brisket boiled with aromatic vegetables and served with a horseradish sauce.

Madame Begue's, opened in 1863, was their only competition, serving a 3-hour "brunch" to the hard-working dock workers. Philibert Guichet (who had purchased Tujague's before the owner died in 1912) and former Begue's employee Jean-Dominic Castet joined forces, in 1914, to purchase Begue's old property. It has been the home of Tujague's ever since. At one of the city's original "stand-up bars", Philibert Guichet Jr reputedly created the Grasshopper. It won second place in a New York cocktail contest which was held in 1928, during the depths of Prohibition. Others say that the competition occurred in 1919, just before Prohibition was enacted.

Cooling off with a Grasshopper at its birthplace in Tujagues.

During Prohibition, Tujaque's waiters carried contraband bottles in their aprons. It is reported that Federal Agent Isadore Einstein arrived in New Orleans to test how easily liquor was accessible and when he walked into Tujague's he got a drink in 37 seconds! The place has one of the most impressive collections of miniature spirits bottles ever seen, extending from the downstairs dining rooms through the upstairs.

GRASSHOPPER
¾ oz crème de menthe, ¾ oz crème de cacao, ¾ oz light cream or milk. Shake with ice and strain into a cocktail glass.

A SIDETRIP BELOW CANAL STREET

22 The Sazerac Bar and The Blue Room at the Roosevelt Hotel, 123 Baronne Street

Though it is renowned as the only place you could get a proper Sazerac, since 1949, the Sazerac Bar is not the only point of interest for cocktailians. The hotel's Blue Room was the location of the Ramos Bar, prior to Prohibition, when the Ramos Gin Fizz was shaken according to the original recipe with equal pride.

23 Former site of the Sazerac Bar, 300 Carondelet Street

WPA writers featured a few of the city's nightlife spots, clubs, and bars in its famous 1938 guide. One of them was the Sazerac Bar, which was "the only bar in the city where the famous 'Sazerac Cocktail' is mixed from a famous

The Sazerac Bar before it was moved the the Roosevelt Hotel.

recipe. The doors are open from 8 AM until 9 PM. Ladies are served only one day a year—Mardi Gras."

After Sazerac Coffee House owner Aaron Bird died, in 1869, a former clerk who worked for Sewell Taylor named Thomas Handy purchased the place. Four years later, he altered the Sazerac, using American rye whiskey instead of brandy and adding a splash of absinthe to the mix. When absinthe was banned in the United States, the ingredient was replaced with a New Orleans substitute, Herbsaint. The tradition carried on until the bar was relocated, in 1949, to the Roosevelt Hotel.

24 Former site of the Imperial Cabinet Saloon, corner of Gravier & Carondelet Streets

Author Stanley Clisby Arthur documented in his 1937 book *New Orleans Drinks and How to Mix 'Em* that Baton Rouge native Henry C Ramos invented the Ramos Gin Fizz (or New Orleans Fizz) the classic, creamy concoction that was like "drinking a flower".

Henry Charles Ramos, a first generation Louisiana native—his parents emigrated from Germany—arrived, in 1888, in New Orleans from Baton Rouge. He purchased the Imperial Cabinet Saloon at the corner of Gravier and Carondelet streets from Emile Sunier. He also bought a house on Rampart Street at the edge of the French Quarter for his growing family, and he set to work.

The saloon shared space with The Old Hickory Restaurant. (Some historians say that the invention took place at Meyer's Restaurant, but no one seems to give a location for this place.) There he remained until, in 1907, he purchased The Stag Saloon (712-714 Gravier Street), across the street from the Gravier entrance of the St Charles Hotel. In a city where business is built on friendships and connections, it isn't too much of a surprise that he bought it from a fellow member of the Elks, Tom Anderson.

It was there that Ramos's "New Orleans Fizz" gained notoriety. Customers patiently waited up to 20 minutes to observe and savour the creations that were shaken by his army of up to 35 "shaker boys".

When an old-time bartender with a few decades experience walked into the Ramos Brothers' bar around the turn of the century, he couldn't fail to be impressed. Frank Stutsman, whose President Cocktail became the talk of Chandler Brothers in Minneapolis (before both the drink and the bar faded into history), recorded his observations of the New Orleans Fizz—as they called the Ramos Gin Fizz back in 1909—and speculated on the recipe. He could nail down the parts of the preparation that took place in front of him. But what was in that bitters bottle? Here's Frank's guess, and his recipe:

The New Orleans Fizz

The New Orleans Fizz is a drink that we must only guess at. It is one of the most talked of drinks in the country. Ramoses' Place, New Orleans, is the home of this fizz and has been very popular for a good many years. When he, the sightseer or tourist, goes to New Orleans, he has not completed this trip without going to Ramoses' Place to get one of the great drinks; once drank, they never forget it. I will give it as near as can be gotten to it by guess. I don't think it has ever appeared in a book of this kind before.

The Mixture	The Fizz
Equal parts,	In a mixing glass put–
Orange Bitters,	Two or three cubes of ice,

Orange Flower Water,
Extract of Vanilla.

The juice of half a small lemon,
One large tablespoon of sugar, making it
very sweet,
The white of one fresh egg,
One teaspoonful of the mixture,
One jigger of Tom gin,
Two jiggers of cream or rich milk,
Shake at least two minutes,
Strain into stem goblet, and serve.

RAMOS GIN FIZZ

1 tb superfine sugar, 3-4 drops orange flower water, juice of ½ lime, juice of ½ lemon, 1 oz dry gin, 1 egg white, 1 oz of cream, 1 squirt seltzer water, 2 drops vanilla extract. Shake over ice for about 12 minutes and strain into a collins glass.

Beignets and café au lait at Café di Monde.

Now if you've managed to make your way to all of these cocktail landmarks, the sun has probably peeked its first rays in your direction. Time to head along Decatur Street back to the French Market for a café au lait and a plate of Beignets at Café du Monde. The staff has been serving revellers 24 hours a day since 1862, except for Christmas Day and when the occasional hurricane passes through.

CHAPTER 3

A SPIRITED A TO Z OF COCKTAILS

The Tales of the Cocktail® Way

Folks who have been attending Tales of the Cocktail® over the past decade have learned a lot about spirits, cocktails and mixed drinks, as well the history of the industry and the major players who sculpted the profession.

Want to know how much knowledge is exchanged at TOTC's events? Want to know how to talk cocktailian like a veteran? Here's an abridged A-to-Z—from absinthe to Zombie—of what's discussed, who is who, how to make some of the drinks to get you up to speed in a hurry.

Abou-Ganim, Tony

He learned bartending from his cousin Helen David at the Brass Rail Bar in Port Huron, Michigan. After graduating from college, Tony Abou-Ganim worked at Jack Slick's Balboa Café in San Francisco. In 1990, he assisted with the opening of Harry Denton's. Moving to New York City, in 1993, he worked at Po with chef Mario Batali. Two years later, Tony was back in San Francisco as part of the opening team for Harry Denton's Starlight Room.

Tony was hand-picked by Steve Wynn, in 1998, to create the cocktail program for the 22 bars at the Bellagio Resort & Casino. Currently operating his own beverage consulting firm that specializes in bar staff training, product education, and cocktail development, Tony also won the 2007 Iron Chef America "Battle Mango" competition with Mario Batali and released his first DVD *Modern Mixology: Making Great Cocktails at Home*. He also appeared on the Fine Living Network *Raising the Bar: America's Best Bar Chefs* TV series.

Helen David was born, in 1915, in an apartment above the storefront that would one day become her bar in Port Huron, Michigan. Her father passed away when she was 21, leaving her and her mother to run an ice cream parlor. Helen's mother took a bold, almost unheard-of step for a woman at that time, and converted it into a bar, the Brass Rail. Helen would run the bar for the next 70 years, serving beers, mixing Tom & Jerrys throughout the cold mid-western winters, and classic cocktails year round. She earned the moniker "First Lady of Port Huron" though her community activism, her caring, and her mentoring. One future bartender she inspired was her young cousin Tony Abou-Ganim. After Helen passed away in 2006, Tony created the Helen David Lifetime Achievement Award to honor her memory and to honor those who, like her, have given their lifetimes to the profession. The winners are as follows: 2008 Dale Degroff, 2009 Peter Dorelli, 2010 Brian Rea, 2011 Dick Bradsell.

As the National Ambassador of the US Bartenders Guild, and Associate Member of the Museum of the American Cocktail, Tony continues to educate about the history and lore of cocktails and lead the bar industry into continually improving the art of the cocktail.

Absinthe

Legend has it that absinthe was created by Dr Pierre Ordinare, a travelling physician fleeing the French Revolution and settling in the Neuchâtel region of Switzerland, where in 1792, he developed his distillate of anise, wormwood, and other botanicals. Some stories say that he gave his formula to the Henriod sisters who produced and sold the spirit as a medicinal elixir. Others reverse the transfer.

Eventually the secret passed into the hands of Major Dubied, who in 1797 with his son Mercellin and son-in-law Henry-Louis Pernod opened the first commercial absinthe distillery in Couvet. Overwhelming success instigated, in 1805, the building of a second distillery in Pontarlier, France. The product was renamed Pernod et Fils, which became the leading absinthe distillery and remained so until a freak fire started by a bolt of lightning and the 1915 French ban on absinthe production forced the manufacturer to reformulate its product into an anise spirit—a popular absinthe substitute along with pastis.

Alcohol

Alcohol means many things to many people. In this instance, we're talking about beverage alcohol—ethyl alcohol (aka: ethanol). This is the potable alcohol that is commonly distilled from fermented fruits, vegetables, sugar cane, or grains and then diluted with water to make it palatable, usually to about 30-50 percent alcohol by volume.

The molecular structure of ethanol looks like this (but smaller):

$$
\begin{array}{l}
\text{H} \\
\text{H3C-C-O-H} \\
\text{H}
\end{array}
$$

Alcoholics Anonymous, Al-Anon, Alateen

Alcoholics Anonymous (AA) is an international mutual aid movement that declares that its "primary purpose is to stay sober and help other alcoholics achieve sobriety." Now claiming more than 2 million members, AA was founded, in 1935, by Bill Wilson and Dr Bob Smith in Akron, Ohio. With early members, Wilson and Smith developed AA's Twelve Step program of spiritual and character development.

Al-Anon and Alateen—known as Al-Anon Family Groups—is an international "fellowship of relatives and friends of alcoholics who share their experience, strength, and hope in order to solve their common problems." They "help families of alcoholics by practicing the Twelve Steps, by welcoming and giving comfort to families of alcoholics, and by giving understanding and encouragement to the alcoholic." Alateen is part of Al-Anon and is their Twelve-step program of recovery for young people affected by another's drinking, generally aged 13 to 19 years (varies depending on each group). "Alateen groups are sponsored by Al-Anon members."

Al-Anon was formed, in 1951, by Lois Wilson, wife of Alcoholics Anonymous (AA) cofounder Bill Wilson. She recognized the need for such an organization as family members living with AA members began to identify their own pathologies associated with their family members' alcoholism.

Algonquin Round Table

Gathering initially as part of a practical joke, members of "The Vicious Circle," as they dubbed themselves, met for lunch each day at New York's Algonquin Hotel from 1919 until roughly 1929. At these luncheons they engaged in wisecracks, wordplay and witticisms that, through the newspaper columns of Round Table members, were disseminated across the country. Daily association with each other, both at the luncheons and outside of them, inspired members of what became known as the Algonquin Round Table to collaborate creatively. The entire group worked together successfully only once, however, to create a revue called No Sirree! which helped launch the Hollywood career of Round Tabler Robert Benchley.

Charter members of the Round Table included: Franklin Pierce Adams, columnist; Robert Benchley, humorist and actor; Heywood Broun, columnist and sportswriter (married to Ruth Hale); Marc Connelly, playwright; George S Kaufman, playwright and director; Dorothy Parker, critic, poet, short-story writer, and screenwriter; Harold Ross, *The New Yorker* editor; Robert E Sherwood, author and playwright; John Peter Toohey, publicist; and Alexander Woollcott, critic and journalist.

Membership was not official or fixed so many others moved in and out of the Circle. Some of these included: Tallulah Bankhead, actress; Edna Ferber, author and playwright; Raymond Austin, author and playwright and screenwriter; Margalo Gillmore, actress; Jane Grant, journalist and feminist (married to Harold Ross); Ruth Hale, journalist and feminist; Beatrice Kaufman, editor and playwright (married to George S Kaufman); Margaret Leech, writer and historian; Harpo Marx, comedian and actor; Neysa McMein, magazine illustrator; Alice Duer Miller, writer; Donald Ogden Stewart, playwright and screenwriter; Frank Sullivan, journalist and humorist; Deems Taylor, composer; and Peggy Wood, actress.

Anise Spirits, Anisette

Anisette is a sweet liqueur made by macerating neutral grain spirit with aniseed and about 16 other botanicals, and sweetening it with sugar. Its alcohol content is 25 percent ABV. Its popularity rose after the ban of absinthe, being first made as a legal alternative to absinthe. It is sweeter and less alcoholic then absinthe, pastis, or anisette.

Anise Spirits, Ouzo

An anise-based distillate, ouzo is the national spirit of Greece. Although its history is said to go back many centuries, ouzo's popularity escalated before the First World War, due in part to the ban on absinthe that was imposed in many countries. Pastis, raki, and sambuca also experienced a market surge around this time.

The word "ouzo" has a vague background. One theory states that it is derived from the Greek term "uzum" [grapes]. The second claims that the word descends from a term once stamped on crates of exported silkworm cocoons: "uso Massalia" [for use in Marseilles], which became known as a statement of quality.

Ouzo production is simple. Anise seeds are macerated with 96 percent ABV grape-spirit. Some producers also add star anise, cloves, coriander, or cinnamon to the mixture. The maceration is distilled into what is called "ouzo yeast"—a somewhat misleading term since fermentation and yeast culture are not involved in the process beyond the initial fermentation of the grapes to make the grape spirit. Ouzo was awarded a geographic designation of origin, in 2006, by the European Union.

Anise Spirits, Pastis

In French, the word "pastis" means "mixture". An extremely popular summertime drink in France, pastis is consumed diluted to a 5:1 ratio with water. Once the water is added to the pastis, the drink "louches" which means it turns a milky white color. (This occurs when hydrophobic essential oil droplets from the botanicals that were concentrated in the ethanol during distillation are released by additional water.) Another popular serve is known as "tomate", which adds a splash of grenadine syrup to the drink.

Pastis was first created as an alternative to absinthe once the ban on its production was enacted in 1915 in France. This distillate possesses the same anise-based formula as absinthe. However it is made without wormwood (Artemisia absinthium) and is much lower in alcohol by volume, being diluted to 40-45 percent ABV. Of the dozens of pastis brands available, two are major players: Ricard and Pernod, the

original commercial producer of absinthe. The two brands
are very different in style. Pernod is made by distillation
rather than maceration, and contains no liquorice, imparting
a lighter character. Ricard is a more traditional pastis and is
the world's most popular pastis.

Anise Spirits, Raki

Raki is an unsweetened, anise-based spirit that is produced
by distilling pomace and then rectifying it with anise seeds
in alembics. It is similar to ouzo, arak, and pastis as well as
anise castellano. In Turkey, raki is the unofficial national
drink. It is mixed with water to create a louching that
turns the clear liquid an opaque milk-white. This drink is
popularly called "aslan sutu" or "arslan sutu" [lion's milk].

Anise Spirits, Arak

Arak or araq is a clear, colourless, unsweetened anise-based
distillate that is popular in the Near East, especially in the
Levant, and North Africa. This spirit is not to be confused
with arrack, which is a popular spirit in Southeast Asia
produced from coconut, sugar cane, and other sweet bases,
even though the Balinese arrack is spelt "arak". Sometimes
this spirit is also confused with "aragh" which is the
Armenian term for vodka. In some regions, arak is mixed
with tea or juices instead of water. As an apéritif, arak is
served with mezza such as olives, bread and hummus, or nuts.

Apéritif

Apéritifs are traditionally consumed before a meal to
stimulate the appetite. Bitter botanicals that stimulate
digestion are part of every formula. The most famous
apéritif is Campari, but the category includes products such
as Picon, Aperol, Dubonnet, and Suze. Low to medium in
alcohol strength, apéritifs are made by macerating botanicals
with spirit and/or wine plus sugar.

Cocktails can be imbibed as apéritifs. So can specific
wines and beers. The key factor is that to be called an
apéritif, the beverage has to be very dry to whet the appetite.
The word "apéritif" derives from the Latin term "aperire"
which means "to open".

Aperitivo

From the Latin aper, aperitivo literally means "to prepare
the stomach". Traditionally lower in alcohol than a cocktail

and containing bitter elements, aperitivi were historically thought to stimulate digestive juices. Also called aperitif, this category includes countless mixed drinks as well as fortified and bittered wines. The most prominent aperitif wine is vermouth.

Apple Juice

Filtered apple juice is transparent with a distinctive golden hue. All apple juice must be refrigerated after opening. Some apple juice is sold refrigerated, but it not necessarily different from UHT packaged or bottled pasteurized juice. Apple juice can be made fresh in a fruit and vegetable juicer, but it oxidizes quickly and turns brown. Stirring in about 10 ml lemon juice for each apple will slow the color change. Unfiltered apple juice is commonly called cider in North America. In Europe, cider is a fermented alcoholic beverage produced from apple juice.

Aquavit

Aquavit or akvavit (meaning "water of life") is distilled from either grain or potatoes. It is flavoured with herbs such as caraway seeds, anise, dill, fennel, coriander, or grains of paradise. One rare exception is made in Aalborg, Denmark, which distills its spirit with amber. Clear aquavit is called taffel.

The earliest known written reference to aquavit is found in a 1531 letter from the Danish Lord of Bergenshus castle, Eske Bille, which was sent to Olav Engelbrektsson, the last Archbishop of Norway which mentions that the accompanying package contained "some water which is called Aqua Vite [aquavit] and is a help for all sort of sickness which a man can have both internally and externally." Popular belief throughout Scandinavia has it that aquavit is an aid to the digestion. Traditionally, the spirit is taken with Christmas lunch. It is also consumed with regular meals as well, especially with starters such as pickled herring or smoked fish.

Armagnac

Locals used to joke that when crows travelled over the Armagnac region they flew upside down so they couldn't see how poor the area was. A loyalty to old traditions surrounding the Armagnac industry is one of many reasons the spirit continues to embrace respect.

Armagnac is historically the oldest style of French brandy. Some historians allege that Arnaud de Ville-Neuve created Armagnac in the mid-1300s. What is documented is that the spirit went into full-scale production throughout the Armagnac region by 1411 and was registered as a commercial product three years later in Saint-Sever. It was a popular therapeutic remedy, particularly to calm the nerves.

The key difference between Armagnac and cognac is the grape selection. Armagnac is distilled from traditionally-produced, unfiltered, natural white wines of Ugni Blanc, Folle Blanche, Bacozza, and Colombard grapes. Distilled in a traditional two-column continuous still (alambic armagnacais) or a pot-still (alambic charentais), Armagnac is distilled only once to 54-60 percent ABV which produces a more intense fruit character and a rustic palate. The collection is lower than that of cognac, which is 72 percent ABV. Distillation takes place during the winter following the harvest and by law must be completed by early March after the harvest. The spirit is then aged for long periods in oak from the Monlezun forest in Bas Armagnac which imparts a subtle hue and complex palate.

Arrack

A popular spirit in South and South East Asia, arrack is one of the world's oldest spirits. The distillate is made with various base elements depending on the region: fermented fruit, grain, sugarcane, sugar palm, or coconut palm sap. One of the most famous styles, Batavia arrack is produced in Indonesia, using red rice and a local yeast as activators. The sugarcane juice is fermented before being distilled in a Chinese style of pot still.

Distilled from coconut palm sap, Lambanog is a style that is unique to the Philippines.

Asian Flush (aka: alcohol flush reaction)

Evolution happens faster than we previously thought. At least in the case of the Asian Flush this may be the case. This super annoying, cancer causing, alcohol inhibiting gene may have arisen from mankind's inability to consume alcohol in moderation after it was first discovered that it offered a pleasurable reaction. It was recently discovered that the populations of southern China were the first to ferment grain into potable alcohol. Rice wine must have caused a serious threat to survival in a land that depends on rice cultivation as a major food source. A variant gene arose that degrades alcohol to a chemical that is not intoxicating but makes nearly one third of all people of East Asian descent turn red in the face when they drink alcohol.

Aviation Cocktail

The first printed mention of the Aviation Cocktail was found in *Recipes for Mixed Drinks* (1916), by Hugo R Ensslin, a New York bartender at the Hotel Wallick in Times Square. It became one of the top cocktails during the age of aviation when greats like Lindbergh were national heroes. The drink became very well known from the version in *The Savoy Cocktail Book* (1930) written by Harry Craddock of London's American Bar at the Savoy Hotel.

AVIATION COCKTAIL
2 oz dry gin, 1/4 oz maraschino liqueur, 1/2 oz fresh lemon juice, dash of creme de violette. Pour the ingredients into a cocktail shaker filled with ice. Shake well. Strain into a chilled cocktail glass. Garnish with a flamed lemon twist.

B

Bacardi Cocktail

Some cocktails have multiple recipes. Some cocktail recipes have multiple names. The Daiquirí has both multiple recipes and multiple names, while the Bacardi Cocktail has only multiple names. Originally, the Bacardi Cocktail may have been the same drink as the Daiquirí. That is, a combination of Cuban rum, fresh lime juice and sugar, without additional fruit or juice.

The Bacardi Cocktail became famous during a legal dispute, in 1936, in which the Bacardi Company sued the Barbican Hotel for serving a Bacardi Cocktail that was made using a rival rum brand. The New York Supreme Court sided with the brand, stating that a Bacardi Cocktail could not be made without using Bacardi rum.

BACARDI COCKTAIL
1 1/2 oz Bacardí silver rum, 3/4 oz lemon juice, 1 tsp grenadine syrup. Shake ingredient over ice. Strain into a glass and serve.

Baker, Charles H.

Documentor of the cocktail's broad global appeal in his 1939 seminal two-volume seminal work *The Gentleman's Companion: Being an Exotic Cookery and Drinking Book*, American journalist Charles H. Baker Jr spent much of his life travelling around world and chronicling food and drink recipes in his "Here's How" column, which appeared in *Esquire* during the 1940s. His work also appeared in *Town & Country* and *Gourmet* magazines.

Bananas Foster

A luscious flambéed dessert of bananas spiced with cinnamon, dark rum, butter, and banana liqueur that's topped with a generous scoop of ice cream, Bananas Foster was born when Owen Brennan of Brennan's Restaurant challenged his chef Paul Blange to create a new dessert with one of New Orleans' major imports—bananas. (During the early 1950s ships bearing the fruit from Central and South America docked in the Crescent City as the major port of entry.) Named after Brennan's friend Richard Foster, nearly 35,000 pounds of bananas are served up in this decadent form at the restaurant every year.

Bar Spoon

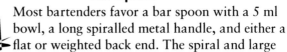
Most bartenders favor a bar spoon with a 5 ml bowl, a long spiralled metal handle, and either a flat or weighted back end. The spiral and large back end are useful for building layered drinks such as a Pousse Café, a Shooter, or a Champagne float. The weighted back end of the spoon can also be used for light muddling, and for cracking ice. The modern bar spoon is a direct descendant of the French medicine spoon (aka: culliére de medicament). The second most common bar spoon has a fork in place of the muddler. This spoon/fork traces back to Germany in the Middle Ages, though its name is the result of its popularity in Elizabethan England. The Queen enjoyed a dessert called sucket, consisting of fruit cooked in syrup. The fork was used to eat the fruit, while the spoon was used to eat the syrup. Thus it became a "sucket fork" or "sucket spoon".

Baum, Joe

Joseph Harold Baum (August 17, 1920 – October 5, 1998) was an American restaurateur and innovator responsible for creating the country's first themed restaurants, including masterpieces such as The Four Seasons Restaurant, Windows on the World, and the restored Rainbow Room. He was the first restaurateur to bring the finest contemporary architects, artists and designers into his restaurant designs. He was best known in the later part of his career for renovating and reopening the Rainbow Room in New York's Rockefeller Center, in 1987, and for the redesign of Windows on the World, in 1996, at the World Trade Center. Baum was inducted into the Culinary Institute of America Hall of Fame in 1995.

Bax, Matthew

Cofounder of Tippling Club and a world renowned mixologist, Matthew Bax discovered his talent for bartending during his days as an artist in Germany. Returning to Melbourne, in 2001, he opened his bar Der Raum (meaning "the space" or "the room", in German). The establishment quickly became an incredible success, giving Matt the opportunity to pursue his career as an artist by day and as a mixologist by night. Der Raum won the 2009 Australian Cocktail List of the Year at the Sydney Bar Awards.

Matt established the Melbourne Temperance Society, in 2005, which now also boasts a successful chapter at the Tippling Club in Singapore. Through regular master class events the Society helped establish Melbourne as one of the world's leading cocktail cultures.

Bax hopes to repeat that same success with the Singapore chapter, which hosts regular interactive and fun master class events and brings international experts to present and unlock the mysteries of fine mixing and spirit appreciation.

Tippling Club has secured numerous accolades. In 2009 alone, it received: World's Top 20 Bars in 2009 (Asia Pacific, *Bartender Magazine*), 4 Stars by *IS Magazine*, and GOLD at the Awards of Excellence for Singapore Parties 2009.

Beaumont, Stephen

While best known for his six books and countless articles on beer, Stephen is also recognized and respected as a writer and authority on spirits from artisanal absinthe to small batch bourbons. He has even written extensively about the pairing of spirits with food, dating back to long before such ideas were at all fashionable.

A regular contributor to ten magazines and three blogs, Beaumont also consults with hospitality groups on beer and drinks menus, teaches servers and consumers alike everything they need to know about beer and spirits— but may have been afraid to ask. He also hosts tastings, tutorials, and dinners across North America and around the world.

Beer, Ginger

Made by fermenting a combination of fresh ginger, sugar, water, lemon juice, and a yeast-laden fungus known as the ginger beer plant, ginger beer is widely available in North America and Europe, but is most popular in Britain and Greece. Ginger ale is an acceptable substitute. But a better option is to use fresh ginger muddled with simple syrup and a touch of lemon juice, then topped with sparkling water. Ginger beer and any substitute for ginger beer should be fizzy.

Beignets

The rest of the US has doughnuts, but New Orleans has Beignets. This deep-fried French pastry (aka: choux pastry) liberally dusted with confectioners' sugar are pure perfection. Introduced by French colonists during the 1700s, these are an early morning or late morning treat when served piping hot and accompanied with café au lait or chocolate milk.

Bellini

The Bellini was created around 1934 and named in 1948 by Giuseppe Cipriani, founder of Harry's Bar in Venice, Italy. Because its unique pink-peach color reminded Cipriani of the color of a saint's toga in a painting by 15th-century Venetian artist Giovanni Bellini, he named the drink after the artist to pay homage to a retrospective exhibit that took place in Venice that year. The drink started as a seasonal speciality at Harry's Bar, a favorite haunt of Ernest Hemingway, Sinclair Lewis, and Orson Welles. Later, it also became popular at the bar's New York counterpart. After an entrepreneurial Frenchman set up a business to ship fresh white peach pureé to both locations, the Bellini has become a year-round favorite.

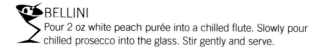

BELLINI
Pour 2 oz white peach purée into a chilled flute. Slowly pour
chilled prosecco into the glass. Stir gently and serve.

Bénédictine DOM

Benedictine (aka: DOM) is believed to be one of world's
oldest liqueurs. Created at the Benedictine abbey of Fecamp,
France, around 1505, by Venetian monk Don Bernardo
Vincelli, this "elixir of health" blends 27 botanicals
including thyme, cinnamon, coriander, nutmeg, hyssop,
angelica and cardamom. Macerated in spirit, distilled in
copper stills, and aged separately in oak for three months,
the liqueur marries four separate extractions that are again
aged before bottling.

The Burnley Miners' Club in Lancashire is the world's
largest single consumer of Benedictine liqueur, after
Lancashire military regiments acquired a taste for it during
the First World War.

Cocktails using Bénédictine besides the B & B include the
Frisco, Derby, Singapore Sling, Vieux Carré, and Monte Carlo.

DERBY COCKTAIL
2 oz bourbon, 1/4 oz Bénédictine, dash Angostura bitters. Stir
over ice and strain into a cocktail glass. Garnish with a lemon
twist.

Bergeron, Trader Vic

It all started when Victor Jules Bergeron was a waiter at
San Francisco's Fairmont Hotel and owned a grocery store
on San Pablo Avenue in Oakland. His son—Victor, Jr—
grew up loving the food business, living with the family in
an apartment above the store and helping out downstairs.
A childhood accident cost him a leg, but left him with a
penchant for telling colorful stories.

With a nest egg of $700 and carpentry help from his
wife's brothers—plus his mother's pot-bellied stove and
oven—Vic built a cosy pub across the street from the store,
in 1932, calling it Hinky Dink's. He was a popular host.
And after trips to the South Seas and Havana, two years
later, his tropical drinks lured San Francisco celebrities such
as Herb Caen to cross the bay. He served up Americanized
adaptations of Polynesian/Chinese dishes with flair, adding
to the delights of the place. By 1936, the transformation was
complete—Trader Vic's was born.

Herb Caen affectionately commented, "The best

restaurant in San Francisco is in Oakland."

Trader Vic's cocktail legacies include his version of the Mai Tai, invented in 1944, and the Starboard Light. The world had beaten a path to Vic's door by the end of the Second World War, prompting journalist Lucius Beebe to write in an introduction to the 1946 *Trader Vic's Book of Food and Drink*: "Trader Vic's is ... more than an Oakland institution. Its influence is as wide as the Pacific and as deep as a Myrtle Bank punch. Vic's trading post is long on atmosphere, and it is possible for the ambitious patron with a talent for chaos to get into more trouble with obsolete anchors, coiled hausers of boa-constrictor dimensions, fish nets, stuffed sharks... Hawaiian ceremonial costumes, tribal drums, boathooks and small bore cannon than the waiters can drag him out of in a week."

Berries, Black

High in ascorbic acid, blackberries bring a tart sweet-and-sour flavour to a cocktail as well as a deep purple color. Frozen and very ripe berries release more color than other berries. Blackberries may be placed in a shaker and shaken with a drink. This is faster than muddling and allows you to strain out the seeds.

Berries, Raspberries

Sweeter than blackberries and with a lighter color, raspberries bring soft fruit and floral notes to a drink as well as a blush color similar to white zinfandel wine. Frozen and very ripe berries release more color than other berries. Raspberries may be placed in a shaker and shaken with a drink. This is faster than muddling and allows you to strain out the seeds.

Berries, Strawberries

Strawberries differ in size, shape, and color as there are approximately twenty different varieties of strawberries are grown commercially around the world. Frozen and very ripe berries release more color than less ripe specimens. Strawberries may be placed in a shaker and shaken with a drink. This is faster than muddling and allows you to strain out the seeds.

Berry, Jeff

(aka: Beachbum Berry) One of *Imbibe* magazine's "25 Most Influential Cocktail Personalities of the Past Century," Jeff Berry is the author of five books on vintage Tiki drinks and cuisine. He's been profiled in *The New York Times*, Salon.com, *Wine Enthusiast*, New Orleans' *Times-Picayune*, and Miami's *Sun-Sentinel*. He's also been featured in the *Washington Post, Wall Street Journal, New York Post*, and *W* magazine.

Jeff created the cocktail menu for the Luau in Beverly Hills and co-created the "Tiki+" drink app for iPhone and iPad, which *Macworld* magazine called "beautifully rendered".

His original cocktail recipes have been printed around the world, most recently in *Bon Appetit* and *Fine Cooking* magazines, *Food & Wine Cocktails 2010*, and the 67th edition of the *Mr. Boston Official Bartenders Guide*.

Jeff has appeared on Martha Stewart Living Radio and Radio Margaritaville, has written for *Saveur* and *Caribbean Travel & Life* magazines, and currently conducts tropical drink seminars and tastings across the US and Europe. He serves on the advisory board of the Museum of The American Cocktail.

Bitters, Angostura

A digestive aid developed by German physician Dr Johann Gottlieb Benjamin Siegert, Angostura bitters was named after the town in which he was based while working in Venezuela as a surgeon general for Simon Bolivar's army. Siegert began to sell his bitters produced from local ingredients, in 1824, establishing a full-scale distillery six years later. The product was exported beginning in 1853 to Britain, Europe, and North America. In 1875 the distillery was moved from Angostura to Port of Spain, Trinidad, where it remains today. The exact formula is a closely guarded secret, with only five people knowing the whole recipe.

Bitters, Aromatic

Alcoholic beverages that are heavily infused with botanicals. Originally created to harness the medicinal properties of various herbs, spices, and barks to relieve digestive ailments, aromatic bitters are a key ingredient in many cocktails. Once a hugely popular category, bitters usage died out until recent times—with only the largest brands surviving the blows of Prohibition in the US, shifting public taste, and the development of better treatments for digestive distress during the 20th century. Due to their highly bitter nature, a dash or two is all that is needed to add complexity and to balance the sweetness of a mixed drink. Angostura, Peychaud, and Fees are some of the oldest brands still available. Modern mixologists are not only rediscovering the value of this ingredient, they are custom-blending their own aromatic bitters formulas.

Bitters, Digestive

There are many somewhat sweeter bitters that are often classed as liqueurs or digestifs such as Carpano, Punt e Mes, Cynar, or Becherovka. These are usually consumed as an after-meal drink to aid digestion. Digestive bitters were traditionally consumed in a small glass or used as a primary ingredient in a mixed drink. Examples of digestive bitters are Campari, Aperol, Suze, Jagermeister, and Underberg.

Bitters, Orange

There are a number of brands of orange bitters on the market today including Regan's Orange Bitters, Bitter Truth Orange Bitters, Fee Brothers Orange Bitters, and Angostura Orange Bitters. A simple orange bitters can be made by steeping the peel from one whole orange and stick of cassia bark in 500 ml of blended whisky for about 24 hours or to taste.

Bitters, Peychaud's

Created around 1830 by Creole pharmacist Antoine Amédée Peychaud, this is a gentian-based bitters that possesses a lighter body, sweeter character, and a more floral aroma than Angostura bitters. Its primary flavours are bitter cherry and almond. Peychaud's Bitters is a key component of the Sazerac cocktail. Today, it is produced by the Buffalo Trace Distillery of Frankfort, Kentucky.

Blending a Drink

Place ingredients in an electric blender with ice. Ensure the top is securely closed. Turn the blender on. If ice prevents the blades from spinning, turn the blender off. Remove the blender cup from the blender, and use a bar spoon to reposition the contents. Close the lid securely and try again. Blending a drink generally takes from

20 to 30 seconds. A hand blender cannot be substituted for a standard blender to make frozen drinks as it cannot properly crush the ice.

Blood & Sand Cocktail

A cocktail made with blended Scotch whisky, it was introduced in 1922 by Harry Craddock in London. The red juice of the blood orange (aka: sanguinello) in the drink helped link it with the recently released film that the cocktail was named after, Rudolph Valentino's bullfighter movie *Blood and Sand*. The recipe first appeared in the 1930 *Savoy Cocktail Book*. A variant combines all ingredients in a collins glass, adding another splash of orange juice then flaming an orange twist over it.

BLOOD & SAND COCKTAIL
3/4 oz blended Scotch whisky, 3/4 oz Cherry Heering, 3/4 oz Italian sweet vermouth, 3/4 oz blood orange juice. Shake over ice and strain into a cocktail glass.

Bloody Mary

Born in Paris on 18 February 1900, Ferdinand "Pete" Petiot was a bartender in the right place at a very auspicious time. Tomatoes had been used in cooking since the 1730s. Tomato juice was on French menus as early as 1914, as a temperance drink. When Smirnov's vodka arrived in Paris, in 1920, Petiot had just landed a job at Tod Sloane's New York Bar at Cinq Rue Daunou.

Petiot's obituary that appeared in the 8 January 1975 edition of the *San Francisco Chronicle*, states: "Petiot was said to have been experimenting with vodka after having been introduced to it in Paris in 1920. He settled on a mix of half vodka and half tomato juice...." Now remember: we are talking about French tomato juice, a bit sweeter than British and considerably sweeter than the first American tomato juice brands.

The name Bloody Mary? In a January 1972 interview with *The Cleveland Press* reporter Al Thompson, Petiot explained that the first two customers to try his creation "were from Chicago, and they say there is a bar there named the Bucket of Blood. And there is a waitress there everybody calls Bloody Mary. One of the boys said that the drink reminds him of Bloody Mary, and the name stuck."

Moving to the US, Petiot married and eventually took a post at the King Cole Bar in new York's St. Regis Hotel. His tomato creation went on the bar menu as the Red Snapper and then as the Bloody Mary, hyped up with Tabasco sauce, salt, lemon juice, and Worcestershire sauce.

Bloody Mary variations include: Frozen Bloody Mary; Bloody Margaret; Flaming Bloody Mary; laming, Frozen Bloody Mary; Bloodless Mary; Screw Mary; Bloody Mary-land, or Crabby Mary; Slutty Mary; Bloody Milo; and Bloody Charlie.

BLOODY MARY
1 1/2 oz vodka, 3 oz tomato juice, 1/2 oz fresh lemon juice, dash Worcestershire sauce, dash Tabasco sauce, salt, pepper. Build in a highball. Stir gently. Garnish with a celery stalk or a lemon wedge.

Bootlegger

Some historians believe that the term "bootlegging" originated during the Civil War, when soldiers would sneak liquor into army camps by concealing pint bottles within their boots or beneath their trouser legs. By Prohibition, the word was applied to a person who smuggled liquor over land as opposed to a rum-runner, who illegally transported alcoholic beverages by water.

Boston Shaker

See Shaker, Boston.

Bottled Cocktail

There are two different definitions for the term "bottled cocktail". One refers to drinks pre-bottled by bartenders in their establishments for service. These days we call these batched cocktails. The other describes a mixed drink commercially produced for at-home consumption. The Heublein Company introduced the concept of premixed drinks aimed at consumers during the late 1800s. The public bought these premixed cocktails that didn't require shaking with ice because water was added to achieve dilution. All the purchaser had to do was chill the bottle and pour it into a glass.

There was only one problem: Any drink that contained citrus had a limited freshness life. Thus, the category largely died out during the mid-1960s. Yet, because of its content, Campari still sells its iconic bottles of Campari and soda in Italy with great success. Boutique, single-serve, bottled cocktails are being offered at bars and by low-volume producers that offer better quality than was previously possible.

Bourbon

A barrel-aged American whiskey that is primarily distilled from corn, bourbon's name is derived from its location—Old Bourbon in what is now Bourbon County, Kentucky. The county itself was named after the French royal House of Bourbon. Produced by the descendants of Scots-Irish immigrants during the 1700s who exported their whiskey tradition with them, many of these emigrant families settled in Kentucky and Tennessee to escape the 1790s Whiskey Tax imposed by President George Washington, who built a whiskey distillery after he left office. Possessing a sweeter character than its Irish and Scots counterparts, bourbon and its close sibling Tennessee rye whiskey feature in a number of early American cocktails.

Brandy

Derived from the Dutch word "brandewijn" [burnt wine], brandy is a distillate made from wine, pomace, or fruit. There are numerous terms used to describe brandies distilled from wine or pomace that vary from region to region: Armagnac, Cognac, brandy de Jerez, sherry, pisco, and lourinha are just a few. Many are aged in casks to achieve an amber to dark hue.

Fruit brandies follow a similar regional pattern. American applejack and French calvados are distilled from apples. French eaux-de-vie as well as German and Austrian schnapps are made from a wide variety of stone fruits including cherries and plums.

Briar, Jacob

The 42 BELOW "Vodka Professor" and the 7th most famous bartender in New Zealand, Jacob's cocktails have been featured in the *Motueka Guardian*, the *Levin Chronicle*, and the *Bangkok Post*. His cocktail training once led the news on Fiji's national television. But then it is a very small country.

Jacob is famous for being a mine of mostly completely useless information about spirits and cocktails and other pointless trivia. He is the only bartender who can claim to equally love vodka and Fernet Branca.

Brown, Jared & Miller, Anistatia

(aka: The Historians) Award-winning drink historians Jared Brown and Anistatia Miller launched their website *Shaken Not Stirred®: A Celebration of the Martini*, on Halloween night 1995, which led, in 1997, to the publication of their book of the same name by HarperCollins and, in 1998, by Europa Verlag. Their homage to bubbly, *Champagne Cocktails*, was published in 1999 by ReganBooks.

This inseparable couple has written some breakthrough findings in drinks history for *Mixology* (Germany), *Imbibe* (UK), *CLASS Magazine*, *Wine Spectator*, and *Cigar Aficionado*. They are contributing editors of the World's Best Bars web site and cocktail history gurus on Drinkology. com. They also write for *The Guardian* and *Observer Food Monthly* in Britain.

During their 20-year collaboration, they have written and published over 30 books, including *Cuba: The Legend of Rum* and *The Mixellany Guide to Vermouth & Other Apéritifs*.

Brown and Miller founded Mixellany® Limited, in 2004, which publishes not only their own books but original works by other esteemed cocktailians including Geraldine Coates, Charles Vexenat, Dave Broom, Nick Strangeway, Gary Regan, and Mardee Haidin.

Their two-volume work *Spirituous Journey: A History of Drink*, won Best Drink History in the UK awards in both 2009 and 2010 from the Gourmand International Cookbook Awards. They were honoured with the 2010 *CLASS Magazine* Award for Best Drinks Writing and the coveted 2011 Communicators of the Year Award from the International Wine & Spirits Competition.

In their spare time, the couple documented and preserved the 10,000-bottle private wine and spirits collection, Exposition Universelle des Vins et Spiritueux, from 2006 through 2009, on Île de Bendor, France.

Brown is also the master distiller for the award-winning Sipsmith Independent Spirits—the first copper-pot based distillery to start up in London in 189 years and one of only four gin distilleries located within the city limits.

Building a Drink

All ingredients are combined in a glass without shaking, stirring, or straining. This technique is most often used in sparkling drinks such as highballs and Champagne cocktails where it is desirable to preserve the effervescence. In this case, it is not necessary to shake or stir as the motion created by the rising bubbles will mix the drink.

Bull Shot

The Bull Shot is a snapper that uses beef bouillon or beef consommé in place of tomato juice. It may also contain salt, pepper, lemon juice, Tabasco sauce, and Worcestershire sauce.

Other snapper variations on the Bloody Mary theme include: The Bloody Bull with both bouillon and tomato juice, the Caesar, Bloody Caesar, Bloody Clam, Clam Digger, Red Wings or Clammy Mary (Clamato replacing tomato juice, much more popular in Canada than the traditional Bloody Mary) and the Commander White (pineapple juice replacing tomato juice).

BULL SHOT
1 ½ oz vodka, 3 oz chilled beef consommé, dash Worcestershire sauce, dash Tabasco sauce, celery salt, salt, pepper. Shake ingredients over ice. Strain into a highball glass filled with ice.

Bum's Rush

Giving someone the bum's rush: It's a common turn of phrase used to describe the act of a bar bouncer, security guard, or some authority figure forcibly removing a person (the "bum") from a location by twisting said person's arm behind his back and pushing the forearm skyward while rapidly pushing ("rushing") the body toward an exit. A similar term is "86-ing" or being "86-ed", which originated in soda fountains where it was a code for an item out of stock, and was later broadened to mean anything or anyone whose presence in the establishment was at an end.

Bureau of Alcohol, Tobacco, Firearms

The Bureau of Alcohol, Tobacco, Firearms and Explosives (formerly abbreviated to BATF)—now called the Alcohol and Tobacco Tax and Trade Bureau or TTB—is a division of the US Department of Justice that investigates the unlawful use, manufacture, and possession of firearms and explosives, acts of arson and bombings, and illegal trafficking of alcohol and tobacco products. The agency also regulates the sale, possession, and transportation of firearms, ammunition, and explosives in interstate commerce. It also regulates the content of alcoholic beverages produced and imported to the US, including ingredients, labelling, and safety warnings.

Cachaça

The national spirit of Brazil, cachaça is distilled from fresh sugarcane juice. It differs from rum in that rum is made with molasses, and rhum agricole is distilled from boiled sugarcane juice. The spirit can vary in strength from 38 percent to 51 percent ABV. It can be bottled aged or unaged. By law up to 6 grams of sugar can be added after distillation.

Cachaça is distilled in two different ways, yielding two different spirit styles: Made in column stills, it is known as "industrial cachaça", then sold to bottling companies who may adjust the spirit to their own specifications. Made in pot stills, it is known as "artisanal cachaça", which is considered to be a better quality of spirit. These spirits are often aged in a broad variety of woods to achieve a more complex character.

Brazilians consume nearly 99 percent of all cachaça that is produced—about 8 litres per capita annually. Most cachaça is made into the national cocktail, the Caipirinha.

Caipirinha

Caipirinha is Brazil's national drink, made with cachaça, sugar, and lime. While both rum and cachaça are made from sugarcane-derived products, most rum is made from molasses. Specifically with cachaça, the alcohol results from the fermentation of fresh sugarcane juice that is afterwards distilled. The Caipirinha itself is closely related to the Draque, Draquecito, and Mojito, as all contain citrus, sugar, and sugar-based spirit components.

CAIPIRINIHA

2 ½ oz cachaça, 3 tsp superfine sugar, 1 ½ limes chopped into cubes. Place the lime cubes and sugar into a mixing glass. Muddle the fruit and sugar into a rough paste. Add the cachaça and a few ice cubes. Shake about 6 times. Pour into a highball glass without straining and serve.

Calvados

Distilled from fermented apple cider, calvados is one of the three great French brandies and originates from Basse-Normandie in northwestern France. In order to protect the quality and ensure its provenance, the region was awarded an AOC [Appellation d'Origine Controlée], which means it can only be made in a designated area and according to specific regulations to be called calvados. This spirit gained its greatest popularity during the phylloxera plague that decimated the French wine making industry during the mid-1800s.

Spin the Liqueur Bottle (at the Farmers Market)

Mixologists with a DIY streak love to make their own mixers and flavourings. Which ingredients would you pluck from the farmers market to flavour your own liqueur, syrup or brandy? Spin the bottles so they point to the correct picks. (*Answers below*)

Liqueur	ANSWER	Ingredient
1. Chambord		A. apple
2. Calvados		B. pomegranate
3. Triple sec		C. blackcurrant
4. Cynar		D. raspberry
5. Grenadine		E. artichoke
6. Frangelico		F. orange
7. Crème de Cassis		G. hazelnuts

Answers:
1. D; 2. A; 3. F; 4. E; 5. B; 6. G; 7. C

Casey, Kathy

Celebrity chef, mixologist, entertaining expert, and pioneer in the bar-chef movement, Kathy is a savvy spotter of what's hot on the culinary and cocktail scene. She is a frequent TV and radio guest and speaker on trends and entertaining. She is also the presented on *Kathy Casey's Liquid Kitchen*™ on the Small Screen Network.

An accomplished writer, she is the author of nine cookbooks, including Sips & Apps. Casey also blogs as Ask the Expert Mixologist for Food Network Canada and Amazon's Al Dente. In 2010 she was lauded as one of the 50 Best Twitter Chefs by Guide to Culinary Schools; her blog Dishing with Kathy Casey was included in Saveur.com's "Sites We Love".

Kathy owns Kathy Casey Food Studios®—Liquid Kitchen™ a food, beverage and development agency. She also owns Dish D'Lish® Cafés and a few speciality products.

Castellon, Fernando

Starting his career as a bartender at London's Quo Vadis members' club, in 1994, Fernando then worked in places such as Maxim's in Brussels and the gastronomic restaurant Léon de Lyon in Lyons. He joined the LVMH group, in 1999, to work as a brand ambassador and has travelled to more than 25 countries to study drinking habits and train bartenders.

Fernando chose the French gastronomic capital of Lyons to establish Bar Expertise, in 2002, which is his independent training center. That same year he published a facsimile of the 1887 edition of Jerry Thomas' *How to Mix Drinks*. He was one of the first to recognize the value of reprints for educating a new generation of bartenders.

He published a complete cocktail timeline in 2004, in his own book *Larousse Cocktails*, which was translated into seven languages. He also wrote, in 2006, *Grand Livre du Bar et des Cocktails*, classifying for the first time cocktail recipes by main flavours to suit a cocktail wheel that was specially created for the book.

Cate, Martin

Owner of Smuggler's Cove San Francisco, which features over three centuries of rum cocktails, Martin is a certified IBA Spirits Professional and member of the United States Bartenders Guild. He is a tasting judge for rum competitions across the US, Europe and the Caribbean, and has conducted seminars at Tales of the Cocktail, The Hukilau, Bourbon and Branch's Beverage Academy, and Tiki Oasis.

Smuggler's Cove was named North American Cocktail Lounge of the Year at the 2011 Nightclub & Bar Awards, and one of the ten best cocktail lounges in America by *Travel + Leisure Magazine*.

Named by *The San Francisco Chronicle* as one of six Bay Area bartenders "essential in defining cocktail culture here and across the country," Martin and his original cocktails have been featured in *The New York Times, San Francisco Magazine, Food & Wine, Huffington Post, USA Today*, the *Today Show*, and more.

Celery

The ubiquitous garnish on the Bloody Mary since it first appeared during the 1960s on the Bloody Marys served at the Pump Room in Chicago's Ambassador East Hotel, the celery stalk can be split lengthwise or partially peeled to create a more delicate looking garnish. Along with green peppers and onions it is part of the "holy trinity" of Creole cuisine.

Champagne Cocktail

The Champagne Cocktail dates back at least to the Civil War era in the United States, when it appeared in Jerry Thomas's 1862 book *How to Mix Drinks*. The effervescent drink was also chosen by *Esquire* magazine as one of the Top 10 Cocktails of 1934. Although its popularity has waned, it still has unflagging adherents, especially among select sophisticates, who still believe that it is the definitive cocktail.

CHAMPAGNE COCKTAIL
1 white sugar cube, 2 dashes Angostura bitters, ¾ oz cognac, 6 oz champagne. Place the sugar cube onto a spoon and add the bitters. Drop the soaked sugar cube into a champagne flute and add the cognac. Slowly fill the glass with champagne, and serve.

Charming, Cheryl

(aka: Miss Charming™) She's been tending bar for over 25 years. She has a popular info-rich website, a blog, a 5000 question iPhone drink trivia app, a beverage consultation business, and more. Cheryl has tended bar around America, on a Caribbean cruise ship, and at Walt Disney World. While working at WDW she became the bar trick/bar magic instructor for Disney's F&B training program "Quest for the Best".

She has authored fourteen books including *Miss Charming's Guide for Hip Bartenders* and *Wayout Wannabes*, and a series of books on Martinis, Margaritas, Sangrias, and tropical drinks.

Cheryl created her bar and cocktail related website, www.misscharming.com, during the late 1990s. Her main focus today is building the site's Master Mixology section, which will eventually be seen at MasterMixologyStore.com. She's involved with hosting and participating in events for Tales of the Cocktail®, the Annual Cocktail Film Fest, and teaching "edutaining" cocktail classes for Royal Caribbean Cruise Line passengers. She is also a member of The Bartenders Guild and The Museum of the American Cocktail.

Chartreuse

A French liqueur made since the 1740s by Carthusian monks, Chartreuse is a distilled alcohol aged with 130 herbal extracts. Named after the monks' Grande Chartreuse monastery, located in the Chartreuse Mountains near Grenoble, France, Chartreuse gives its name to a distinctive tint. It is one of a handful of liquors considered to age and improve in the bottle.

There are two styles: Chartreuse Verte (55 percent ABV), which is a naturally green liqueur made from 132 plants. Its colouring comes from the botanicals' chlorophyll; and Chartreuse Jaune (40 percent ABV), which has a milder and sweeter character and aroma.

Cherries, Cocktail

Originally made by macerating any of a variety of cherries (commonly Royal Ann, Rainier, or Gold) in a calcium chloride or sulphur dioxide brine solution and then bottled with a sugar syrup, tinted with food colouring, and fortified with preservatives. Artificially colored and flavoured red cocktail cherries frequently replace the classic dark-red maraschino cherries in cocktails.

Cherries, Maraschino

Made by macerating Morello cherries in maraschino liqueur made from Marasca cherries. The cherry stones are crushed in the process of making maraschino liqueur, releasing a subtle almond flavour. The fruits are then lightly sweetened and bottled without additives.

Chersevani, Gina

Gina began bartending in the Washington DC area while attending college. After graduation, she landed her first martini-making gig at Penang. She helped design the beverage program at 15 Ria and consulted with Poste Moderne Brasserie in the Hotel Monaco, designing an imaginative cocktail menu that secured her reputation in the nation's capital.

Ashok Bajaj hired Chersevani as his master mixologist for Rasika, in 2006, where she began experimenting with exotic ingredients like saffron, cloves, and lotus. She assumed the role of the Bar Chef for the Neighborhood Restaurant Group, in 2008, stationed primarily at gastropub EatBar and the upscale neighborhood restaurant Tallula.

Chersevani was named in 2008 as one of *The Beverage*

Journal's "10 Mixologists to Watch" and won Absolut
Vodka's 2008 "Best Martini" competition.

After taking over the beverage program at Chef Peter
Smith's PS7's Restaurant, in 2009, Chersevani and Smith
launched a Food and Cocktail Pairing Menu, available full
time at the bar—a first of its kind. The pair has hosted a
number of dinners for liquor company launches, including
Plymouth Gin, Balvenie 17, Blue Coat Gin and Vieux Carre
Absinthe, and Del Maguey Mezcal Dinner.

Chinese Spirits

Formerly known as "Shao Jiu" and "Sorghum Spirit",
Chinese spirits are a difficult category to classify. There are
two strength categories. The first, "spirits with low alcohol
content" range in strength from around 20 percent up to
38 percent ABV. The second, "spirits with high alcohol
content" range in strength from 41 to 65 percent ABV.
The latter spirits are traditionally more popular in colder
northern China regions. Since the late 1940s these spirits are
also classified by fermenting agent and distilling base; and
by different flavour groups (such as Maotai or "soy sauce
flavour").

Clarke, Paul

A contributing editor to Imbibe magazine, Paul Clarke is
the spirits and cocktails columnist for SeriousEats.com and
a frequent contributor to the *San Francisco Chronicle*. His
articles have appeared in *The New York Times*, *Wine &
Spirits*, *Seattle Met*, and other publications.

Clarke has documented his exploration of fine spirits
and mixology, since 2005, on The Cocktail Chronicles: one
of the internet's first exclusively spirits-and-cocktail-related
blogs. Clarke is also the founder and moderator of Mixology
Monday, a monthly online cocktail party that has attracted
scores of participants world wide since its 2006 debut.

Profiled on Salon.com and in the *Seattle Post-
Intelligencer*, Clarke's blog has been declared an "Online
Find" by the *Boston Globe*, designated a "Favorite Blog"
by *PC Magazine* in 2009 and 2010, and selected as a
spotlighted "Pick" by Yahoo! Paul has been quoted in
articles on spirits and cocktails in publications, including
The New York Times, *Washington Post*, *Seattle Times*,
Pittsburgh Post-Gazette, and *Tiki Magazine*. He has
discussed spirits and mixology on National Public Radio and

on the Seattle NBC affiliate's *Evening Magazine*.

Classic cocktail

A classic cocktail, in this case, is defined as a cocktail that appears after the publication of Jerry Thomas' 1887 *Bar-Tender's Guide* but before the 1933 repeal of Prohibition in the United States. This is distinct from a traditional cocktail from pre-1887 or a modern cocktail from after the end of Prohibition, but created before 1990.

Clift, Ryan

Cofounder of Tippling Club, Ryan Clift took an early interest in cooking, leaving school at an early age to work his way up the kitchen's career ladder.

Ryan moved to Australia, in 1999, and excelled as Head Chef of Vue de Monde with Shannon Bennett, winning three hats in The Age Good Food Guide. He met Matthew Bax in Melbourne and they became close friends, sharing an interest in all things epicurean. Before long, they started to discuss business ideas and eventually decided to pursue the Tippling Club in Singapore.

Matthew and Ryan started up the Tippling Club, located at Dempsey Hill in August 2008 and correlated their expertise to present an impeccable degustation menu. Matthew creates a unique cocktail to match every dish prepared by Ryan, complementing the tastes on the palate. Within its first year of opening, the Tippling Club has been hailed as one of Singapore's top restaurants, and *Appetite* magazine, in its annual roundup of the region's top 100 establishments, declared Tippling Club as Asia's no. 1 venue.

Cocktail hour

The cocktail hour has been used as a marketing technique by restaurants and hotels as a means of attracting patrons during the hours between 4 PM and 6 PM. It is similar to the Italian tradition of aperitivo, which is a daily ritual that occurs between the hours of 5 PM and 7 PM.

Cocktail lounge

While most Americans in the post-World War II boom years would never achieve the high-life of a Kennedy, they could easily escape to a cocktail lounge and lead an imagined glamorous—even libertine—lifestyle, if only for a couple of hours. Commuter trains and increased automobile usage meant the neighborhood tavern was no longer the only place to drink in public. Cocktail lounges became the ultimate escape—an outpost located far away from home and neighbors. Music, fashion, and interior styles grew around this carefree environment, where cocktails stimulated a carefree, sophisticated lifestyle.

Cocktail party

Although many believe the inventor of the cocktail party to be British novelist Alec Waugh, who in 1924, found a need for this pleasant interlude before a dinner party, an article in a May 1917 edition of the *St Paul Pioneer Press* credits Mrs Julius S Walsh Jr of St Louis, Missouri as the originator. Mrs Walsh invited 50 guests to her house on a Sunday at high noon for a one hour fête. "The party scored an instant hit," the *St Paul Pioneer Press* declared. And within a matter of weeks, cocktail parties became "a St. Louis institution". (Alec Waugh noted that the first cocktail party in London was hosted, in 1924, by wartime artist Christopher Nevinson.)

Cocktail shaker

A device used to mix beverages by shaking. Ice is put in the shaker along with cocktail ingredients and the whole is manually agitated. It quickly cools the mixture and adds necessary dilution via the melting ice. There are at least three varieties of cocktail shakers: Boston shaker; cobbler shaker; and French shaker. (See shaker, Boston; shaker, cobbler; and shaker, French.)

Coconut

A key ingredient in the Puerto Rican Piña Colada, sweetened cream of coconut has become, since the 1950s, a mainstream bar ingredient. Cream of coconut is made by simmering the shaved or grated flesh from a mature coconut in an equal part of water (or coconut water) until it is frothy. The resulting "milk" is strained through a cheese cloth, and the "cream" is gathered once it rises to the top. Packaged in tins, the contents begins to turn bad a few days after it is opened. The most popular brand of commercial cream of coconut is Coco Lopez.

Coconut milk and green coconut water have recently

joined the commercially-sweetened cream version as part
of the bartender's repertoire, adding more flavour and less
sugar to drink recipes.

Coffee

Coffee should always be served fresh. For mixing
in cocktails, it should be used within a few hours.
One caution: hot coffee will melt a lot of ice. It
can be refrigerated prior to use in a cocktail to reduce the
amount of dilution it brings to a drink. Whether coffee is
used in a hot or cold drink it should be brewed as strong as
possible.

Coffee, Espresso

Espresso is a special roast of coffee that is
compressed in an espresso machine. Once it is
positioned, steaming hot water is forced through
it under pressure to release intense flavour with as little
water as possible. For this reason, espresso is called for
specifically in many recipes such as the Vodka Espresso. If
a drink made with espresso is to be shaken, shake it harder
and a little longer than a normal drink. You have done it
properly when the espresso creates a dense creamy froth on
top.

Coffey, Aeneas

Born in Calais, France in 1780, Aeneas Coffey moved with
his family to their ancestral home in Dublin, where he was
educated at Trinity College. After he finished his studies, he
worked as a gauger in Dublin for a quarter of a century. This
afforded him ample opportunities to observe all manner
of still designs. Legend has it that he was severely beaten
by moonshiners when he attempted to shut down illegal
distilling operations in his territory. Because of his job, he
knew how much alcohol could be produced in a given period
of time. He also knew that the new continuous stills had a
flaw: to obtain a higher proof spirit, receiving vessels had to
be changed so multiple distillations could take place.

Tired of either his government job or the beatings
that came with it, Coffey opened the Dock Distillery on
Grand Canal Street in Dublin. The main feature of his
operation was a customized still of his own design—or
rather Robert Stein's design for a patent still with a minor
modification. Coffey inserted two pipes into Stein's column

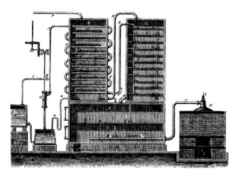

still that allowed a greater portion of the aqueous vapors to re-circulate into the still instead of flowing into the receiver with the spirit, thus eliminating the need for multi-distillation and producing a spirit with a higher proof and lighter character. In 1830, he was granted Patent #5974 for his second design, a two-column continuous still.

Within five years of receiving his patent, Coffey had enough orders to warrant the establishment of Aeneas Coffey & Sons in London. (The company is still in operation today under the name John Dore & Co Limited) He closed Dock Distillery four years later and devoted all of his time to building and installing stills in others' distilleries.

You could say that Coffey merely trumped Stein's original concept by perfecting it. But without Coffey's improvements and the overwhelming popularity of his column still, the Scotch whisky market might never have grown by the leaps and bounds it did during the two decades that followed his achievement.

Cognac

One of the three major French brandies—along with Armagnac and calvados—Cognac is distilled from white wines in two chauffes—that is, in two separate heatings, using a special Charentais copper still. The Cognac distillation season closes on March 31ˢᵗ following the harvest.

The cognac production area was delimited by the decree of 1 May 1909. Based on the soil features described by the geologist Henri Coquand in 1860, six Cognac growing areas (crus) were delimited and then ratified by decree in 1938: Champagnes (Grande and Petite Champagne), Borderies, and Bois (Fins Bois, Bons Bois, and Bois à Terroirs). The Crus received their names when the local forests were cleared at the beginning of the 19th century.

Collins

Back in 1874, people in New York, Pennsylvania, and elsewhere in the United States would start a conversation by saying: "Have you seen Tom Collins?" After the listener predictably reacts by explaining that they did not know a Tom Collins, the speaker would assert that Tom Collins was talking about the listener to others (often saying bad things) and that Tom Collins was "just around the corner", "in a [local] bar," or somewhere else near. If a man walked into a bar looking for Tom Collins, the bartender would claim he had just left and send him on to the next place.

The conversation about the nonexistent Tom Collins was a proven hoax of exposure. In The Great Tom Collins hoax of 1874 as it became known, the speaker would encourage the listener to act foolishly by reacting to patent nonsense that the hoaxer deliberately presents as reality. In particular, the speaker desired the listener to become agitated at the idea of someone talking about them to others such that the listener would rush off to find the purportedly nearby Tom Collins. Similar to The New York Zoo hoax of 1874, several newspapers propagated the very successful practical joke by printing stories containing false sightings of Tom Collins. The 1874 hoax quickly gained such notoriety that several 1874 music hall songs memorialized the event.

The recipe for the Tom Collins first appeared in the 1876 edition of Jerry Thomas' *The Bartender's Guide*. Since Manhattan-based Thomas would have known about the widespread hoax, and the contents of the 1876 published book were developed during or right after The Great Tom Collins hoax of 1874, the hoax event is the most plausible source of the name for the Tom Collins. Popularity reached such a frenzy that just about any spirit was mixed in the same fashion and given a new first name followed by the Collins sobriquet (Ron, John, Jock, etc). A new drink family was born.

TOM COLLINS
2 oz gin, 1 oz fresh lemon juice, 1 tsp gomme syrup, soda water. Build the gin, juice, and syrup in a collins glass filled with ice. Top up with soda water. Garnish with a lemon twist.

Column Still

Invented in 1826 by Robert Stein, the column still (aka: continuous still or patent still) behaves like a series of pot stills by forming a long vertical column that allows vapour to pass through each successive stage at a progressively declining temperature. The result: the vaporized alcohol content is twice that of a pot still, reaching 96 percent ABV, instead of 40-50 percent ABV. It also increases the output capacity of the distillation process with a single charge (load of fermented mash and water). This system radically changed the Scotch whisky business, allowing producers to distil great amounts of lighter, smoother spirit and gave birth to the blended Scotch whisky industry.

The column still eventually transformed the way that Cuban-style rum and vodka were produced before the turn of the century, especially after improvements made by Aeneas Coffey further increased output and reliability.

Coquetier

The French term for an egg cup, *coquetier* was once thought to be the origin—through mispronunciation—of the word "cocktail". In its own right, it is most historically famous as the presumed vessel of choice into which 19th century New Orleans pharmacist Antoine Amédée Peychaud is said to have mixed his proprietary bitters with cognac, creating a signature drink which would one day evolve into the Sazerac.

Cordials

In the United States, liqueurs are sometimes called cordials: spirits that are infused with fruits, nuts, botanicals, and creams that are then sweetened. In Britain, the term refers to a non-alcoholic syrup-like beverage made from similar ingredients that is commonly served diluted with water or soda water. The most famous is Rose's Lime Cordial, which Americans call Rose's Lime Juice. Ribena, a blackcurrant cordial, is also an extremely popular British cordial brand.

Cosmopolitan Cocktail

The Cosmopolitan Cocktail (aka: Cosmo) seems to have evolved from the Kamikaze, with cranberry juice cocktail added to give it a rosy hue. Its origins are disputed. It is likely that the drink was created independently by different bartenders since the 1970s. Cheryl Cook claims to have created it in a South Beach bar in Miami, around 1985, where she added cranberry juice cocktail to a Kamikaze made with Absolut Citron. (The product was officially launched in 1988.) The recipe was also made with regular vodka in numerous regions including San Francisco and Vancouver. The internationally recognized version of the Cosmopolitan was created by Melissa Huffman and Toby Cecchini, using fresh lime juice instead of lime cordial and replacing the triple sec with Cointreau. Dale DeGroff popularized the drink when he introduced a variation at New York's Rainbow Room and served it to Madonna.

One thing is sure: The Cosmopolitan has become a modern classic that entered the mainstream thanks to the TV series *Sex and the City*.

COSMOPOLITAN COCKTAIL
1 ½ oz citron vodka, ½ oz Cointreau, ½ oz fresh lime juice, 1 oz cranberry juice cocktail. Shake ingredients over ice. Strain into a cocktail glass. Garnish with a lime wheel.

Cosmopolitan Daisy

The forgotten parent of the Cosmopolitan Cocktail (aka: Cosmo) is made with gin, lime juice, raspberry syrup, and triple sec. It was called the Cosmopolitan Daisy in the 1933 book *Pioneers of Mixing Gins at Elite Bars*. Essentially, a Daisy is a Sour that contains a dash of grenadine or raspberry or other red-hued syrup or juice. Originally, it finished with a splash of soda water. But this option seemed to disappear in some recipes such as the Cosmopolitan Daisy. In Latin American Spanish, the word margarita means daisy.

COSMOPOLITAN DAISY
2 oz Beefeater Gin, 1/2 oz triple sec, 1/2 fresh lemon juice, 1 oz fresh raspberry syrup. Shake ingredients over ice and strain into a cocktail glass.

Cosmopolitan Magazine

Cosmopolitan (aka: Cosmo) is a women's magazine that is published around the world. First appearing in the United States, in 1886, the publication started its life as a family magazine and later transformed into a literary magazine. Under Chief Editor Helen Gurley Brown, author of *Sex and the Single Girl*, the magazine was transformed into a women's publication in true 1960s style, featuring articles on relationships and sex, health, careers, self-improvement, celebrities, as well as fashion and beauty. Published by Hearst Magazines, *Cosmopolitan* has 63 international editions, printed in 36 languages, which are is distributed in more than 100 countries.

Craddock, Harry

In the 2 May 1927 edition of the *Marion Star* newspaper from Marion, Ohio, a curious note appeared: "The last legal cocktail in America is reputed to have been mixed at the old Holland House on Fifth Avenue by a Harry Craddock. Word drifts back from London that Craddock is now frosting the shakers at the Savoy. He took a boat the next morning pouting and has never returned."

Harry Craddock is a legendary figure in the cocktail world. Arriving in the United States, in the 1890s, he learned his trade in some of America's most famous bars including Chicago's Palmer House Hotel as well as Manhattan's Holland House and Knickerbocker Hotel before Prohibition.

Returning to Britain with his American wife and daughter, in 1920, he took the position of head bartender at the Savoy's American Bar throughout the 1920s and 1930s. He is best known for writing the 1930 *Savoy Cocktail Book*, the most important cocktail book since Jerry Thomas. Creator of the White Lady, Blood & Sand, and the White Cargo, Craddock is credited with the invention of over 250 cocktails before moving to the bar at London's Dorchester Hotel from which he retired in 1947.

Cranberry Juice

A key ingredient in the Cape Codder and the Cosmopolitan Cocktail, cranberry juice is pressed from cranberries, and then heavily sweetened as cranberries are nearly as tart as lemons. The most common sweeteners used are apple juice and white grape juice. White cranberry juice is made by pressing cranberries that have not fully ripened. The flavour is virtually identical to regular cranberry juice.

Cream, Double

Slightly heavier than American heavy cream and whipping cream (both of which may be used as substitutes), double cream has a butterfat content of around 48 percent. In comparison, whipping cream contains 30-40 percent butterfat. It is sold fresh and must be refrigerated prior to use.

Cream, Ice

As with all drink ingredients, the best quality ingredients produce the best cocktail. Ice cream may seem inappropriate in a balanced cocktail, but the contents of ice cream: sugar, cream, egg, are all ingredients in many traditional and classic mixed drinks such as flips. The White Cargo, Mi Amante, and Soyer au Champagne simply use ice cream as a premix of these ingredients. A portion of ice cream equal to the amount of spirit will provide a proper balance of sweetness.

SOYER AU CHAMPAGNE

1 tbs French vanilla ice cream, 6 dashes maraschino liqueur, 6 dashes orange curaçao, 6 dashes brandy. Build ingredients in a champagne flute or coupe and fill with champagne. Garnish with an orange slice and a cherry.

Cream, Single

Comparable to half-and-half in the United States, single cream has 10-12 percent butterfat and is frequently used in drinks such as the Alexander.

Cuba Libre

This Highball is often referred to as a Rum and Coke in the United States and Canada, where the lime juice is optional. Despite tales told about the drink's invention during or after the 1898 Spanish-American War, the Cuba Libre (meaning "free Cuba") does not appear in print in reference to this particular recipe until the 1960s. Prior to that time, Cuba Libre was the name of a drink that was very similar to a Daiquirí or a Cancháncharra.

CUBA LIBRE

1 ½ oz dark or white rum, juice of half a lime, cola. Build the ingredients in a highball filled with ice. Garnish with a lime wedge.

Cucumber

A widely cultivated gourd, the cucumber is not savoury but neutral in flavour and is very similar to the flesh of a watermelon close to the rind. In Britain, cucumber replaced borage blossoms and leaves in the Pimm's Cup for many years. However, British bartenders are reintroducing these lovely purple blossoms as a garnish in traditional Pimm's Cups. Like all fruit and vegetables meant for consumption, cucumbers should be washed before cutting and serving them.

Daiquirí

The Daiquirí is one of six basic drinks listed in David Embury's 1948 classic The Fine Art of Mixing Drinks. Daiquiri is at its essence a Rum Sour made with Cuban rum, key lime juice, and sugar. There are several versions, but those that gained international fame are the ones made at El Floridita in Havana, Cuba—the Daiquirí Floridita and the Papa Doble (aka: Hemingway Daiquirí). The origins of this drink have been in constant dispute since it gained popularity in the 1900s.

A direct descendant of the Cancháncharra (aka: Cuba Libre), some sources say that during the 1898 Spanish-American War, US General William Shafter—"an inveterate gourmet"—discovered the Cuban patriots' cancháncharra when he landed near Daiquirí, commenting that "only one ingredient is missing: ice."

The most common story about the Daiquirí's birth involves a meeting between Jenning Stockton Cox, Jr and Frederico Domenico Pagliuchi. A New York mining engineer, Cox was appointed, in 1896, to the general managership of the Spanish-American Iron Company. Frederico Domenico Pagliuchi was an engineer as well as a *Harper's Monthly* war correspondent, and a Cuban Liberation Army commander.

When bartender Emilio "Maragato" González—famous for popularizing the Daiquirí in Havana—passed away a number of years later, it was Pagliuchi who documented the incident of the drink's invention. The editor of El Pais newspaper made a mistake in writing Maragato's obituary, crediting the late bartender with the Daiquirí's origination. Pagliuchi sent a correction stating: "At the conclusion of the war of independence of Cuba [in 1898], ...I obtained American capital to reactivate the old El Cobre copper mines...of which I was the director. ...I had occasion to go to Daiquirí to speak with mister Cox. Concluding the matter that I took to Daiquirí, I asked mister Cox if he was going to invite me for a cocktail. In the sideboard of the mine's dining room, there was not gin nor vermouth; there was only rum, lemons, sugar, and ice. With these elements we did a very well shaken and very cold cocktail that I liked much. Then I asked Cox: — and this: how is it called? He answered: 'Rum Sour'. In the United States there is a drink that is called a 'Whisky Sour', which is made with whisky, sugar, lemon juice and ice". But I said to him: "This name is very long, why not call it Daiquirí?"

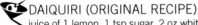

DAIQUIRI (ORIGINAL RECIPE)
juice of 1 lemon, 1 tsp sugar, 2 oz white rum, 1 splash mineral water. Shake ingredients over ice. Strain into a cocktail glass.

Daiquiri, Floridita

A variation on the original Daiquirí that has become the icon of the drink is the Floridita Daiquirí. A Catalan bartender took over the famed Havana bar-restaurant La Florida, in 1918, four years after his arrival in Cuba and after he first started working behind the restaurant's bar. Thanks to him—Constante Ribaliguia Vert—the Daiquirí Frappé (aka: Daiquirí No. 4 or Floridita Daiquirí) became the toast of the town, immortalized by novelist Ernest Hemingway, who once scribbled a note that read: "My Daiquirís at Floridita, my Mojitos at Bodeguita." What most people don't realize is that during Constante's reign at El Floridita (aka: "the Cradle of the Daiquirí), he developed five versions of this Cuban classic.

FLORIDITA DAIQUIRI NO. 1
2 oz white rum, 1 tsp sugar, juice of half a green lemon (key lime). Shake over cracked ice and strain into a cocktail glass.

FLORIDITA DAIQUIRI NO. 2
2 oz white rum, several dashes curaçao, 1 tsp orange juice, 1 tsp sugar, juice of half a green lemon (key lime). Shake over cracked ice and strain into a cocktail glass.

FLORIDITA DAIQUIRI NO. 3
2 oz white rum, 1 tsp grapefruit juice, 1 tsp maraschino liqueur, 1 tsp sugar, juice of half a green lemon. Shake over cracked ice and pour into a cocktail glass. Serve frappé.

FLORIDITA DAIQUIRI NO. 4 (HOWARD AND MAE)
2 oz white rum, 1 tsp maraschino liqueur, 1 tsp sugar, juice of half a green lemon (key lime). Mix in a blender with cracked ice. Serve frappé.

FLORIDITA DAIQUIRI NO. 5 (PINK)
2 oz white rum, 1 tsp maraschino liqueur, 1 tsp sugar, 1 tsp grenadine syrup, juice of half a green lemon (key lime). Mix in a blender with cracked ice. Serve frappé.

We won't discuss the obvious facts about the El Floridita Daiquirís. Thanks to author Ernest Hemingway, these are the Daiquirís that had the longest legs. They resonated with the A-list celebrity set, who were introduced to them by Hemingway, for the most part, until he left Cuba.

Daiquiri, Frozen

A modern variation of the Floridita Daiquirí, the Frozen Daiquirí takes fresh fruit such as strawberries and blends it with rum, sugar, and lime juice into a thick frappé. A favourite of 1920s singer/actor Rudi Vallee, the Frozen Strawberry Daiquirí was the first in a long line of fruit-based Daiquiris, including Banana Daiquirí, Pineapple Daiquirí, Mango Daiquirí...

FROZEN STRAWBERRY DAIQUIRI
2 oz white rum, 2 fresh strawberries, 1 oz fresh lime juice, 2 tsp superfine sugar. Mix ingredients with cracked ice in a blender. Pour into a cocktail glass. Serve frappé.

Daiquirí, Hemingway

See Papa Doble.

DeGroff, Dale

(aka: King Cocktail) Dale developed his extraordinary techniques tending bar at New York's famous Rainbow Room, where in the late 1980's he pioneered a gourmet approach to recreating the great classic cocktails.

He has been credited with reinventing the profession of bartending and setting off the cocktail explosion that continues to transform the industry.

DeGroff is a founding partner of Beverage Alcohol Resource (BAR), a partnership of six of the world's leading spirits and cocktails authorities who provide training and credentialing in distilled spirits and mixology.

Industry awards include: the 2009 James Beard Wine & Spirits Professional Award, the 2009 Lifetime Achievement Award from *Nightclub & Bar Magazine*, 2008 TOTC Helen David Lifetime Achievement Award, and the 2007 Cheers Beverage Industry Innovator of the Year with his partners, for Beverage Alcohol Resource.

DeGroff is the author of The Essential Cocktail (Random House), winner of the 2009 Tales of the Cocktail® Spirited Award® Ceremony, and *The Craft of the Cocktail* (Random House), winner of the 2002 IACP Julia Child Award.

Dale is also the founding President of The Museum of the American Cocktail, located in New Orleans.

Dietsch, Michael

Bartender and cocktail columnist for *Edible Rhody*
magazine, when Michael's not mixing cocktails, he's usually
smoking huge chunks of meat, cycling, or enjoying a fine
cigar, but rarely all three at once.

Digestif

A digestif is a drink that is consumed after dinner to aid the
digestion process. Many spirits come under this category,
such as Cognac, whisky, and calvados. However there is also
a set of liqueurs that also come under this category which
contain a particularly high quantity of bitter herbs that help
prevent or ease the formation of gas in the gastrointestinal
tract. One example is Fernet Branca, a famous Italian after
dinner drink.

Diners Club

Diners Club International, founded as Diners Club in 1950,
is a charge card company formed by Frank X McNamara,
Ralph Schneider and Matty Simmons. It was the world's
first independent credit card company. The first credit card
charge was made on February 8, 1950, by the company
founders at Major's Cabin Grill, a restaurant adjacent to
their offices in the Empire State Building. McNamara was
bought out two years later by department store heir Alfred
Bloomingdale, who resigned several years later. Schneider
died in the early 1960s. Simmons resigned in 1967 to form
the publishing company that became National Lampoon.
During that approximately 20-year period, these four men
were the only major participants in Diners Club's operations.

Don the Beachcomber

Donn Beach (February 22, 1907 – June 7, 1989), born
Ernest Raymond Beaumont Gantt, is the acknowledged
founding father of tiki restaurants, bars and nightclubs. The
many so-called "Polynesian" restaurants and pubs that have
enjoyed great popularity are directly descended from what
he created. After years of being called Don the Beachcomber
because of his original bar/restaurant, Gantt changed his
name several times, using Donn Beach-Comber, Donn
Beachcomber, and finally settling on Donn Beach.

Gantt, a Texas native, left home in 1926 and travelled
around the world, scouring many of the islands of the
Caribbean and the South Pacific. He found himself in

Hollywood, in 1934, where he opened Don's Beachcomber Cafe at 1722 N McCadden Place. The place moved across the street three years later. Don the Beachcomber customers ate what seemed like wonderfully exotic cuisine, but in truth, were mostly standard Cantonese dishes served with exuberant flair. The first "pu pu platter" was probably served there. He is best known for creating the Zombie.

Duff, Philip

After more than a decade bartending in his native Dublin, followed by London, New York, the Cayman Islands, Rotterdam and the Hague, Duff chose the life of a brand ambassador/cocktail consultant. He and his firm, Liquid Solutions have trained about 17,000 people in 60-odd countries across every continent. Philip has presented at every even halfway-decent bar show in the world and is much in demand by the better sort of drinks brands. They hire him to train their staff, for new product development, to design and execute on-trade communications and bartender-targeted initiatives.

An in-demand writer, Philip writing includes columns in *Australian Bartender* and regular articles in *Mixology* (Germany). His columns and recipes have also appeared in *Food & Wine* (USA), *Playboy, FHM, CLASS* magazine, *Bar & Beverage* (Canada) and others.

Dutch Courage

Dutch courage (aka: liquid courage) refers to bravado gained from intoxication by alcohol. The phrase has its origins in the bracing ration given to troops before they went into battled during the Dutch War for Independence (1566-1609) and the Thirty Years War (1618-1648). Dutch troops were provided with a daily ration of jenever in addition to this prebattle drink. British troops were sent to aid the Dutch in their fight for freedom and immediately embraced the practice. "Dutch courage" has also been used as nickname for gin.

Doc Eason

For 20 years, Doc Eason was the featured bar magician at John Denver's World Famous Tower Comedy/Magic Bar in Snowmass Village, Colorado. The 37th Annual Academy of Magical Arts Awards Show, held in 2004, at Hollywood's Magic Castle, named him Bar Magician of the Year.

Doc was instrumental in establishing the WC Fields bar located in the Magic Castle's Inner Circle as a performing venue while also working at The Magic Castle at the same time. Doc is widely recognized as one of the premier bar magicians of our time.

Eau-de-Vie

The French term eau-de-vie [plural: eaux-de-vie] literally translates to "water of life" and was coined by alchemist Arnaud de Ville-Neuve, the first European to construct and operate, in the 1200s, an alembic still based on the Arab al-ambiq device. The names of many spirit categories are derivative of the "water of life", including whisky, akvavit, and vodka.

Today the term eau-de-vie refers to a dry-style of brandy, commonly made from fruit. However, sometimes the term also applies to brandy distilled from wine as it did back in the days of de Ville-Neuve.

Eaux-de-vie are not usually aged, meaning they have no colour. Although the term is a French one, there are many French eaux-de-vie (often sold in clear Alsatian style bottles), other countries developed national eaux-de-vie: for example, schnapps from Germany, palinka from Hungary, coconut arrack from Sri Lanka, rakia from the Balkan states, slivovitz from central Europe.

Eaux-de-vie are made by harvesting ripe fruit, fermenting the juice and then double distilling the liquid. The alcohol is usually bottled around 40 percent ABV.

If distilled from pomace (the stems and stalks of grapes) it is called pomace brandy, eau de Marc or simply Marc.

Egg, Whole

A whole egg adds froth, creaminess, density, plus a light but distinctive flavour. Although raw eggs are banned by health codes in some parts of the United States there is still debate as to whether salmonella, the food-borne pathogen associated with raw eggs can survive the levels of alcohol or citric acid found in most drinks that call for an egg. In any case, pasteurized eggs may be used as a substitute.

As the size of eggs varies, most cocktail recipes are standardized to use large eggs. If you are employing medium or extra large eggs, there will be minor differences. Eggs should be as fresh as possible, and the shells should be clean and unbroken.

Egg White

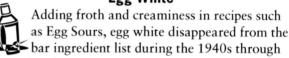

Adding froth and creaminess in recipes such as Egg Sours, egg white disappeared from the bar ingredient list during the 1940s through 1990s, replaced in many cases with artificial foaming agent. Although raw egg whites are banned by health codes in some parts of the United States there is still debate as to whether salmonella the food-borne pathogen associated with raw eggs can survive the levels of alcohol or citric acid found in most drinks that call for egg whites. Pasteurized egg whites may be safely used as a substitute.

When shaken, beaten, whisked or blended, egg whites become foamy. The best example in cooking is meringue. The best example in mixed drinks is the Ramos Gin Fizz. Egg whites have a distinctive aroma, thus the Pisco Sour uses Angostura bitters to mask this.

Egg Yolk

A surprising number of classic drinks called for an egg yolk. Egg yolk does not foam like egg white. It is much richer in texture and adds a golden hue to drinks such as the Golden Fizz.

Einstein, Izzy and Smith, Moe

American agents of the US Prohibition Unit operating in New York City, Izzy (Isidor/Isadore) Einstein (circa 1880 – 17 February 1938) and Moe Smith (circa 1887–1961) are best known for successfully shutting down hundreds of speakeasies in all of the boroughs. With no education in law enforcement but a talent for languages, Izzy was the first agent to be signed up to the unit after Prohibition was enacted. He asked his friend and fellow Mason to join him. Although neither man believed in temperance, they did believe that the law was the law.

Well- known for using disguises and making 4932 arrests of which 95 percent ended in convictions of bartenders, bootleggers, and bar owners, the pair did too well and got too much publicity for their efforts. They were laid off along with 36 other agents in November, 1925, by higher officials who called for a reorganization of the unit. The pair both went into the insurance business.

Ekus-Saffer, Lisa

With more than 27 years experience managing a culinary-focused public relations firm that has trained hundreds of cookbook authors, chefs and spokespeople, including Emeril Lagasse, Charlie Trotter, Sara Moulton, Marcel Desaulniers, Barbara Lynch, and Ana Sortun, Lisa Ekus-Saffer holds regular media training seminars in her professional studio kitchen as well as on-location trainings around the country for corporate restaurant groups. Lisa speaks regularly at a wide range of conferences and events, including the International Association of Culinary Professionals, Women Chefs and Restaurateurs, The Symposium for Professional Food Writers, Les Dames d'Escoffier, Edible Communities, and the Traverse Epicurean Classic. In addition to her work as media trainer and publicist, Lisa is also a respected literary agent, representing both new and established authors to publishers around the globe.

Ellis, Tobin

Most recognized for his recent appearances on *Throwdown with Bobby Flay, On the Rocks: The Search for America's Top Bartender*, and the *Food Network Challenge*, Tobin has logged 19 years behind the wood in New York, DC, and Las Vegas, including as head bartender for Caesars Palace.

A 15-time finalist in national and world bartending competitions, Ellis Tobin has titles that include 2009 Tales of the Cocktail® USBG National Champion and has organized as well as judged many major competitions including NBC's *On the Rocks, Legends of Bartending*, and Hendrick's Cocktail Competition. He has also been a technical consultant for NBC, A&E, Travel Channel, and Food Network.

The principal consultant and owner of BarMagic of Las Vegas, established in 1997, his company provides concept and cocktail development, training, operations, and special event bar catering for resorts, casinos, restaurant groups, and major spirit brands on four continents. The company has won a slew of accredited awards and has been featured on a number of television networks around the world.

Embury, David

A New York attorney who earned his place in the Cocktail Hall of Fame, David Embury wrote the 1948 encyclopedia of cocktails titled *The Fine Art of Mixing Drinks*. More detailed in defining the styles of drinks, glassware, bar equipment, and types of spirits used in drinks than any other book up to that time, this non-bartender investigated every single aspect of his true passion. He produced an industry-changing book by changing the way people looked at the structure of drinks.

English, Camper

A San Francisco-based freelance cocktails and spirits writer and consultant, Camper English has visited more than 70 distilleries, blending houses, and bodegas in fourteen countries and has judged cocktail contests both locally and internationally. Camper is a member of the United States Bartenders' Guild, passed the prestigious B.A.R. course, and was a finalist in the Best Cocktail Writing award category at the Tales of the Cocktail® 2009 Spirit Awards.

Camper is the Contributing Spirits Editor for *7x7 Magazine*, the cocktail blogger for Fine Cooking Magazine, and a regular contributor to the *Los Angeles Times Magazine, San Francisco Chronicle, Mixology Magazine* (Germany), and *SilverKris* (Singapore Airlines).

Alcademics.com—his blog about cocktails, spirits, bars, and bartenders—has been mentioned in publications such as the *Wall Street Journal, Washington Post*, VillageVoice. com, the Associated Press, *Zeit* (Germany) and *Vinos y Restaurantes* (Spain).

English, Jennifer

One of America's most exciting and articulate culinary personalities, Jennifer English and her company Brandnewmedia LLC became the first national talk radio network dedicated exclusively to the delicious, entertaining

Name That Cocktail

None of these popular cocktails would stump Joe the Bartender, but can you name that cocktail...

1. Vodka + Beef Bouillon + Worcestershire Sauce

= _____

2. Tequila + Orange Juice + Grenadine

= _____

3. Light Rum + Lime Juice + Cola

= _____

4. Vodka + Lemonade

= _____

Answers:
1. Bull Shot; 2. Tequila Sunrise;
3. Cuba Libre; 4. Bull Frog

and dynamic world of food, wine and the good life.

Launch in December 1999, *The Food & Wine Network Show* won the 2002 James Beard Foundation/ Viking Range Best Radio Show About Food Award. With James Beard Foundation Award nominations again in 2003 and 2004, her show is now established in reputation and practice as the "best in the business."

Prior to founding the Food & Wine Radio Network, Jennifer was a senior executive and strategic marketing consultant for several prominent advertising and public relations agencies such as Cone Communications and Gearon & Hoffman.

Today Jennifer's professional affiliations include the Foundation for American Women in Radio & Television, Women Chefs & Restaurateurs, Slow Food International, The American Institute of Wine & Food, and the James Beard Foundation, and Culinary Guild of New England, The Professional Advisory Board of the Aspen Center for Integral Health, and the National Advisory Board of CIRA, and the Museum of the American Cocktail.

Esquire Magazine

Appearing for the first time in October 1933, *Esquire* magazine evolved rapidly over the years, becoming a men's magazine with a fashion and literary bent with contributions by Ernest Hemingway and F Scott Fitzgerald. The magazine published both the "10 Worst" and the "10 Best Cocktails of 1934", earning it a reputation for cocktail knowledge in those very early days. The editorial staff was also responsible for publishing a number of books on party planning, cocktails, and food over the decades.

A precursor to Playboy, the publication's Vargas girls sent circulation during the 1940s soaring. And by the 1960s, the magazine was the vehicle for such new literary talent as Norman Mailer, Terry Southern, Tom Wolfe, and Gay Talese.

In 2007 *Esquire* launched the Napkin Fiction Project,

in which 250 cocktail napkins were mailed to writers all over the country by the incoming fiction editor, in a playful attempt to revive short fiction — "some with a half dozen books to their name, others just finishing their first." Esquire received over a hundred entries.

Étoufée, Crawfish

Similar to gumbo in its seasoning with sassafras and bay leaves, Crawfish Étoufée is a rich, hearty stew that derives its name from the French term "to smother". The roux of flour and oil is not browned for as long as the one used in gumbo, giving its a lighter colour and a distinction character. Crawfish tails are combined with bell peppers, onions, spring onions, and celery in this sauce which is served over rice.

Filé powder

Finely ground sassafras leaves are the essence of filé powder (aka: gumbo powder). Used as a seasoning—along with bay leaves—and as a thickening agent in Gumbo, Étoufée, and other Creole dishes, filé powder cane be purchased in shops. But the best version is homemade from sassafras leaves found deep in Louisiana, which are picked when they are young and tender, dried, and pulverized.

Finter, Sean

Sean Finter has spent his entire life in the hospitality industry, working his way from dishwasher to multi-site restaurant owner. He quickly gained a reputation for turning struggling businesses around at a remarkable pace by focusing primarily on business reporting and management/ staff training. His holistic approach of working with restaurant owners, management teams and front line staff has attracted the attention of some of the top venues in the world, which are now among his clients.

Currently, Sean runs Barmetrix, a consulting practice committed to teaching the tools and methodologies that underpin the best businesses in the world. Barmetrix assists restaurant and bar owners in the USA, Canada, Australia, and Britain. From re-engineering business strategies to developing world-class cocktail programs, Barmetrix tackles a myriad of restaurant operations challenges by starting with the core belief that "you can't improve what you can't measure." The company's success is attributed to their ability to coach their clients to healthier profits and happier, more focused staff/management.

Sean continues as CEO of this small company with big plans. With his revolutionary custom-built software suite and talented team of consultants, Barmetrix is determined to change the hospitality industry.

Fizz

A Fizz is a variation on the Sours family that adds soda water to the mix. The first printed reference to a Fizz is in the 1887 posthumous edition of Jerry Thomas' Bartender's Guide. The Fizz became widely popular in America between 1900s and the 1940s. There are numerous variations. A Silver Fizz adds egg white while a Golden Fizz uses egg yolk. The Royal Fizz includes a whole egg. A Diamond Fizz replaces the soda water with sparkling wine or champagne. And a Green Fizz adds a dash of green crème de menthe. The most famous Fizzes are the Gin Fizz and especially the New Orleans classic—the Ramos Gin Fizz or New Orleans Fizz.

Flaming Drinks

Flaming mixed drinks contain flammable distilled spirits or high-proof liqueurs. Ignited prior to service they add a bit of excitement to the presentation and to caramelize some of the ingredients. The most famous flaming cocktails are the Blue Blazer and the New Orleans' favorite—Café Brulot. Sambucca is commonly ignited prior to service, and the Czech absinthe ritual calls for lighting the absinthe-soaked sugar cube (many purists do not approve of this).

CAFE BRULOT
1 orange peel, cut into 1 by 1/8-inch strips; 1 orange, peel cut into 1 long, intact spiral; 1 lemon peel, cut into 1 by 1/8-inch strips; 4 sugar cubes; 6 whole cloves; 1 cinnamon stick; 4 oz Cointreau; 2 cups freshly brewed, hot black coffee. Light the burner under a brulot bowl or chafing dish and adjust the flame to low. Place the orange and lemon peels, sugar, cloves, cinnamon stick and orange liqueur into the bowl. Cook for 2 minutes, stirring constantly with a long-handled ladle. When the mixture is warm, stir in the hot coffee, and ignite it with a match. While the mixture is still burning, hold the spiralled orange peel with the prongs of a fork over the bowl, and ladle the flaming mixture down the peel several times into the bowl. Ladle the mixture into demitasse cups, being careful to leave the peels, cloves, and cinnamon in the bowl. Serve immediately.

Ford, Simon

Currently the Director of Brand Education and Trade Outreach for Pernod Ricard USA—a role that has him visiting bars across the USA—Simon Ford previously was the International Brand Ambassador for Plymouth Gin. With more than sixteen years in the spirits industry, Simon has a range of experience from running a wine shop to opening a cocktail bar, judging spirits in competition, and marketing some of the biggest brands on the planet.

Simon received the 2009 award for Best US Brand Ambassador at the Tales of the Cocktail® Spirit Awards® and was also honoured with the 2007 Best International Brand Ambassador. He founded the annual Cocktail Funeral at Tales of the Cocktail and cohosts the annual Plymouth Bartenders' Breakfast.

Fortified Wine—Sherry

A fortified wine made from white grape varietals (Palomino, Pedero Ximenex, or Moscatel) that grow near the Spanish town of Jerez, sherry is a protected designation of origin beverage. After fermentation of the wine is complete, a dosage of brandy and sometimes sweetener is added before it is barrel aged in North American oak, using the solera system. This method employs new wine that is progressively decanted into a series of 3 to 9 barrels, taking extra care not to damage the layer of flor in each barrel.

There are six styles of sherry:

Fino: The driest and palest style, the wine is aged in barrels under a cap of flor yeast to prevent oxidation.

Manzanilla: An especially light variety of fino sherry produced near Sanlúcar de Barrameda.

Amontillado: A style that is first aged under flor but then allowed to oxidize, producing a sherry that is darker than a fino but lighter than an oloroso. Naturally dry, they are sometimes sold lightly sweetened.

Oloroso: This style is allowed to oxidize for a long time, producing a darker and richer wine with a higher alcohol content. They are often sweetened.

Palo Cortado: A rare form of sherry that is aged like an amontillado, but then subsequently develops a character closer to an oloroso.

Sweet Sherries: Made from Pedro Ximénez or Moscatel grapes, the wines produce an intensely sweet dark brown or black wine. Cream Sherry is a common type of sweet sherry made by blending different wines.

Fortified Wine—Vin Doux Naturel

Vin Doux Naturel [naturally sweet wine] was defined as a specific wine category in 1898 by the Brousse Law in France. Originally developed by alchemist Arnaud de Ville-Neuve in the 1200s, the term refers to a fortified wine in which natural level of sweetness is maintained by fortification with a spirit before the end of the fermentation process, resulting in a wine sweetened by residual grape sugars.

The discovery of this method, called mutage, is attributed to de Ville-Neuve, a doctor of medicine at the University of Montpellier.

Several wines are made according to this method, some red, some white. This category is associated with the Rousillion area of France, where Rivesaltes and Muscat Rivesaltes are made. These are the world's oldest known fortified wines. The hot, dry and windy climate helps to concentrate the sweetness in the grapes.

Most vins doux naturel, excepting Muscat Rivesalte, are aged in old oak barrels, and sometimes exposed to the sun in demijohns to concentrate flavours.

Fortified Wine—Vermouth

The concept of aromatizing wine with herbs and spices has been around for at least 3,000 years. Archaeologists excavating in Anyang, China uncovered vessels of rice and millet "wines" that were macerated with wormwood, chrysanthemum, China fir, elemi, and other herbs and flowers.

The Greek alchemist Hippocrates is credited with first infusing wormwood into wine as a digestive remedy. In Germany, Britain, and elsewhere, wormwood wine was a common beverage. Queen Elizabeth I is said to have enjoyed a daily glass. During the 1660s, diarist Samuel Pepys noted on more than one occasion consuming or serving wormwood wine as a digestif.

Credit for perfecting the mutage [fortification] process goes to French alchemist Arnaud de Ville-Neuve, who used the method, in the 1200s, to halt fermentation and preserve sweetness of wine called vin doux naturel. This is also a traditional method of adding sweetness to vermouth, using spirits to halt fermentation before the yeast can consume all the sugars in the fermenting juice.

The invention of what is now called "vermouth" is said to date to 1786, when it was born in a liquor shop below the porticoes of the Piazza della Fiera (now Piazza Castello) on the corner with Via della Palma (now Via Viotti) in Torino, Italy. Signor Marendazzo hired a helper named Antonio Benedetto Carpano, who moved from Bioglio Biellese. Carpano had it in his mind to create an aromatic wine from moscato, adding the same spices and herbs used by the monks in his native valley. The 22-year-old apprentice macerated more than 30 ingredients including wormwood to the sweet wine and fortified it with distilled spirit.

Marendazzo let him sell it in the shop. It became an immediate hit with the ladies and then the gentlemen. Popular lore tells us that Carpano had a passion for Goethe's poetry and named his new drink after the German word for wormwood, "wermut" (pronounced vair-MOOT).

One might expect vermouth formulas to be as legendarily guarded as Chartreuse or Angostura Bitters. However, a visit to Noilly Prat in Marseillan, France, or Martini and Rossi in Pessione, Italy, includes a comprehensive tour of their herbs and spices. The formulas are well protected by the sheer number of ingredients, their proportions, and the skill required to gather and store them in peak condition, and to marry them during the lengthy production process.

To make vermouth, up to 40 herbs and spices are gathered such as locally grown artemisia absinthium [wormwood], gentian, chamomile, lavender, juniper, citrus peel, and mint as well as imported exotics including cloves, cassia, cinchona, nutmeg, and tumeric.

In traditional Italian vermouth the flavour is captured from the botanicals by macerating them in alcohol for up to a week. This extract is then blended with a base wine (almost always a white wine regardless of whether dry or sweet vermouth is being produced). Caramel and sugar are added along with a small proportion of alcohol, fortified wine, or fruit liqueur to help preserve the flavour by raising the ABV.

By the late 1800s, vermouth was an essential ingredient in dozens of drinks from the Martinez, Martini, and Manhattan to the Addington and Americano. No bar anywhere in the world was considered complete without imported Italian and French vermouth.

Argentines and Chileans like vermouth so much that their cocktail hour is called "l'hora del vermut" [the vermouth hour]. In parts of Spain every bodega sports a barrel of vermouth for doling out after-work aperitivos.

Fresh vermouth brings complexity to a Martini, spice and strength to a Manhattan, softness to a Negroni, and balance to all. However, it does not need to be mixed. It is also delicious on the rocks. Few summer drinks are as quenching as equal parts sweet vermouth (a lighter one like Cinzano) with fresh squeezed orange juice.

Fortified Wine—Vin de liqueur

Similar to vin doux naturel, vin de liqueur is a sweet, fortified wine that is unique to France. However, the term "vin de liqueur" is also used by the EU to refer to all fortified wines including vermouth and vin doux naturel.

There is a difference between vin doux naturel and vin de liqueur: the latter is fortified just prior to fermentation and is sweeter, with more character achieved from the added brandy.

Fortification takes vin de liqueur to an alcohol level of 16 percent to 22 percent.

Vins de liqueur are available in many regional styles. Grapes from the Champagne region are used for making ratafia. The Rhone region makes a rinquinquin. The Languedoc region produces cartagene. The Jura wine region produces Macvin du Jura, which uses marc as the fortifier. In Cognac, Pineau des Charentes uses Cognac and in Gascony, Floc de Gascogne is made with Armagnac.

Fortified Wine—Port

A fortified wine made in the Douro Valley of Portugal, port has a European Union Protected Designation of Origin. Established in 1756, it is the third oldest protected wine region after Hungary's Tokaj-Hegyalja and Italy's Chianti regions.

Mostly produced from the wines of the Tinta Barroca, Tinta Cão, Tinta Roriz (Tempranillo), Touriga Francesa, and Touriga Nacional grape varietals, there are over a hundred varietals that are sanctioned from port production. For example, white ports are produced from white varietals such as Esgana-Cão, Folgasão, Malvasia, Rabigato, Verdelho, and Viosinho.

Unlike sherry, port wine is fortified before fermentation is completed to retain its natural sweetness. Distilled grape spirit called aguardente is use as the fortifier.

There are numerous styles of port, but broadly they are categorized as barrel-aged ports (Tawny, Colheita, and

Garrafeira) and bottle-aged ports (Ruby, Reserve or Vintage, Pink, White, Late Bottled Vintage [LBV], Crusted, and Single Quinta Vintage).

Free Lunch

The phrase "free lunch" refers to a tradition once common in saloons throughout the United States. It frequently appeared in print in the US between 1870 to 1920, as establishments offered a "free" lunch, varying from rudimentary to quite elaborate with the purchase of at least one drink. Typically the lunch was worth far more than the drink. The saloon-keeper relied on most customers buying more than one drink, and that the practice would build patronage for other times of day. Thus, free lunches were often highly salted to encourage thirst.

Free food or drink is sometimes supplied in contemporary times, often by gambling establishments such as casinos.

The saying "there ain't no such thing as a free lunch", often abbreviated to TANSTAAFL, refers to this custom, meaning that things which appear to be free are always paid for in some way.

Freeman, Eben

Eben Freeman has been bartending for over two decades. During this time he has worked in blender bars, beer bars, hotel bars, clubs, dives and fine dining establishments. Widely credited with leading the Molecular Mixology movement in the United States, Freeman also possesses a thorough understanding of the classics, as seen in his Emmy-nominated series of bartending tutorials on Epicurious.com. After spending a year in Asia consulting and travelling, Eben is back home in New York working with Michelin-starred Chef Michael White as the Director of Bar Operations & Innovation for his AltaMarea group of restaurants.

Fruit Brandy

Fruit eaux-de-vie or fruit brandies are made by harvesting ripe fruit, fermenting the juice, and double distilling the liquid. The alcohol is usually bottled around 40 percent ABV.

Eaux-de-vie are usually not aged, meaning they have no colour. Although the term is a French one, there are many French eaux-de-vie (often sold in clear Alsatian style bottles), other countries developed national eaux-de-vie: for example, schnapps from Germany, palinka from Hungary, coconut arrack from Sri Lanka, rakia from the Balkan states, slivovitz from central Europe.

Fruit Wine

A familiar beverage in countries with cooler climates, fruit wines are made from a wide variety of fruits. The fruits used are often lower in sugar content, meaning the juices must have additional sugar or honey added to them to be converted into alcohol. This is called chaptalization.

Unlike making wine from grapes, where there is a natural balance of yeast to sugar to water, there must often be considerable adjustments made to the juices during fermentation.

In Britain fruit wines are traditional, often made at home and rested over the winter. Fruit wines are best consumed within a year of making and do not usually improve with bottle ageing. With once plentiful local fruit sources dwindling and changes in drinking fashions, the custom of bottling fruit wines died out somewhat in the twentieth century.

Fruit wine can be made from almost any edible berry or fruit. Common British fruit wines include damson, elderberry, cherry, strawberry, plus a spice wine: ginger, of which Stone's Green Ginger Wine is still bottled and sold commercially.

In Finland a traditional fruit wine named "Lappish Hag's Love Potion", "Lappish Grandmother's Love Potion", "Lappish Mother's Love Potion" or "Lappish Love Potion", it is made by packing whole blueberries into a bottle with a little water, then adding a little more water to the bottle over the course of a month. This helps the yeasts that are present on the berry skins to ferment the mixture.

Japan's famous plum wine, Umeshu, also falls into this category as does the pineapple wine found in Hawaii, Florida, and Japan.

Gantt, Ernest Raymond Beaumont

See Don the Beachcomber.

Garver, William

(aka: Garv) Cinema enthusiast William T. Garver has shared his knowledge of cocktail-related film since 2006 through feature articles in *Modern Drunkard Magazine*. He is also the creator of the popular movie review website Booze Movies: The 100-proof Film Guide that explores the role alcohol has played in motion pictures from the silent era to the present day. His goal is that his readers will find the world of film more intoxicating than they ever imagined. Garv's website has been recommended or cited in several print and online publications including *The New York Times*, *The Sacramento Bee*, and *The San Diego Reader*.

Genever

Genever (aka: Hollands Gin or jenever) is the precursor to gin. Belgian physician Philippus Hermanni was one of the first to record, in 1552, the recipe for making a malted grain eau-de-vie, called eau-de-genever [aka: juniper water]—a widely recognized kidney tonic.

　　Thanks to successful colonization of Asia, the Americas, and Africa, Dutch chemists and distillers had a veritable cornucopia of exotic ingredients at their fingertips. University of Leyden professor, Dr Sylvius de Bouve, capitalized on this bounty, in 1565, creating a kidney tonic and lumbago remedy by rectifying a grain spirit with juniper berries. Word got around about this medical marvel and its pleasant pine aroma. Not that the locals were suffering from an epidemic of kidney problems and back pains. They liked sipping what was now dubbed genever simply for pleasure. (Many people cited Dr Franciscus "Sylvius" de la Böe as the mastermind of genever, but he was a neurologist who lent his name to the Sylvian Fissure in the brain a century later, when genever was already flowing like water throughout the Netherlands.)

　　Within decades, around 200 genever distilleries popped around the Netherlands to meet a growing demand. Lucius

Bols became especially successful with this venture, when in 1602, he was commissioned to supply the Dutch East India Company's officers and crew with a daily ration of a half pint of his genever. The fortifier that became known as "Dutch courage" when British troops came to the aid of the Dutch during the Dutch War of Independence and the subsequent Thirty Years War made its way across the English Channel, where King William of Orange encouraged its production on British soil and gave birth to gin.

Today, there are three styles of genever: Oude, Jonge and Korenwijn. It is a common misconception that the Oude (old) and Jonge (young) refer to age statements. In fact these terms refer to the distillation style. Oude is made from at least 15 percent malt wine but not more than 20 grams of sugar per litre. Jonge contains no more than 15 percent malt wine and 10 grams of sugar per litre. Korenwijn is a very old style, which contains between 51 percent and 70 percent malt wine and up to 20 grams of sugar per litre. It is then often aged for a few years in oak casks, giving it a heavy full flavour that could be called an acquired taste.

Gibson

Although Charles Dana Gibson is often said to be responsible for the creation of the Gibson (a dry martini with a pickled onion as the garnish), the details are debatable and several alternate stories exist. In one story, Gibson challenged Charley Connolly, the bartender of the Players

Club in New York City, to improve upon the martini's recipe, so Connolly simply substituted an onion for the olive and named the drink after the patron. Other stories involve different Gibsons, such as an apocryphal American diplomat who served in Europe during Prohibition. Although he was a teetotaller, he often had to attend receptions where cocktails were served. To avoid an awkward situation, Gibson would ask the staff to fill his cocktail glass with cold water and garnish it with a small onion so that he could pick it out among the gin drinks. A similar story postulates a savvy investment banker named Gibson, who would take his clients out for proverbial three-Martini business lunches. He purportedly had the bartender serve him cold water, permitting him to remain sober while his clients became intoxicated; the cocktail onion garnish served to distinguish his beverage from those of his clients.

Another version now considered the more probable story comes from Charles McCabe of the *San Francisco Chronicle*. In 1968 he interviewed Allan P Gibson (1923–2005) and included the story in his 9 December 1968 column, as well as in his book *The Good Man's Weakness*. AP Gibson remembered that when he was a boy, his great-uncle, prominent San Francisco businessman Walter DK Gibson (1864–1938), was said to have created the drink at the Bohemian Club in the 1890s. Eric Felton, writing in the *Wall Street Journal*, in his 30 May 2009 article "A Thoroughly Western Cocktail" considers this version to be correct, citing Ward Thompson, a Bohemian Club member whose mention of it in 1898 as the first recorded in print. Although bartenders' guides sometimes gave the recipe as 50/50 gin and vermouth, Gibsons in the early days were much drier than other Martinis.

A third version, supported by Kazuo Uyeda in his book *Cocktail Techniques*, states that Gibsons started as very dry Martinis garnished with a cocktail onion to distinguish them from traditional martinis, but as the fondness for drier Martinis became popular the onion became the only difference.

GIBSON
1 1/2 oz gin, 3/4 oz French vermouth. Stir ingredients over ice and strain into a cocktail glass. Garnish with 2 cocktail onions.

Gimlet

The Gimlet was defined in Raymond Chandler's 1953 novel *The Long Goodbye* as "half gin and half Rose's lime juice and nothing else." The recipe has had just about as many variations as the Martini. As of the 1990s, maybe earlier, bartenders often answer requests for the Gimlet with a Vodka Gimlet. As the Gimlet was director Edward D Wood, Jr's favorite cocktail, he often used the pseudonyms "Telmig Akdov" or "Akdov Telmig" (Vodka Gimlet spelled backwards) when writing his adult novels.

But where did the Gimlet originate? Some tell tales that after Rose's Lime Cordial was first patented, in 1867, in answer to the British Royal Navy's call to provide seamen and officers with limes as a scurvy preventative, Surgeon General Sir Thomas D Gimlette came up with the bright idea of mixing the cordial with gin to get them to take their medicine, so to speak. Fresh limes had been supplied to the navy since the 1700s, added to the daily rum ration and the officers' daily gin ration. Laughlin Rose's patented lime cordial combined juice and sugar, making the product easier to store and use on board, even though it was later discovered that lemons had more of the valuable Vitamin C than their green cousins. Today, most bartenders make Gimlets with fresh lime juice and sugar syrup.

GIMLET
1 1/2 oz gin, 3/4 oz Rose's Lime Cordial. Stir ingredients over ice and strain into a cocktail glass. Garnish with 2 cocktail onions.

Gin

The British descendant of genever, gin is a neutral grain spirit that is predominantly flavoured with juniper berries. It is one of the most famous spirits used in the making of classic cocktails, appearing in such drinks as the Martini, Gin Fizz, and Tom Collins.

Produced since the 1600s in Great Britain, there are a number of ways gin can be made. Compound gin is made by flavoring grain neutral spirit with juniper berries without rectifying (re-distillation). Distilled gin is produced by rectifying neutral grain spirit with juniper and other botanicals, with the juniper as the dominant flavour.

The most popular style, however, is London dry gin, which is produced by macerating juniper berries along with citrus and botanical elements such as bitter lemon, bitter orange, anise, angelica, orris root, liquorice, coriander, cassia, bitter almond, and cardamom. The liquid is then rectified.

Gin, Damson

Damson gin is a liqueur made by infusing damson plums into gin and then sweetening the strained liquid. Damson gin is another traditional Christmas gift and toast in Britain along with Sloe gin.

Gin, Plymouth

The first spirit to be designated as a "dry gin", back in 1798 when distiller Thomas Coates at the Black Friars Distillery in Plymouth, England came up with the recipe, Plymouth gin is produced according to a similar method as London dry gin, but does not include the bitter botanicals in its maceration. It is the only gin to be granted a Geographical Designation (similar to an AOC in wine culture) by the European Union.

Gin, Sloe

Sloe gin is a liqueur made by infusing ripe sloes (the fruit of the blackthorn tree, a cousin of the plum) into gin, usually for about three months, and then sweetening the strained liquid. It was the replacement ingredient in the Blackthorn Cocktail after it became impossible to acquire Irish whiskey during the Irish War for Independence (1919-1921). Sloe gin is a traditional Christmas gift and toast in Britain.

Gin Act

First imported from the Netherlands and then produced in Britain thanks to encouragement from Britain's only Dutch monarch, William of Orange, gin became an extremely popular drink during the 1700s. Cheaper than beer to produce and to purchase, gin may have helped the grain farmers upload surplus grain, but it also turn an entire nation into alcoholics. In 1721, nearly 2,000,000 gallons of gin was produced in London. Politicians and religious leaders began to argue that gin drinking encouraged laziness and criminal behaviour. Parliament increased the tax on gin with the Gin Act of 1729 and the Gin Act of 1736, leading to complaints that culminated in the 1743 Gin Riots. The government responded by reducing duties and penalties, claiming that moderate measures would be easier to enforce. Yet gin drinking and uncontrolled—sometimes lethal—gin distilling continued to be a scourge. By the 1740s the British were consuming 8,000,000 gallons a year. It was estimated that in the City of London over a quarter of the houses were gin shops. Parliament finally took action effective action, with the Gin Act of 1751. Distillation was controlled by expensive licensing—one for distilling the spirit, one for rectifying it was botanicals—and heavy excise taxes on the final output. The sale by distillers and shopkeepers was equally controlled. The "Gin Craze" was finally over.

Ginger Ale

Ginger ale developed as a carbonated soft drink that was inspired by the importation of British and German ginger beer as well as Irish ginger ale to the United States. The first American soft drink, James Vernor developed his distinctive, aged recipe around 1866, which was sold at drugstore soda fountains. A blend of ginger, vanilla, and other flavours in a syrup base that is charged with carbonated water, ginger ale became a popular

Highball mixer in drinks such as Jameson & Ginger and Ginger Whisky.

Ginger Beer

Brewed from ginger, sugar, water, lemon juice, and ginger beer plant, ginger beer is a fermented beverage that is a key ingredient in the Dark 'N' Stormy and Moscow Mule. Popular in Britain and the Ionian islands in Greece, one of the oldest brands of commercial ginger beer is Crabbie's Original Alcoholic Ginger Beer (producers of Crabbie's Ginger Wine since 1801), although many more non-alcoholic versions were manufactured on a small, local scale throughout Britain.

Ginger Wine

When the Finsbury Distilling Company first opened, in 1740, it produced as one of its offerings green ginger wine: a fortified wine made from raisins and ground ginger. In accordance with a 1751 law, the company built a retail network that included Joseph Stone, a prominent grocer in High Holburn. Obviously he liked the product and sold enough of it to warrant proprietary labelling: Stone's Green Ginger Wine.

It became the flagship of the company's domestic wines division. Sales soared into the stratosphere when word spread that ginger was an effective preventative against cholera. An epidemic of disease first struck East London on 12 February 1832. And although only 800 people died from the water-born pathogen (fewer than died of tuberculosis and other diseases associated with poverty in the same district), it was enough to strike fear in the rest of the nation.

Two decades later British military forces and colonists living in South Asia during the British Raj found themselves facing cholera, malaria, typhoid, and other "tropical" ailments. Legend has it that a certain Colonel Macdonald who was stationed in India devised the drink there in hopes of averting cholera.

Because of his Scot background, it is more than likely that the original Whisky Macdonald was made with Crabbie's Green Ginger Wine. Produced since 1801 in Leith, this particular product is made with raisins that are flavoured with cowslips, elder flowers, cinnamon, cloves, lemons, and oranges, then blended and flavoured with ginger.

But the name Whisky Macdonald was a bit long for even the lightest drinker. In Scotland and throughout the UK, it became known as Whisky Mac.

Who's Your Daddy, Where's Your Mommie

What city claims parentage of these cocktails?
(And if you know the originating bar, hotel, or restaurant, mix yourself a cocktail on the house!)

Cocktail	City Hint	ANSWER
1. Singapore Sling	It's an island city-state	
2. Mai Tai	It's not in Asia	
3. Bellini	It's famous for pre-Lenten celebrations	
4. Black Russian	It serves as capital of the European Union	
5. Hurricane	It has French roots (but the cocktail source is Irish)	
6. Mary Pickford	It's a former movie star playground	
7. Piña Colada	It's a capital city on an island with Creole roots	

Answers:
1. Singapore; 2. Oakland, CA; 3. Venice, Italy; 4. Brussels, Belgium; 5. New Orleans, LA; 6. Havana, Cuba; 7. San Juan, Puerto Rico

Gintellectuals

During Prohibition in the United States, speakeasies ranged from single-rooms in tenement dwellings to "posh" establishments such as the Cotton Club, the Stork Club, El Morocco and the 21 Club.

For the first time, these nightclubs offered food, drinks, dancing and entertainment to their clientele. They were patronized by not only the wealthy and dissipated; but also by Broadway stars and the New York intelligentsia (dubbed "gintellectuals, by Walter Winchell, the pioneer of American celebrity journalism.)

Glass, Cocktail

A cocktail glass (aka: Martini glass) is a stemmed glass that has a cone-shaped bowl placed upon a stem above a flat base. Its form derives from the fact that all cocktails are traditionally served chilled and contain an aromatic element. The stem allows the drinker to hold the glass without affecting the temperature of the liquid, and the wide bowl places the surface of the drink directly under the drinker's nose, ensuring that the aromatic element has the desired effect.

Glass, Collins

Designed to serve Tom Collins and other Collins family drinks, a collins glass is a tumbler that is as tall but narrower than a highball glass and has a capacity of about 10 to 14 fluid ounces (300 to 420 ml).

Glass, Champage Coupe or Coupette

A champagne coupe (aka: champagne saucer) is a stemmed glass with shallow, broad-bowl placed upon a stem above a flat base. The coupe reached the height of fashion during the 1930s, when legends abounded about the bowl being modelled after the breast of Marie Antoinette or Madame du Pomapdour. Yet the truth is the coupe originated in Britain, in 1663, long before these famous French royals were born. Coupes were the champagne glass of choice well into the 1960s. Today, the coupe had replaced the cocktail glass in many classic cocktail bars. The ideal size holds about 5.5 fluid ounces (165 ml). As for the story about the breast-shaped glass? It does exist. It was made from Marie Antoinette's breast, but for a much more appropriate beverage: milk.

Glass, Champagne Flute

The ideal glass for maintaining the temperature of a dry sparkling wine, the champagne flute is a stemmed glass with a tall, narrow bowl, which retains the natural carbonation more effectively than a standard wine glass or a coupe. This design has largely replaced the use of coupes in the service of sparkling cocktails and wines. The ideal size holds about 6 fluid ounces (180 ml). High quality Champagne flutes often have a fizz mark, a rough spot etched into the glass at the deepest point, allowing the bubbles to cling to the glass and rise from that point. You can add a fizz mark to any champagne flute with an etching pen.

Glass, Cordial

Smaller than a wine glass, the diminutive stemmed cordial glass was sometimes called a "pony glass" because of its size.

Coming in both round and straight bowl shapes, the cordial glass is used to serve liqueurs and cordials, holding about 2 to 3 fluid ounces (60 to 90 ml). Some modern cordial glasses are stemless.

Glass, Highball

Designed to serve long drinks such as Highballs Bloody Marys, a highball glass is a tall tumbler that is taller than an old-fashioned glass and wider than a collins glass, holding about 8 to 12 fluid ounces (240 to 350 ml).

Glass, Martini

See Glass, Cocktail.

Glass, Noah

Noah Glass is the founder and CEO of GoMobo, a mobile and online ordering provider to major restaurant chains, including Applebee's, Cold Stone Creamery, and Five Guys Burgers & Fries. GoMobo, dubbed "Fandango for Food" by *New York Magazine*, allows customers to place orders online or from a mobile device, so that they can Skip the Line® at their restaurant of choice.

Glass was recognized as a "New M-Commerce Baron" by *Businessweek* in 2006 and named to the "Silicon Alley 100" by *Silicon Alley Insider* in 2009. He and GoMobo have been featured in "ABC World News," *Advertising Age*, Bloomberg TV, CNN, *Entrepreneur Magazine*, "Good Morning America," *New York Magazine, The New York Times, USA Today*, and the *Wall Street Journal*.

Glass, Old-Fashioned

Designed to serve mixed drinks or straight liquor "on the rocks" the old-fashioned glass (aka: rocks glass or tumbler) is shorter and wider than either a collins or highball glass. These days, old-fashioneds come in two sizes. The regular glass holds about 6 to 10 fluid ounces (180 to 300 ml), while the double old-fashioned or American old fashioned holds 12 to 16 fluid ounces (350 to 440 ml).

Glass, Rocks

See Glass, Old-Fashioned.

Glass, Shot

A short tumbler used to measure or serve alcohol has been dubbed a shot glass at least since the 1930s. Depending on the country, shot glasses do vary in size for liquor service. For example in the US, a small shot is equal to 1 fluid ounce (30 ml) while a single shot is equal to 1 1/2 fluid ounces (45 ml). In Britain, shots of spirits that are sold on premises must be either 25 or 35 ml (3/4 fluid ounce or 1 fluid ounce plus a splash).

Glass, Tumbler

Flat-bottomed tumblers come in all shapes and sizes for serving everything from juice to beer to mixed drinks to iced tea. In the cocktail world, there are four types of tumblers that you should know about: old-fashioned glass, collins glass, highball glass, and shot glass.

Grape

Many varieties of grapes can be used as garnish or muddled into a drink. For garnish, seedless varieties are preferable. Grapes can also be frozen individually or on stems of three or four grapes. Brushing them with egg white and dipping them in confectioners sugar make a particularly striking garnish.

Grapefruit

These days, grapefruit are cultivated in a few varieties, ranging from white to pink to ruby. Each has a different level of sweetness and sourness. Always squeeze grapefruit juice fresh, if possible. There is no form of prepackaged grapefruit juice that approximates the flavour of fresh juice. 50 ml is generally equal to half a grapefruit. A close relative of the grapefruit, the Southeast Asian pomelo is also entering the bartending repertoire. It has a mellower character.

Grappa

An Italian spirit originally formulated to utilize the stalks and skins (called pomace) that are left over during the wine making process, grappas are generally distilled from a single grape variety, bottled to between 37.5 percent and 60 percent ABV. They are usually bottled unaged. There are a small number of grappas that are rested in wood to achieve a more complex character.

Due to its increased popularity in recent decades, some grappas are now being produced from "prima uva" [whole grape] instead of pomace.

Legend has it that grappa originated in Bassano del Grappa. Another theory holds that the term stems from the Latin name for pomace spirit, which is traceable throughout northern Italy.

Consumed as a digestif accompanied by espresso, grappa has achieved a sort of cult status among aficionados for its artisanal distillations and ornate glass packagings.

Greene, Philip

An attorney, writer and cocktail historian, Philip Greene is one of the founders of the Museum of the American Cocktail, serving as treasurer, legal counsel, and member of the Board of Directors. He has deep ancestral roots in New Orleans: Among his Orleanian ancestors is Antoine Amédée Peychaud, the creator of Peychaud's Bitters and the original Sazerac.

Phil manages the Museum's monthly cocktail seminar program in Washington DC and also has been a guest presenter for the Smithsonian Institute, Tales of the Cocktail®, the Polished Palate RumFest, the Manhattan Cocktail Classic, Miami Rum Renaissance, the Distilled Spirits Council of the US, and other organizations.

He is also a Brand Ambassador for Domaine de Canton French Ginger Liqueur, and does outreach, cocktail design, consultation, staff training, guest bartending, and other duties for Maurice Cooper et Cie LLC.

Additionally, Phil is working on a book titled *To Have and Have Another: The Hemingway Bartender's Companion*, and presented a cocktail seminar at the Ernest Hemingway Home in Key West in 2010.

Grenadine

Used to flavour and to give a reddish hue to mixed drinks, grenadine syrup was originally prepared from pomegranate juice or cherry juice, and sugar. In French, the word grenade means "pomegranate".

The food industry, however, has widely replaced grenadine fruit bases with artificial ingredients. Rose's Grenadine Syrup is by far the most common grenadine brand in the United States, formulated entirely out of a corn syrup base mixed with flavoring and colouring agents.

Grenadine can be created by simmering pomegranate juice for 15 minutes on the stove, then adding superfine sugar. Grenadine can also be quickly prepared "cold" by adding superfine sugar to cold pomegranate juice, then shaking vigorously for a few minutes.

Grenadine syrup is commonly used to mix Cherry Cola (aka: Grenadini or the Roy Rogers), pink lemonade, Shirley Temple cocktail, Tequila Sunrise, Cherry Bomb, and to color cocktail cherries.

Gumbo

A comfort food stew served over rice that's seasoned with sassafras and bay leaves, gumbo's key ingredient is okra. In fact, the West African name for okra—*kimgombo*—is said to be the basis for this New Orleans classic's name. Chicken, andouille sausage, ham, prawns, crayfish, and other seafoods are added to this rich, saucy base. No one person in the Crescent City makes gumbo exactly the same way, it is a personal dish that deserves to be sampled everywhere and anywhere in New Orleans.

Haigh, Ted

(aka: Doc Cocktail) Ted Haigh is one of the most visible "cocktail pundits" on the scene today, writing a forgotten cocktail column for Imbibe, he owns CocktailDB.com: the Internet Cocktail Database. Ted is also the designer and curator of the Museum of the American Cocktail. He played the bartender in the movie *Superbad* and loves Zubrowka, Corenwyn, good Cognac (and more!) The newly revised and expanded deluxe hardback edition of his celebrated tome, *Vintage Spirits & Forgotten Cocktails*, is published by Quarry Books.

Hair of the Dog

Premised on the quaint notion that the best thing for what ails you is more of what ails you, "hair-of-the-dog-that-bit-you" cures have been popular since the time of Shakespeare (before that, the phrase referred quite literally to a method of treating dog bites).

The Bloody Mary is still touted as the ideal morning-after pick-me-up. Other reputedly effective concoctions popularly believed to relieve the symptoms of a hangover include Black Velvet, Corpse Reviver, and the New Orleans favorite, the French 75. (Of course, there is no truth to the idea that further alcohol consumption cures a hangover.)

FRENCH 75

1 1/4 oz gin, 1/4 oz simple syrup, 1/4 oz fresh lemon juice, champagne. Shake gin, syrup, and juice over ice. Strain into a flute. Slowly fill champagne. Garnish with a cherry.

Hamilton, Edward

After more than a decade of scouring the Caribbean for the finest examples of the distiller's art, Ed Hamilton published *Rums of the Eastern Caribbean* and *The Complete Guide to Rum*. His research has appeared in *Caribbean Travel and Life, Yachting, Drinks,* and *Nightclub & Bar.* He has appeared on NBC's *Today Show* and in *Time* magazine. An industry consultant as well, Hamilton also owns the Ministry of Rum website —just Google the word "rum".

Hangover

A Victoria expression that described unfinished business the term hangover took on a new life, in 1904, when it surfaced as a way of expressing "the morning after-effect of drinking too much". Symptoms of an alcohol hangover include dehydration, fatigue, headache, body aches, vomiting, diarrhoea, flatulence, weakness, elevated body temperature and heart rate, difficulty concentrating, sweating, anxiety, dysphoria, irritability, sensitivity to light and noise, erratic motor functions (including tremors), trouble sleeping, severe hunger, increased libido, halitosis, and lack of depth perception. Despite numerous so-called remedies ranging from the "hair of the dog" to Marmite on toast, Prairie Oysters, and Eggs Benedict, the best cure for a hangover is plenty of water and time.

Happy hour

Happy hour is a marketing term employed to describe a period of time in which a restaurant or bar offers discounts on alcoholic drinks. It typically takes place during the late afternoon Monday through Thursday, between 4 PM and 7 PM. Some bars also offer a late-night happy hour for afternoon-shift workers from 10 PM - 1 AM. The term is also used to describe the gathering of coworkers at a restaurant or bar after business hours.

Harry's Bar

Harry's Bar was opened in 1931 by bartender Giuseppe Cipriani. According to the company history, Harry Pickering—a rich, young Bostonian—had been frequenting Hotel Europa in Venice, where Giuseppe Cipriani was a bartender. When Pickering suddenly stopped coming to the hotel bar, Cipriani asked him why. Pickering explained that he was broke because his family discovered that he was drinking and cut off his funds. Cipriani loaned him 10,000 lire (about $5,000 US) to travel home. Two years later, Pickering returned to the hotel bar, ordered a drink, and gave Cipriani 50,000 lire in return. "Mr. Cipriani, thank you," he said, according to the Cipriani website. "Here's the money. And to show you my appreciation, here's 40,000 more, enough to open a bar. We will call it Harry's Bar." Harry's Bar is home of the Bellini.

Harry's New York Bar

A former American jockey Henry McGee went into partnership with a Manhattan bar owner known simply as Clancy. They dismantled Clancy's bar and wood-panelled walls and transported the entire assembly Paris. On Thanksgiving Day that year, The New York Bar opened its doors at 5 Rue Daunou in the Opèra district. A Scot bartender named Harry MacElhone was on the opening team, but he didn't stay. He went to New York instead.

The place filled with racing car enthusiasts and American tourists making grand tours of Europe. For a couple of years during the First World War, the place was managed by another former American jockey Tod Sloan. In fact, it was known for a while as Tod Sloan's Bar.

Then it faltered until Henry's ex-wife Nell McGee bought the place, in 1917, at the height of American involvement on the Western Front. She hired Charlie Herrick as manager and renamed it The New York Bar. A haven for British and American troops, the joint was hopping once again.

By 1923, McGee was tired of hosting rich kids and disillusioned ex-doughboys who hadn't gone home after the war. She offered Harry MacElhone The New York Bar. He accepted.

Novelist F Scott Fitzgerald had his first Dry Martini there along with a host of MacElhone's original creations and drinks that he popularised such as the Monkey's Gland Cocktail. Composer George Gershwin put the finishing touches on his "An American in Paris Suite" on the downstairs piano. When he wasn't behind the bar, Harry played towel holder to novelist-adventurer Ernest Hemingway when he boxed at the Montmartre Sportif. Everybody who was anybody ended up at "Sank Roo Doe Noo."

Today the bar still looks about the same as it did when it opened, complete with hot dog machine. The place still conducts a straw poll during the US presidential election. Thus far, every single election since the 1910s has come out just as the bar expats predict, save for four of them.

Harvey Wallbanger

The Harvey Wallbanger was reputedly invented in 1952 by Donato "Duke" Antone, who named the drink after a Manhattan Beach surfer who was a regular patron of Duke's Blackwatch Bar on Sunset Boulevard in Hollywood. Among Duke's other cocktail creations were the Rusty Nail, the Flaming Caesar, the White Russian, the Freddie Fudpucker, and the Godfather. The drink outstripped the popularity of the ubiquitous Screwdriver during the 1970s.

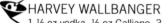HARVEY WALLBANGER
1 ½ oz vodka, ½ oz Galliano, 3 oz fresh orange juice. Build the ingredients in a highball glass. Stir and garnish with an orange slice.

Havana

Known as the "Little Paris of the Caribbean" by authors such as Basil Woon, Havana is the capital city, major port, and leading commercial center of Cuba. It is also the birthplace of numerous cocktails including the El Floridita Daiquirí, Papa Doble or Hemingway Daiquirí, Mojito, Mary Pickford, and El Presidente. It was also home to American novelist Ernest Hemingway until 1959.

The city and its drinking spots inspired Trade Vic Begeron and others to explore tropical drinks, especially those made with rum or gin, and introduce them in American bars after Prohibition.

Hemingway, Ernest

Born in Oak Park, Illinois, Ernest Hemingway (1899-1961) started his career as a newspaper reporter in Kansas City at the age of seventeen. After the United States entered the First World War, he joined a volunteer ambulance unit attached to the Italian army. Serving at the front, he was wounded, was decorated by the Italian Government, and spent considerable time in hospitals. After his return to the United States, he became a reporter for Canadian and American newspapers and was soon sent back to Europe to cover such events as the Greek Revolution.

During the 1920s, Hemingway joined a group of American expats in Paris, which he described in his 1926 novel *The Sun Also Rises*. Returning from the horrors of the Spanish Civil War, in 1938, Ernest Hemingway escaped to Havana and settled into room 511 at the Hotel Ambos Mundos on 153 Calle Obispo, where he began to write his novel *For Whom the Bell Tolls*. The story goes that Hemingway took a break one day and stopped into El Floridita at the other end of the street near Parque Central, where he ordered a Daiquirí from Constante.

In spite of the opinions of his doctor friends, Hemingway was convinced that he had diabetes. Consequently, he excluded all sugar from his diet, though he was never concerned about his alcohol consumption. Constante offered him a sugar-free Daiquirí with a double dose of Cuban rum. This Daiquirí del Salvaje, soon became the Daiquirí a la Papa, then Daiquirí Como Papa.

Enamoured with his new discovery, Hemingway returned every day at 11 AM dressed in Bermudas, short-sleeved shirt and espadrilles. He always sat on the same bar stool and downed a couple of his special Daiquirís. Sometimes he would return at 5 PM to consume a dozen more.

Later, cantinero Antonio Meilan modified the recipe by adding grapefruit juice and immortalized it under the appellation "Hemingway Special" or "Papa Doble".

Forced to leave his beloved Cuba after the fall of the Batista government, Hemingway moved to Ketchum, Idaho, where he committed suicide in 1961.

Herbsaint

The name Herbsaint originates from "Herbe Sainte" (Sacred Herb), the French/Creole term for Artemisia absinthium (aka: Grand wormwood). It is an anise-flavoured liquor currently produced by the Sazerac Company and originally made in New Orleans.

Herbsaint first appeared in 1934, the creation of JM Legendre and Reginald Parker, who learned how to make absinthe while serving in France during First World War. It was unique in its category as an absinthe substitute, having a different character than pastis. Herbsaint was originally labelled "Legendre Absinthe", although it didn't contain Artemisia absinthium. The Federal Alcohol Control Administration objected to term "absinthe", so the name was changed. The Sazerac Company bought the company in June 1949.

Hermansson, Per

A sensory analyst for more than 30 years, Per Hermansson has spent the last fourteen years using his keen sense of smell and taste to develop unique, quality spirits for the The Absolut Company. Per is the go-to source for pinpointing the variation of flavours among different vodka brands and is passionate about analysing consumer perceptions. Based at Absolut headquarters in Sweden, Per is credited with building the Sensory Laboratory/Department. Today, he is responsible for staying abreast of the latest developments within the spirits industry and consulting with the Research & Development department to seize opportunities for market growth. He provides both internal and external training sessions around the world that crystallize how different spirits achieve their unique tastes.

Hess, Robert

(aka: Drinkboy) Robert B Hess is a cocktail expert, a cofounder of the Museum of the American Cocktail, and a technology evangelist for Microsoft. He is the author of the 2008 book *The Essential Bartender's Guide: How to Make Truly Great Cocktails*. He is also host of "The Cocktail Spirit," an online video series distributed by the Small Screen Network. Along with several other well-known cocktail personalities, he founded The Chanticleer Society in 2008, which is a "worldwide organization of cocktail enthusiasts." He also writes the "Classic Cocktails" column for the bi-monthly fine beverage publication, *Mutineer Magazine*.

Highball

A category of mixed drinks that combines spirit with a non-alcoholic component such as ginger beer, soda water, fizzy lemonade, juice, or soft drink that are served on ice in a tall tumbler glass, Highballs are a direct descendant of Collinses, gaining prominence during the 1890s, introduced from Britain to America. Patrick Gavin Duffy in his 1940 book *The Official Mixer's Manual* suggested that the drink was imported, in 1894, by British actor and film star Edward J Ratcliffe. Familiar Highballs include Dark 'N' Stormy, Gin & Tonic, Moscow Mule, Rum & Coke (aka: Cuba Libre), Pimm's Cup, and the Screwdriver.

Honey

 A sweet food made by bees from flower and blossom nectar, honey is one of the world's oldest sweeteners. In mixed drinks, it can may be used alone or half and half with a more neutral sweetener such as simple syrup. In Britain, there are a couple grades of honey: runny honey (thin) and set honey (containing beeswax). Just like sugar, not all honeys taste the same, imparting distinctive characters and levels of sweetness depending on the type of flowers the honeybees pollinated. One drink that employs honey as both a sweetener and a primary flavour is the 1930s Orange Blossom Special: equal parts gin and fresh orange juice are shaken with runny honey and strained into a cocktail glass.

Ice

 What's the most important element in a bar after quality spirits, fresh juices, and fresh garnishes? Ice. Cubed, carved, shaved, cracked, or crushed, ice chills mixed drinks and adds a very critical component—dilution. Without dilution, the balance of flavours, alcohol strength, and aromas cannot be achieved. Frederic Tudor (aka: the Ice King) is to be thanked for introducing the world,

ICE PAIL.

ICE TONGS.

in 1806, shipping crystal, clear ice from Wenham Lake, Massachusetts to the far reaches of Havana and Calcutta. The numerous inventors of commercial ice-making machines and ice-storage units are owed a toast as well. And a deep bow of appreciation and reverence goes to today's Japanese bartenders for showing the rest of us how to make magical presentations with these simple chunks of frozen water.

International Bartender Association

The International Bartenders Association—often confused with the International Bar Association—was founded on 24 February 1951 in the Saloon of the Grand Hotel in Torquay, England. An offshoot of the United Kingdom Bartenders Guild, the IBA reputedly represents the world's best bartenders.

The World Cocktail Competition (WCC) and World Flairtending Competition (WFC) are annual events organized and presented by this organization. The IBA also sanctions a list of official cocktails that are measured in centilitres (cl) rather than the more commonly used millilitres (ml).

Irish Coffee

It all started with a boat—a flying boat. Back in the day, the fastest way a civilian could cross the Atlantic Ocean was aboard a flying boat airliner. (You know what they looked like. Indiana Jones hopped one, the China Clipper, across the Pacific on his way to Tibet in the film Raiders of the Ark.)

If you could afford the $674 USD return fare (about $8,400 USD, today) the Pan Am Clipper fleet offered you all the comforts of an ocean voyage and cut travel time from five days down to one. However, there were a few drawbacks.

Pan Am's Boeing B-314—affectionately known as the Yankee Clipper—was so huge that it could not be landed at a conventional airport. That meant landing in out-of-the-way spots with few or no services during layovers. If you were headed from New York to London between 1939 and 1942, it meant you stopped to refuel in Botwood, Newfoundland, and the port town of Foynes, County Limerick, Ireland at the mouth of the River Shannon.

Even when the crossing was pared down to a gruelling 25 hours, 40 minutes, nonstop, in 1942, you still landed at

Foynes before heading on to London because famed flyer
Colonel Charles Lindbergh determined the tiny Irish port
town was the perfect place to build the European Terminal
for all transatlantic air services.

That same, year Foynes Air Terminal began offering
food and refreshment to cold and weary passengers in the
Pier Lounge, opened by Brendan O'Regan. He hired Chef
Joe Sheridan to run the kitchen.

As the story goes, late one night just after it opened, a
group of chilled-to-the-bone passengers walked in. They had
left Foynes bound for Botwood ten hours earlier. But the
flying boat was turned back by wretched weather. The group
ordered coffee. Looking at the frazzled assembly, Sheridan
thought they needed a little something more. He added
a "little drop" of Irish whiskey to a cup of strong coffee,
sweetened it with sugar and topped it with thick whipped
cream.

"Hey buddy! Is this Brazilian coffee?" one surprised
passenger enquired.

"No. That's Irish Coffee," Sheridan replied with a
smile.

Word had gotten out about Sheridan's Irish Coffee,
all the way to the Buena Vista Café on Hyde Street in San
Francisco. Jack Koeppler and George Freeberg had taken
ownership of the place, which had become a favourite
watering hole for the *San Francisco Chronicle*'s two Pulitzer
Prize winning journalists Herb Caen and syndicated travel
writer Stanton Delaplane.

Delaplane frequently crossed the
"Pond" to London, stopping as one
did at Foynes. On the night of 10
November 1952, he asked Koeppler to
re-create Sheridan's Irish Coffee. The
pair didn't succeed in replicating the
taste or getting the cream to float on
the top.

Koeppler himself took a
pilgrimage to Foynes soon after
and upon his return made a few
adjustments to the recipe. This time, he and
Delaplane used the proper whiskey—Irish
whiskey. But the cream still wasn't right.
Four years later, the pair went to San
Francisco's mayor George Christopher

for advice: His honour owned the Christopher Dairy on Fillmore Street. He told Koeppler to stop using farm-fresh cream. It needed to age for at least 48 hours before it could be whipped to the right thickness and float on the surface.

With this final success, Delaplane started pushing the virtues of the café's Irish Coffee in his nationally-syndicated columns. Koeppler quickly ordered a bunch of crystal clear, six-ounce, heat-treated goblets to serve the signature drink, which was an "overnight sensation". Today, the Buena Vista Café serves up to 2000 Irish Coffees each and every day!

IRISH COFFEE
Fill a heat-proof goblet or Irish Coffee mug with boiling hot water. Wait a few minutes and then empty it. Pour in strong-brewed, hot coffee to about three-quarters full. Add two sugar cubes and stir to dissolve. Pour in 1 ½ oz Jameson's Irish Whiskey. Top with a dollop of lightly whipped cream, pouring it gently over a spoon to make it float. Serve while it is still piping hot.

Jack and Charlie's

New York City alone reputedly sported over 10,000 hidden watering holes by the late 1920s. And the city's 21 Club was one of the first.

Originally named the Red Head, the speakeasy was opened in Greenwich Village, in 1922, by cousins Jack Kreindler, a Fordham University pharmacy student, and Charlie Berns, a New York University School of Commerce student. All they wanted to do was earn enough money to pay their tuitions. Their cashier was future writer-producer Mark Hellinger.

The venue was moved three years later to a basement at 88 Washington Place and was renamed the Fronton. The building was condemned to make way for a subway. So the cousins moved the following year to West 49th Street. To confuse officials, a name change to Puncheon Club was amended with alternate names including The Puncheon Grotto, 42, 42 Club, Jack and Charlie's, plus the name they used whenever they got raided—Keyburn Club.

The building of Rockefeller Centre, in 1929, forced the venue's final move to 21 West 52nd Street: from that point the place was known as Jack and Charlie's "21". One raid on the speakeasy turned up the cream of the city's political, social, and business elite.

Today, Jack and Charlie's, now known as the 21 Club, is a preeminent power-lunch spot, and still serves a great drink and the world's finest hamburger.

Jake Leg

At the height of Prohibition, Americans who could not afford to make their way to Cuba to have a drink resorted to numerous alternatives. One of the saddest cases was the imbibing of Jamaican Ginger Extract, which was known as "Jake". An early patent medicine, Jake contained 70-80 percent ABV and in of itself was not dangerous. However, the US Treasury Department noting that Jake had the potential of running afoul of Prohibition laws, required that manufacturers had to add at least 5 grams of ginger solids per cubic centimetre of alcohol. This made Jake difficult to drink.

Some bootleggers simply replaced the ginger solids with a small amount of ginger and either castor oil or molasses to pass inspection. But bootleggers Harry Gross and Max Reisman found their way around the ruling by using a plasticizer called tri-o-tolyl phosphate (TOCP), an FDA-approved additive, instead of ginger solids. It passed the government tests and was more palatable to consumers.

But there was a hitch. TOCP contained an undiscovered neurotoxin. It caused damage to the nervous system. In 1930, large numbers of Jake drinkers lost control of their extremities. Some were paralysed. The terms "jake walk," "jake leg," and "jake paralysis" entered the public consciousness. Within a few months the adulterated Jake was taken off the market.

This did not help the estimated 30,000 to 50,000 victims who were afflicted, many of whom were recent immigrants and even more who were poor or poverty-stricken.

Jambalaya

Containing a zesty mix of tomatoes, onions, bell peppers, celery oregano, bay leaves, thyme, and rice, Jambalaya's origins have a great tale to tell. According to *The Dictionary of American Food and Drink* the dish was born late one night when a traveller walked into the New Orleans Inn long after dinner service had shut down. The inn's cook, Jean, was asked to *"balayez"* ["throw something together"] for the gentleman.

Add a feature ingredient such as andouille sausage or chicken or seafood or use all three and make sure you dash on a healthy dose of hot sauce to make this classic come alive.

Janse, Timo

For the last ten years, Timo Janse has been working in several award-winning bars, buying and reading bartending books, and writing for various digital magazines such as Venuez and Sensez.nl. (His latest post is at Door 74 in Amsterdam.)

When it became the trend in Holland for young children and teens to drink as much alcohol as they could, he saw that there should be something for them that was as complex as a good old cocktail but without the alcohol. For this he created over forty recipes and wrote a non-alcoholic cocktail book for teens titled, Shake It!.

In 2009, he also founded Holland's first non-alcoholic "Shake It!" cocktail competition, which was welcomed with much enthusiasm by the trade and the press. That same year, he won the Best Bartender award from Venuez Hospitality & Style Awards.

Jelly Shots

The Jelly Shot (aka: Jell-O shot or vodka jelly) is a modern descendant of the Punch Jelly introduced by the world's first celebrity chef Alexis Benoit Soyer at London's Reform Club during the 1840s and imported to the United States by Jerry Thomas in the 1860s. Spirit replaces a portion of the water or fruit juice used to make a set gelatin. In the early days, a punch recipe served as the base for this prehistoric molecular presentation.

The American satirist and mathematician Tom Lehrer was rumoured to have been the first to invent the gelatin shot in the 1950s while working for the National Security Agency, where he developed vodka gelatin as a way to circumvent a restriction of alcoholic beverages on base, but the claim that he was first is untrue.

PUNCH JELLY
1 cup boiling hot water, 4 envelopes powdered gelatin, 1 cup London dry gin, 4 oz maraschino liqueur, juice of 2 lemons, grated peel of 1 lemon. 4 oz simple syrup, 1 cup champagne. Mix the gin, liqueur, juice, peel, syrup and champagne in a bowl. Dissolve the gelatin in hot water in a separate container, stirring thoroughly. Strain into a bowl through a fine sieve. Pour into a glass baking dish to about 1 inch deep. Refrigerate overnight. Cut into 1-inch squares.

Jigger

See Measure.

Jitters, Jitterbug

The term jitterbug was used during the early 20th century to describe alcoholics who suffered from the "jitters" (read: delirium tremens). Jitterbug was then associated with swing dancers who danced seemingly without any control and then with a type of swing dance.

Joe Rickey

The Rickey is a category of mixed drinks that closely resemble a highball. Made from spirit, half of a lime squeezed and dropped in the glass, and soda water, little or no sugar is added to the Rickey. Originally created with bourbon in Washington, DC at Shoomaker's Bar by George A. Williamson, in 1883, the drink was purportedly created in collaboration with Democratic lobbyist, Colonel Joe Rickey. Gin Rickeys dominated the cocktail world during the 1890s, eclipsed only by the Mamie Taylor (a Scotch Rickey by any other name).

Since 2008 the DC Craft Bartenders Guild established July as National Rickey Month. The Mojito is a close relative of the Rickey.

Johnson, Harry

Born in Königsberg in German-held Prussia (now known as Kaliningrad, Russia), Harry "the Dean" Johnson (1845-1933) is the second most important American bartender in cocktail history. He was also the first person to document recipes for the Martini and Marguerite, the Morning Glory Fizz and the Blackthorn Cocktail made with Irish whiskey. Working in San Francisco he reputedly wrote a pamphlet in 1860 that recorded some of his recipes, before he relocated to Chicago. After losing his bar to the Great Chicago Fire in 1879, he moved with his wife to New York, where he took at position at Delmonico's.

Asked to write an expanded version of his book, he added about 15 pages on bar operations in this 1882 edition. After opening Little Jumbo on the Bowery, he expanded the operations section to 29 pages for his 1888 illustrated edition. This was also the first book to document recipes for a Martini and a Columbia Skin—predecessor to the Daiquirí.

But it is his 1900 edition of his *Bartenders' Manual* that he recorded his accumulated knowledge of the bar business. 139 to 159 pages covered every aspect from negotiating leases, hiring and training staff, stocking, and service. At the turn of the century, Johnson purchased and operated two Manhattan hotels, the last was the Pabst Grand Circle, with a theatre that premiered the *Wizard of Oz*, banqueting spaces, a night club that had Irving Berlin as a house musician, and an art gallery filled with his personal collection of paintings and sculptures.

During Prohibition, Johnson continued to advise his nephew Paul Henkel, who had opened and managed Keen's Chop House, served as vice-president of the Heart of the New York Business Men's Association, and lobbied in Washington DC for prohibition reforms.

Julep, Mint

The Mint Julep went by another name—Julepum Stomachicum—throughout the British Isles a century before the debate on the exact location of its "birth" in the American South hit its height during the 1800s. In the 1753 edition of John Quincy's *The New Dispensatory* a simple Stomach Julep called for six ounces of "simple mint water" (which the book later describes as a distillation of 1.5 pounds of dry mint leaves and water), two drams of saffron syrup, and two ounces of spirituous mint water made by distilling 1.5 pounds of dry mint leaves and 1 gallon of spirit.

Although the word "julep" is derived from the Arabic *juleb*, the word itself is an old French or Provençale word that came from Latin as a term for a medicinal mixture containing no solids. It is quite likely that the Julep was brought to the New World by French settlers, who first landed in Wisconsin in 1634 and colonized the area north of the Ohio River and east of the Mississippi, from western Pennsylvania to Illinois. The transition from medicine to pleasure was a small step. The Brandy Julep was considered to be an excellent preventative against malaria, and French colonists would have imbibed heavily in the swampy regions of Illinois, Missouri, Kentucky, Tennessee, Arkansas, Mississippi, and Louisiana during the swelteringly humid summertime.

How then did the Mint Julep that British chronicler
John Davis noted in his 1803 travelogue *Travels of Four
Years and a Half in the United States of America* was "a
dram of spirituous liquor that has mint steeped in it, taken
by Virginians of a morning" become a pleasurable morning
drink? (David further commented: "I honestly date my own
love of whiskey, from mixing and tasting my young master's
Juleps.")

The Scot-Irish emigrants who settled along
the eastern seaboard and driven west during
the American Revolution and during the 1791
Whiskey Rebellion imported their whiskey-
making traditions to Kentucky and Tennessee.
This domestic whiskey was quickly embraced
by the newly independent nation. They also
brought their own medical texts, such as *The
New Dispensatory*, which was published in
Dublin. But in the South, where mint is plentiful
almost year-round a simpler formula emerged.
Thus, from all of combined beginnings the Mint
Julep developed into the favoured American
beverage throughout the 1800s and the official
toast of the Kentucky Derby.

MINT JULEP

3 oz bourbon, 6 sprigs fresh mint, superfine sugar, to taste. Place
mint, sugar, and a splash of bourbon into the bottom of a mixing
glass. Gently muddle the mint and sugar, then let stand for a bit to allow
the muddled leaves to release their flavour. Strain and pour into a julep
cup, rotating to coat the sides. Fill with crushed ice, then add the rest of
the bourbon. Garnish with a lightly slapped small mint sprig.

Katz, Allen

Director of Mixology & Spirits Education for Southern Wine
& Spirits of New York, Allen Katz is also the cofounder
of the New York Distilling Company in Williamsburg,
Brooklyn.

Besides presenting food and beverage seminars,
Allen has worked as a business consultant, in cocktail
development, and with Slow Food to develop programming.

Allen was the co-curator of the Jerry Thomas American Cocktail Bar at the inaugural Slow Food Nation (San Francisco, 2008). Most recently he presented The History of Distilling in New York City for The Manhattan Cocktail Classic (2011).

He is a regular speaker at Tales of the Cocktail in New Orleans, the New York Wine & Food Festival, the NASFT's Fancy Food Show in San Francisco, Chicago and New York and The National Restaurant Association's annual convention in Chicago on topics of regional food and beverage heritage in America.

Allen serves on the Board of Advisors for The Manhattan Cocktail Classic and as the Treasurer of the Board of Directors of the New Orleans Culinary and Cultural Preservation Society, the host of Tales of the Cocktail. He is also the Chairman Emeritus (ex officio) of the Board of Directors for Slow Food USA.

King Cake

From Epiphany (January 6) to Ash Wednesday, King Cake can be found in bakeries throughout the city. A braided Danish pastry, laced with cinnamon and iced in the Mardi Gras colours of purple (justice), green (faith), and gold (power), a tiny plastic baby is hidden inside this treat, which also contains fillings such as cream cheese, apple, or strawberry filling. Great at breakfast, dessert, or with café au lait, the tradition of king cake dates back to the Middle Ages when Twelfth Night was celebrated in many European cultures with pageants, special presents for kids, and a celebratory cake—King Cake.

Klemm, Eben

A former research biologist, Eben Klemm encourages knowledge among bartenders concerning the basic chemical and physics principals that affect the materials they use in order to better understand the techniques they use.

Klemm and his cocktails have been featured in such diverse publications as *The New York Times, Wall Street Journal, Food & Wine, Time Out New York, Popular Science,* and *Playboy.* He has also made televised appearances include *The Today Show,* CBS's *Early Show,* and ABC's *20/20.* His outstanding cocktail book for beginners, *The Cocktail Primer,* was published in December by Andrews McNeel.

Knife

 A sharp knife is essential for cutting garnishes. Remember, a knife will not stay sharp for long since the acid from the citrus fruit eats away at the edge of the blade. You can slow this deterioration by rinsing or at least wiping the blade immediately after each use.

Want more precision in your garnish cut? Try using a channel knife: perfect for cutting thin strips of peel.

LaFranconi, Francesco

National Director of Mixology and Spirits Educator for Southern Wine and Spirits of America, Francesco Lafranconi honed his skills at some of the world's leading hotel bars, The Gleneagles (Scotland), The Palace Hotel (Gstaadt, Switzerland), The Intercontinental Hotel (Cologne, Germany), as well as Harry's Bar and Hotel Cipriani (Venice, Italy).

Francesco has several prestigious wins in international cocktail competitions, including The 1998 Bacardi-Martini Grand Prix World Final, Singapore's J. White Course, and two Italian National Finals.

Cofounder of the United States Bartenders Guild (USBG) – Nevada Chapter as well as one of their national ambassadors, Francesco actively participates in the International Bartenders Association. He was named 2008 Mixologist of the Year by Night Club & Bar Magazine and received Tales of The Cocktail®'s 2009 Spirited Award® for Best Presenter. He contributed to the 2010 *Food & Wine Cocktail Guide* and helped develop the first cocktail guide published by *Robb Report Luxury Magazine*.

With his team of eight professional mixologists, Francesco created and conducts the 12-week-long Academy of Spirits and Fine Service.

Lansky, Meyer

Known as the "Mob's Accountant", Meyer Lansky (1902-1983) was a key figure in the development of the National Crime Syndicate: a name given by the media to the multi-ethnic, organized crime consortium that controlled gambling, the alcohol trade, and much of the hospitality and entertainment business in the United States. His influence with the Italian Mafia and membership in the Jewish Mafia helped to consolidate a criminal underworld that had gained strength during Prohibition. He was largely responsible for developing a gambling empire that stretched from Saratoga, New York to Miami to New Orleans to Council Bluffs, Iowa and on to Las Vegas.

Then Lansky set his sights on Cuba. With the sanction of his friend Cuban president General Fulgencio Batista, Lansky and "Lucky" Luciano took control of Havana's casinos, hotels, nightclubs, and racetracks, paying kickbacks to the island's leader.

The day before Fidel Castro marched into Havana on 8 January 1959, Lansky fled to the Bahamas, leaving his network of casinos and hotels to be closed or destroyed. With pressure from the US Treasury on tax evasion charges, Lansky fled to Israel between 1970 and 1972. Deported by the Israeli government, he was acquitted, in 1974, and spent the remaining years of his life in Miami.

Las Vegas

Famed for its casino-hotels, Las Vegas bills itself as the "Entertainment Capital of the World". Established in 1905, the settlement grew into a city within six years. A tolerance for various forms of adult entertainment earned Las Vegas a secondary title—Sin City.

Gambling became legal there in 1931, but it was during the 1940s that its casino-hotel industry burgeoned. Initially, the industry was largely managed and funded by organized crime figures such as Benjamin "Bugsy" Siegel and Meyer Lansky. With the arrival in the late 1960s of business tycoon Howard Hughes, legitimate corporations took over the booming trade and helped to increase tourism. Augmented by federal funding of military installations and the settlement of military personnel in the surrounding area, by 2000, Las Vegas became America's most populous city founded within the 20th century.

Latin Quarter

Not to be confused with the Latin Quarter along Paris's Left Bank, New York's Latin Quarter nightclub was opened in 1942 by Lou Walters—father of Barbara Walters—at 1580

Broadway, near Times Square, the former home of the famed Cotton Club when it moved from Harlem in 1936 until 1940.

The club featured the era's biggest names: Frank Sinatra, Ella Fitzgerald, The Carter Family, Sophie Tucker, Mae West, Diahann Carroll, Milton Berle, The Andrews Sisters, Frankie Laine, and Ted Lewis along with chorus girls, who finished the nightly shows with a high-stepping can-can. After Walters left the business in the 1950s, the club traded hands until, by 1969, it was shut by the authorities for non-payment of rent.

Lemon

A key ingredient in Sours and other cocktails as well as a garnish for even more, lemons are sweeter than limes and less acidic. They also contain more vitamin C than their green siblings. Explorer Christopher Columbus exported the first lemons to the Caribbean, in 1493, and encouraged subsequent cultivation by the Spanish throughout the Americas.

The varieties of lemons used in mixed drinks include the Eureka that is found in supermarkets; Meyer, which is a cultivated cross between a lemon and an orange; and the Yuzu, which is cultivated in Japan and Korea, possessing a character that blends both Meyer lemon and white grapefruit.

Lemon—Crusta twist

Cut the peel from the entire center of a lemon by going around the fruit with a paring knife or vegetable peeler. The twist should be about 3 cm wide.

Lemon—Horse's Neck

This is a lemon twist made from the peel of an entire lemon. To create a horse's neck, begin peeling at the top of a lemon and spiral down to the bottom to create one continuous twist from the entire peel.

Lemon Juice

Always squeeze lemon juice fresh if possible. There is no form of prepackaged lemon juice that approximates the flavour of fresh juice. 3/4 oz (25 ml) is generally equal to half a lemon.

Lemon Peel

Also known as lemon zest or lemon twist. There are two ways to cut a twist. Using a knife or vegetable peeler, lift an oblong strip of the yellow peel being careful to take as little of the white pith as possible. This gives the best, but least economical twist. You can get many more twists from a lemon if you cut the top and bottom off, then separate and remove the pulp with a bar spoon. Cut the remaining piece of lemon skin open lengthwise. Then slice it into strips. These will have a lot of pith and will get squeezed somewhat in the process so they will lose some of the lemon oil which is trapped in the pores of the lemon rind and released the first time a twist is twisted. To cut a very long thin twist, use a channel knife to spiral down the fruit from top to bottom. Twists should only be cut on the day they are used, and preferably cut fresh for each drink.

Lemon Slice

Cut the top and bottom off a lemon. Then cut across the lemon to create 5 - 10 mm thick lemon slices or wheels.

Lemon Twist

See Lemon Peel.

Lemon Wedge

Trim the tips off a lemon. Then cut it in half lengthwise. Cut each half in half lengthwise. Then cut each quarter in half lengthwise. A lemon yields eight wedges. For more economical service and for muddling, wedges can be cut in half widthwise.

Lemon Wheel

Cut the end off the lemon, then cut across the fruit to create a circle between 5 - 10 mm thick.

Lemon Zest

See Lemon Peel.

Lemonade

If you think there is only one style of lemonade, then think again—there are three distinctive styles found throughout the world. Americans and Canadians are accustomed to the mixture of lemon juice, sugar, and still water that the British call "cloudy lemonade". Western Europeans make their *limonade* or "clear lemonade" by mixing lemon juice with soda water. Both the French and the British make their *limonade* or "fizzy lemonade" by combining lemon juice and sugar with soda water. (Although some Brits favor mixing lemon squash (a juice and sugar concentrate with soda to get their share of this citrus refreshment.) In the United Kingdom, lemon-lime soft drinks such as Sprite and 7up are also called lemonade.

In the world of mixed drinks, fizzy lemonade is the topper in a classic British Pimm's Cup.

Leonhard, Alan T.

After retiring from the University of New Orleans faculty, Alan T. Leonhard became a lecturer on New Orleans history and a French Quarter tour guide. His experiences in overcoming the stereotyped images of the city, formed from motion pictures for many visitors, led him to write the 2008 book *New Orleans Goes to the Movies*.

A New Orleans native, Leonhard holds degrees from Tulane University and a PhD in political science from Duke University. While teaching at the university level for over 30 years, he received several grants for research and advanced studies including one from the National Endowment for the Humanities.

Lime

In the same way that not all lemons taste or smell the same, limes come in a variety of characters. They are used as juice in mixed drinks such as Sours, Margaritas, and Collinses as well as garnishes. Limes are more sour than lemons as well as more acidic.

The British Royal Navy ordered ships to carry limes instead of lemons, back in 1867, to prevent scurvy amongst the crew. A powerful lobby by British colonial lime-growers made this happen. (Later it was discovered limes contain significantly less Vitamin C than lemons, much to the dismay of ships' surgeons and economy minded captains.) Yet the British taste for limes found firm ground at home with the invention and commercialization of Rose's Lime Cordial.

Today, bartenders are squeezing more than the standard Persian (or Tahiti) lime found in American supermarkets. Key limes (aka: Mexican or West Indian limes) are the citrus of choice for making Cuban cocktails including the Mojito and Daiquirí. Kaffir limes from Southeast Asia and the mandarin-lemon hybrid—the Rangpur—is being used as a lime replacement because of its high acidity.

Lime Juice

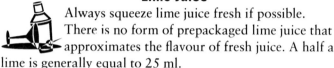

Always squeeze lime juice fresh if possible. There is no form of prepackaged lime juice that approximates the flavour of fresh juice. A half a lime is generally equal to 25 ml.

Lime Slice

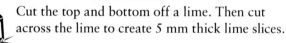

Cut the top and bottom off a lime. Then cut across the lime to create 5 mm thick lime slices.

Lime Wedge

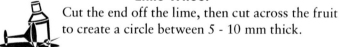

Trim the tips off the lime. Then cut it in half lengthwise. Cut each half in half lengthwise. Then cut each quarter in half lengthwise. A lime yields eight wedges. For more economical service and for muddling, wedges can be cut in half widthwise.

Lime Wheel

Cut the end off the lime, then cut across the fruit to create a circle between 5 - 10 mm thick.

Liqueur

Liqueurs are direct descendants of medieval herbal medicines that were prepared by monastic alchemists. There are still a number of monastic liqueurs in production including Bénédictine and Chartreuse.

Cordials—according to American parlance—are derived from spirit or wine that is blended with sweetened fruit pulp or juice. Because of this broad difference, the ABV of liqueurs and cordials ranges from as low as 15 percent to as high as 55 percent.

Originating from the Latin word *liquifacere* [to liquefy], liqueurs can also be flavoured with fruits, herbs, nuts, barks, spices, flowers, or cream and sweetened with additional sugar. The ingredients are macerated in base spirit for resting periods ranging from a few days to a few months.

There are literally hundreds of liqueurs and cordials produced around the globe, many of which are sold strictly as regional specialities, especially in France, Italy, Spain, and Eastern Europe.

Lounge Lizards

Since its first appearance as American slang in 1917, "lounge lizard" has surprisingly shown up in nearly every decade. A lounge lizard is typically depicted as a well-dressed man who frequents the watering holes of the rich and famous to seduce a wealthy woman with his flattery, deceptive charm, and crocodile shoes. In this sense, the term is almost synonymous with the word "gigolo".

Beat artist Robert Branaman reputedly coined the phrase during the 1950s in Wichita, Kansas as reference to people that spend too much time going from bar to bar, leading to the term being used to described anyone who frequents nightclubs.

In more recent times, lounge lizards has come to mean lounge musicians—most often in a negative sense. (Of course, that's not to say that the New York jazz band, The Lounge Lizards, formed in 1979 by John Lurie is not worth a listen with its eccentric blend of jazz, punk, and new wave.)

McGoram, Simon

Starting out in the alehouses of Surrey, England, New Zealand born Simon McGoram returned home, in 2001, having caught the bartending bug in a big way. Whilst running the award winning Mea Culpa in Auckland, Simon won *New Zealand Bartender* magazine's 2006 Bartender of the Year award and soon became the contributing editor for said publication. Moving to Sydney a year later and doing a stint at the renowned Bayswater Brasserie, Simon joined the *Bartender* magazine team full time working as deputy editor on both the New Zealand and Australian editions. In March

2009, he was appointed editor of *Australian Bartender* magazine.

Mai Tai

An icon of Tiki culture, the Mai Tai's story is truly the tale of two cocktails: one was invented in 1944 by Trader Vic Bergeron, the other created in 1933 by Donn Beach. The recipes are as different as night and day.

Maita'i is the Tahitian word for "good" and thus is the provenance of the drink name. Featured in the 1961 Elvis Presley film *Blue Hawaii*, the best story about the drink's creation comes from Trader Vic, who said he created it one afternoon for some friends who were visiting from Tahiti, including Carrie Guild. When she tasted his creation, she explained: "*Maita'i roa ae!*" (figuratively meaning "Out of this world! The Best!").

MAI TAI (TRADE VIC VERSION)
1 oz white rum, 1 oz dark rum, ½ oz curaçao, ½ oz orgeat syrup, 1 tsp rock candy syrup, juice of a whole lime. Shake all ingredients except for the dark rum over ice. Strain into a cocktail glass and float the dark rum on top. Garnish with pineapple and cherry flag.

MAI TAI (DON THE BEACHCOMBER VERSION)
2 oz water, ¾ oz fresh lime juice, 1 oz fresh grapefruit juice, 1 oz sugar syrup, 1 oz dark rum, 1 ½ oz golden rum, ½ oz triple sec, ¼ oz falernum syrup, 2 dashes Angostura bitters, 1 dash Pernod. Shake all ingredients over ice and strain into a highball glass filled with crushed ice. Garnish with fruits and serve with a straw.

Making a Twist

Twist is not just a noun in cocktail parlance. Twist is also a verb. It is the action that releases the essential citrus oils from the lemon, lime, orange, or grapefruit peel onto the surface of the drink and the inside edges of the glass. A twist is best when it's fresh cut. It may only be twisted effectively one time. After that the oils have been released from the skin's pores. Further twisting will not release any additional flavour. For this reason it is important that a twist properly is twisted.

After cutting a twist, be careful not to fold or twist it until it is directly over the drink, at a distance of about three to six inches above the rim. Hold the twist between the thumb and forefinger on both hands so that you will fold it lengthwise when you squeeze it. Then give the twist one firm squeeze directly over the glass. Afterwards, you may run the twist peel side down around the rim of the glass to intensify its effect. We recommend running it only around half of the rim as the twist is intended to add aroma not taste. Additionally, the twist may be used for garnish or discarded.

Manhattan

One of six basic drinks listed in David A. Embury's 1948 classic *The Fine Art of Mixing Drinks*, the Manhattan Cocktail's history is closely linked with New York's Manhattan Club.

Opened in 1865, the club's archives remind us that the drink was invented there. However, the club secretary was certain that another drink born there was the one destined for immortality: the Sam Ward (yellow chartreuse over crushed ice in a cocktail glass, rimmed with a long thin lemon twist).

What about the whole Samuel Tilden story? There are too many questionable or outright mythical elements for this tale—that young socialite Jennie Jerome created the drink to salute Tilden—to be true. On the evening of 29 December 1874, a party was held at the club for Samuel Tilden and William Wickham, then-governor of New York State and mayor of New York City, respectively. They were the Democrats' great hopefuls. Tilden was also a prominent member of the Manhattan Club.

The club's food and drink was said to rise above the finest New York restaurant of its time, Delmonico's: Save for the ice cream, which they bought directly from Delmonico's. The wine cellar was renowned. So, it would be likely that the club's bar was of the same calibre.

The night of the Tilden event, one Republican reporter raved about the food and drink. Although his exact words are lost, it is very possible he mentioned the Manhattan Cocktail. However, neither he nor anyone else who recorded the evening's events mentioned any member of the Jerome family—or for that matter any woman let alone Jenny Jerome Churchill—attending the event.

If it was born there, the Manhattan would have been created by the club's bartender. Drinks created by members were normally acknowledged. Take for example the Manhattan à la Gilbert (whiskey, French vermouth, and Amer Picon), or the previously-mentioned Sam Ward. The

Manhattan could have made the club's cocktail list as early as 1865 when the club opened or any time prior to 1874.

MANHATTAN COCKTAIL
2 oz bourbon or rye whiskey, 1 oz Italian sweet vermouth, 2 dashes Angostura bitters. Stir or shake over ice and strain into a cocktail glass. Garnish with an orange twist or a cocktail cherry.

Maraschino Liqueur

A bittersweet, clear liqueur derived from Marasca cherries, which are grown in Dalmatia, Croatia, mostly around the city of Zadar and in Torreglia (near Padua in Northern Italy), this liqueur's distinctive character comes from the flesh, the skin, and the pit, which imparts an almond-like flavour. Honey is also part of the ancient recipe. The distillate matures for at least two years on ashwood because it does not lend its colour to the liqueur. The resulting spirit is then diluted and sweetened.

The original recipe created, in the early 1500s, by Dominican monks in Zadar, Croatia, was a cherry rosolio (rosolio being a particular method for making liqueur common to Italy and Croatia). Sometime in the 1700s, the liqueur was named maraschino.

Lending a touch of dryness and fruitiness, maraschino is used to make, amongst other drinks, a Floridita Daiquiri and an Aviation Cocktail.

Marc

Marc—or eau-de-vie de marc—is a spirit distilled from the pomace that remains when the grapes are pressed for wine making. Collected at a high ABV, marc has a very distinctive character when it is well-aged. In Italy, this spirit is called grappa.

The best known marcs are produced in Burgundy, possessing a lighter character than grappa because they are made from white grapes. The most expensive marc originates from this area—Marc des Hospices de Beaune. The lightest marc—and the one possessing the greatest finesse—is produced in France's Champagne region. However, excellent marcs are also produced in Romani-Conti, Musigny, Chambertin, Nuits Saint-Georges, Mersault, Montrachet, and Auvergne.

Margarita

The Latin-American Spanish word for "daisy" lends itself to an extremely popular tequila Daisy—the Margarita. Like the other classic "M" cocktails, there are numerous tales and debates over the Margarita's origins. The list is impressive:

1934: Willie: at the Los Dos Republicos in Matamoros created it for Marguerite Hemery.

1936: Danny Negrete at the Garci Crispo Hotel made it as a wedding present for his sister-in-law Margarita.

1938: Danny Herrera at the Riviera del Pacifico Hotel and Casino in Ensenada, Mexico crafted it for actress Majorie King.

Circa early 1940s: Enrique Bastate Gutierrez of Tijuana, Mexico divined it as an homage to actress Rita Hayworth, whose birth name was Margarita Cansino.

1942: Francisco "Pancho" Morales at Tommy's Place in Juarez, Mexico improvised the drink for a woman who asked for a Magnolia.

1948: Margaret Sames, an Alcapulco bar owner.

One thing is for certain, the drink closely resembles the Picador Cocktail found in William J Tarling's 1937 *The Café Royal Cocktail Book*.

These days, Margaritas can be found in two forms—natural and frozen (that is, frappeéd like a Frozen Daiquirí). And just like its rum sibling, variations abound from Strawberry Margaritas to Pineapple Sage Margaritas.

MARGARITA
2 oz tequila, 1 oz triple sec, 1 oz fresh lime juice. Rim a cocktail glass with a lime slice and coarse salt. Shake ingredients over ice, then carefully pour into the glass. Garnish with a fresh lime.

PICADOR
1 oz fresh lime or lemon juice, 1 oz Cointreau, 2 oz tequila. Shake, strain, and serve.

Margaritaville

A song written and recorded in 1977 by Jimmy Buffett, "Margaritaville" from his album *Changes in Latitudes*, which tells the tale about a drink in Austin, Texas and about the first huge surge of tourists who descended on Key West during the 1970s. In fact, the song was written in Key West. "Margaritaville" reached #8 on Billboard Hot 100 chart,

Cocktail Movers and Shakers

Master bartenders are like gangsters and presidents – their reputations earn them nicknames (like Anthony "Mad Dog" DiPasquale, or Johnny "Sausages" Barbato) or sobriquets (like "Honest Abe" Lincoln). The following list of modern day masters are among the best at the bar. Can you... Match the Mixologist to his Moniker:

Name	ANSWER	Nickname
1. Tony Abou-Ganim		A. Dr Cocktail
2. Dale DeGroff		B. Beach Bum
3. Robert Hess		C. King Cocktail
4. Jeff Berry		D. The Modern Mixologist
5. Ted Haigh		E. Drinkboy

ANSWERS:
1. D; 2. C; 3. E; 4. B; 5. A

topped the Easy Listening (Adult Contemporary) chart at #1, and peaked at #13 on the Hot Country Songs chart. Named for the Margarita Cocktail, its lyrics reflect the laid-back lifestyle of the tropics and subtropics.

Martini

The reigning champion of classic "M" cocktails, whose origin is hotly debated, the Martini (aka: Silver Bullet) is still the subject of controversy when it comes to its making. No two people agree on whether it should be shaken or stirred, made with gin or vodka, with orange bitters or without, with Italian or French vermouth, balanced 2:1, 3:1, 5:1 10:1, 12:1, dashes of curacao, absinthe or crème de noyau. You get it.

One thing is certain about the drink that journalist HL Mencken once called "the only American invention as perfect as the sonnet"and EB White referred to as "the elixir of quietude", the Martini is the greatest test of a bartender's skill—not just in the making of it, but in the ability to give customers what they want.

What is known is that the first documentation of a Martini recipe appeared in Harry Johnson's 1888 revised edition of his *Bartenders' Manual*, along with a Marguerite (aka: Dry Martini) and a Bradford à la Martini. The first time the name "Dry Martini" appeared with a recipe was in Louis Muckensturm's 1906 book *Louis' Mixed Drinks*, directly above a recipe for the Marguerite.

One of six basic drinks listed in David A. Embury's 1948 classic, *The Fine Art of Mixing Drinks*, there is the most serious possibility that the Martini was named after the  brand of vermouth that was used to make the first recipe. Think of the Bacardí Cocktail, the Dubonnet Cocktail, the Chartreuse Cocktail, see what we mean? Jack Townsend in his 1951 book *The Bartender's Book* believed it to be true. Gary Regan (aka: gaz regan) thinks so, too. And after some careful digging in the archives of a well-known brand of vermouth, so do we.

MARTINI
2 oz Plymouth Gin, 1 oz dry vermouth, 1 dash orange bitters. Stir or shake over ice. Strain into a cocktail glass. Garnish with either a lemon twist or an olive.

Martinez

Many historians have attributed the Martini's origins to flamboyant bartender Jerry "the Professor" Thomas' creation—the Martinez. Curiously enough, in the 1862 edition of Thomas' *The Bar-Tender's Guide and Bon Vivant's Companion*, neither the Martini nor the Martinez are listed among the recipes. Only ten cocktail recipes were presented: Bottle, Brandy, Fancy brandy, Whiskey, Champagne, Gin, Fancy Gin, Japanese, Soda, and Jersey.

If Thomas had created the Martinez while working at the Occidental Hotel in San Francisco around 1860, it's strange that he didn't include it in his 1862 first edition. As far as we can reckon, much of the Martinez story was created in the 1960s by San Francisco advertising agency. (But don't let the controversy stop you from making a pilgrimage to Martinez, California, as you can still take a peek at the plaque that pays homage to the eponymous drink.)

Another story tells us that Julio Richelieu created the drink, in 1874, at a bar on Ferry Street in Martinez, California. According to his much younger brother-in-law John "Toddy" Briones, Richelieu divined the libation when a prospector asked him to create a new drink in exchange for a bottle of Jesse Moore whiskey. Or a bag of gold dust. Or a gold nugget. Also according to Briones, Richelieu later opened a bar in San Francisco near Lotte's Fountain.

We wondered why Thomas was credited for so many years with the creation of the Martinez and the Martini.

The conclusion was that journalist Herbert Asbury, author of *Gangs of New York* and writer of the introduction to the 1928 edition of Thomas' book was a writer who didn't always let the truth stand in the way of a good story, and was as convincing as HL Mencken, perpetrator of the Aztec origins of the cocktail and the Great Bathtub Hoax.

MARTINEZ
2 oz Old Tom gin, ½ oz Italian sweet vermouth, 2 dashes maraschino liqueur, 3 drops orange bitters. Shake over ice and strain into a cocktail glass. Garnish with a lemon slice.

Measure

Don't laugh. Measures come in all shapes and sizes behind the bar. Call them what you will—measures, jiggers, shot glasses, pony glasses—measures do one thing: They provide an accurate way to pour the contents of a mixed drink. "Eyeing" or "counting" a portion of liquid (or solid, for that matter) is not the best way to consistently produce a quality creation. Some recipes require accuracy. That's where a measure comes in.

In the US, the standard devices for measuring ingredients are a jigger or shot or bar glass (1.5 fluid ounces or 45 ml). A few decades ago a pony (1 fluid ounce) and a wine glass (2 fluid ounces, at the time, now measured as 4 fluid ounces) were frequently used in recipe books.

Where the metric system is standardised by law, metal measures such as the Bonzer brand from the UK are use to parse out everything from cocktail ingredients to single shots to measured glasses of wine. Produced in a number of sizes, the 25 ml, 50 ml, and 60 ml measures are in just about every bartender's kit. (The underside on most is ideal for measuring 10 ml.)

Menken, HL

American journalist, essayist, magazine editor and satirist Henry Louis Mencken (1880-1956) is regarded as one of the most influential writers during the first half of the 20th century. He was also a notorious trickster, having published an article in 1917 in which he claimed that the bathtub was introduced into the United States as recently as 1842, the first ones having been made of mahogany lined with lead. Some people actually believed it and parroted these "facts". Today, we now know this Mencken joke as "The Great Bathtub Hoax".

Yet to his credit, Mencken provided the perfect description for the Martini when he called it "the only American invention as perfect as the sonnet".

Mescal

Recently, experts have employed the term "mescal" to define any agave-based spirit that is not tequila. By law, tequila must be made from the Blue Webber agave varietal. Mescal, on the other hand, can be distilled from any combination of the 400 agave varieties that grow in Mexico.

Made by almost precisely the same process as tequila, mescal comes in blanco (bottled immediately or rested for up to 2 months before bottling), reposado (aged in barrel for 2 to 12 months), and in añejo (aged in 350-litre barrels or smaller for longer than one year).

Bottled mescals frequently contain a gusano [caterpillar]. There are two types of gusano. The red is considered superior as it lives in the root and heart of the agave. Whilst the blue gusano lives on the agave leaves. Legend has it that the gusano is placed in the mescal bottle to demonstrate its quality. If the gusano died and was preserved in the mescal it proved that it was of sufficient strength and not adulterated.

Milk

The obvious feature in a Brandy Milk Punch, there are a few rules for using milk in a mixed drink. 1) Whole milk tastes and mixes better than skim or semi-skim. 2) Milk is generally not a good substitute for recipes that call for cream.

Miller, Anistatia and Brown, Jared

See Brown, Jared and Miller, Anistatia

Mint

To keep mint fresh, treat it like a bouquet of flowers. Place it in a glass of ice water and store it in the warmest part of the refrigerator. Do not pick the leaves from the stems until you need them. In some parts of the world whole mint plants can be purchased. These remain fresh longer. Dried mint does not work as a substitute.

Mint Julep

See Julep, Mint.

Mixing Glass

Most often the clear glass half of a Boston shaker set (though separate single purpose mixing glasses are becoming more common), a mixing glass should have a total capacity of at least a liter, since you need space for ice, liquid, and for stirring. A mixing glass can have straight or sloped sides. It helps if it has a notched pouring lip so that drinks can be accurately drained into glasses after mixing. The proper strainer to use with a mixing glass is a julep strainer, however a hawthorne strainer will work as well.

Mixologist

The term is not as new as some people may have you think. A new name was coined for creative bartenders who crafted new recipes as they plied their trade coast to coast and across the Atlantic—mixologist. *The Knickerbocker: New-York Monthly Magazine*, literary home to Washington Irving, Robert Louis Stevenson, and Nathaniel Hawthorne, featured in the sixth installment of the fictional serial "The Observations of Mace Sloper" a conversation overheard in a New Jersey hotel, appearing in the July 1856 issue which noted that: "The mixologist of tipiculars directored me to apartment XC, which, being exceedingly weary, I did uncandelized. Yet if you desire illuminosity- . . ."

During the late 1890s, the *Police Gazette*—a champion of the bartending art and its adherents—suggested to its readers that those who stood behind the mahogany should call themselves mixologists to elevate their profession before the public at a time when the divide between a good quality drinking establishment and a down and dirty saloon was widening and the reputation of barkeeps was in jeopardy.

The word disappeared from view at the dawn of Prohibition until the 1990s when it was taken up again by a new generation of bartenders, who wanted to differentiate themselves from flairtenders and people who pour shots and pull pints.

Mocktails

They used to be called Virgin cocktails in the day. Ask for a Virgin Bloody Mary and you get a spiced up tomato juice served with a lemon wedge and a celery stalk—no alcohol.

Just as times change, "click" words change. Today, non-alcoholic beer is called "near beer". And non-alcoholic versions of some cocktails and mixed drinks are called mocktails.

Mojito

A direct descendant of the Draque (a stomach julep made with hierbabuena and cachaça, aguardiente de caña, or rum), the Mojito made its way from the countryside to the city where first appeared in 1910 at the La Concha Bar in Havana's Hotel-Balneario, where a bar attendant called Rogelio crafted a combination of white Cuban rum, ice, pomelo or lemon juice, unrefined sugar, a few dashes of Angostura bitters and soda water. It was baptized with the name "Mojito". The next decade, a simpler Mojito Criollo came on the scene, which was nothing more than a glass of iced rum sweetened with sugar, brightened in a touch of lemon juice, and garnished with hierbabuena (a Caribbean mint that, in terms of flavour, has little in common with the yerba buena plant found in the American west coast). It wasn't until the 1930s when Sloppy Joe's published its familiar recipe and the drink was popularized by Angel Martinez at his La Bodeguita del Medio during the 1940s that the Mojito came into its own.

MOJITO
1 tsp sugar, 1 key lime cut into quarters, 1 oz white rum, sprigs of mint, soda water. Muddle the sugar, a sprig of mint, and lime quarters gently in a highball glass. Add rum and 3 cubes of ice. Stir gently and garnish with an additional sprig of mint.

Molasses

Molasses is a by-product of the sugar-making process: Sugar cane juice is repeatedly heated and cooled to remove sugar crystals and the remaining liquid is molasses. Mild molasses comes from one round of heating. Dark molasses is produced by a second round of heat. Blackstrap is molasses that has been heated and cooled three times to extract as much sugar as possible. Brown sugars contain more of the molasses character than white sugar because of the lack of these heating steps. Molasses itself is used as the fermentable base for making many styles of rum.

Moonshine

Moonshine (aka: white lightning, mountain dew, and hooch) is an illegally produced distilled beverage. The word is believed to have descended from the British term "moonraker" used to describe people living in Wiltshire, which lies on the smugglers' secret routes that started on the southern coast and their customers who lived in London and surrounding counties. The story goes that some local people hid contraband barrels of French brandy from customs officers in a village pond. While trying to retrieve them one night, they were caught by the revenue men, but explained themselves by pointing to the moon's reflection and saying they were trying to rake in a round cheese. The excise men thought they were simpletons, laughed, and went about their business.

Based on this origin, it is no surprise that the illegally distilled whiskey, made largely by Scot-Irish immigrants who had settled in the Applachians and the Canadian Maritime provinces made their spirit by moonlight called it called "moonshine."

Moonshining in the Applachians is usually conducted on makeshift copper or stainless steel three-stage stills fitted with a copper tubing coil used as a condenser. Corn mash is the customary fermentable base that is distilled, although other grains have been known to be used as well.

Muddler

A muddler is a bartender's tool, used like a pestle to mash — or muddle — fruits, herbs, and/or spices in the bottom of a glass to release their flavour. The ideal muddler is made from unfinished or oil-finished wood. Lacquered or painted muddlers tend to chip, leaving bits of lacquer in the drink itself. Food-safe plastic muddlers are also showing up on the market, but do not have the classic look or feel of wood.

Popular cocktails that require the use of a muddler include the Old-Fashioned, Mojito, Caipirinha, and Mint Julep.

Muddling a Drink

Using the muddler end of a bar spoon or a muddler, gently crush the ingredients in the bottom of a glass with a repeated pressing motion combined with a slight twist of the muddler with each downward stroke. This is most commonly applied on wedges of citrus fruit and is essential to release the flavours from the peel, the pulp, and the pith (the white part between the peel and the pulp).

A dozen strokes with the muddler is usually enough. If granulated sugar is being muddled with fruit, adding a splash of water speeds the process of dissolving the sugar. Take care not to press too hard with the muddler as it is possible to break the glass. Also excessive muddling can release unwanted bitterness from citrus fruits as well as chalky traits in fresh mint.

The muddler should always be used in a vertical motion to avoid cracking the rim of the glass as can happen if it is placed into the glass at too much of an angle.

Muffuletta

Most folks know of New Orleans' French and Spanish heritage. But did you know that the city also has a strong bond with Italy? Sicilian immigration began during the late 1880s, and the city's cuisine found a new and enduring influence. Muffuletta—a massive Italian sandwich—is one of those contributions. Invented in 1906 at the Central Grocery, this sandwich is served on an entire round loaf of Italian bread, piled high with Provolone cheese, Genoa salami, and Cappicola ham, topped with chopped, green unstuffed olives, pimientos, celery, garlic, cocktail onions, capers, oregano, parsley, olive oil, red-wine vinegar, salt, and pepper. Around 10 inches in diameter, a Muffuletta is the perfect sharing dish washed down with a Pimm's Cup.

Museum of the American Cocktail

The Museum of the American Cocktail was founded in October 2004 by renowned mixologists, spirits experts, and food and drink writers. The current Board of Directors include Dale DeGroff (president), Jill DeGroff (vice president), Robert Hess (secretary), Ted Haigh (curator), Phil Greene (treasurer), Tim McNally, Brenda Maitland, Ti Martin, Chris McMillian, and Laura McMillian (managing director).

The Museum of the American Cocktail opened, in January 2005, with an exhibit in the New Orleans Pharmacy Museum. After Hurricane Katrina, the museum moved its collection to Commander's Palace in Las Vegas, where it was on display until November 2006. The exhibit included rare books, Prohibition-era literature and music, vintage cocktail shakers, glassware, tools, gadgets, memorabilia, and photographs from the collections of the founders.

The Museum of the American Cocktail publishes a website, and a monthly newsletter as well as events and seminars on a variety of cocktail related subjects. In May 2006, the museum published *The Museum of the American Cocktail Pocket Recipe Guide*, a pocket-sized book of cocktail tips and techniques plus 100 classic recipes every cocktailian should know.

The museum returned to New Orleans, on 16 July 2008, opening in the Southern Food and Beverage Museum at the Riverwalk Marketplace. The permanent exhibit showcases rare spirits and books as well as Prohibition-era literature. In addition to antique cocktail shakers, glassware, recorded music, graphics, paper ephemera, fabrics, and bartending tools, there are examples of the cocktail's impact on broader historical trends.

Nation, Carrie

Arrested more than 30 times between 1900 and 1910, Carrie Nation (1846-1911) would march into a watering hole with a team of women who sang and prayed while she smashed bottles and bar fixtures with a hatchet. The solidly

built, six-foot-tall Nation once described herself as "a bulldog running along at the feet of Jesus, barking at what he doesn't like."

Divorced from Dr Charles Gloyd, a severe alcoholic, shortly before the birth of their daughter Charlien, Nation often attributed her passionate prohibitionist sentiments to her failed marriage. Her second marriage, to Dr David A Nation fared far better. Whilst preaching at a Christian church in Medicine Lodge, Kansas, Carrie operated a successful hotel and established a local branch of the Women's Christian Temperance Union.

Carrie claimed God spoke to her in a vision in June 1900. Responding to this epiphany,

Nation gathered several "smashers" [rocks], headed to
Dobson's Saloon and announced: "Men, I have come to save
you from a drunkard's fate." She decimated the saloon's
entire stock with her arsenal. She proceeded to repeat her
performance at two saloons in Kiowa, Kansas, wielding a
hatchet. Then she performed "hachetations" throughout
Missouri.

She collapsed during a speech, on 9 June 1911, died,
and was buried in an unmarked grave in Belton, Missouri.
The Women's Christian Temperance Union later erected a
tombstone with her epitaph, reading: "Faithful to the Cause
of Prohibition, She Hath Done What She Could." Today,
there are over a dozen liquor stores and bars within a few
minutes drive of her grave.

Negroni

Count Camillo Negroni, who returned, in 1920, from
America to his native Italy had been a cowboy in the
American west a gambler in New York, and a banker in
western Canada in the previous decade. When Prohibition
was enacted, Negroni returned home to Firenze [Florence].
He frequented Caffee Casoni at Hotel Baglioni, where
Fosco "Gloomy" Scarselli was famed for his Torino-Milano
(then called an Americano). One day Negroni asked for his
Americano to be made without soda water and with gin. The
Negroni was born. Or was it?

Recently, a member of the Negroni family, Noel
Negroni, whose brother Héctor has traced their lineage back
to 1092, questioned this oft-told tale of Count Negroni as
there is no evidence in the noble Negroni family tree of his
existence. Also, their cousin François Marquis de Negroni
recalls his grandfather showing him a French newspaper
article from the 1920s crediting a more traceable name with
inventing the drink: Pascale Olivier Count de Negroni. They
are still searching for this article. Until it is found, there
seem to be two competing tales of the birth of this great
apéritif, but it seems either way, it is all in the family.

One of the earliest reports of the drink came from
Orson Welles in correspondence with the *Coshocton Tribune*
while working in Rome on Cagliostro in 1947, where he
described a new drink called the Negroni, "The bitters are
excellent for your liver, the gin is bad for you. They balance
each other."

NEGRONI
1 oz London dry gin, 1 oz Campari, 1 oz Italian sweet vermouth.
Shake ingredients over ice and strain into a rocks glass filled with
ice. Garnish with an orange twist.

Nicholls, Andrew

Born in Zimbabwe, raised in South Africa, Andrew Nicholls
started bartending on the Isle of Man. He was initially a
self-taught bartender. But after moving to the Netherlands,
Andrew joined Ricardo Sporkslede, Tal Nadari, and Misja
Vorstermans at Amsterdam's The Fabulous Shaker Boys.

After four good years with this group, Andrew decided
to start his own company titled Andrew Nicholls Cocktails
& Bartending, focusing on national and international high-
end bartender training, cocktail development, service, and
body language.

Andrew has been involved in bar shows conducted
Amsterdam, Paris, London, New Orleans, Barcelona,
Zurich, and Berlin,. He is also the Netherlands ambassador
for Tres Generaciones Tequila and Geranium Gin. No
stranger to cocktail competitions, he has been awarded
first place in Dutch competitions on five occasions and has
achieved second place in one international final. Currently,
Andrew is behind the bar in Amsterdam's Door 74 and
Vesper.

Nightclub

Between 1900 to 1920, working-class Americans gathered
at honky tonks or juke joints to dance to music played on a
piano or a jukebox.

During Prohibition, these venues went underground
as illegal speakeasies, and became known as "nightclubs".
Harlem's Cotton Club and Connie's Inn were popular venues
for audiences from both uptown and downtown Manhattan,
featuring the talents of Billie Holiday, Bessie Smith,
Cab Calloway, and numerous New Orleans musicians.
With repeal, the concept of the nightclub came into the
spotlight with New York's Stork Club, El Morocco, and the
Copacabana hosting the city's celebrities. The "big band"
era and the careers of numerous jazz singers were partially
fuelled by these music-centric establishments.

Nightclubs were replaced by a new concept that
appeared, in 1947, in Paris when Whisky à GoGo opened.
The owner, Régine, laid down a dance-floor, in 1953, laid
in coloured lights and replaced the juke-box with two

turntables that she operated herself. The discothèque was born. Mark Birley opened a members-only discothèque nightclub, Annabel's, during the early 1960s, in Berkeley Square, London. The Peppermint Lounge in New York City opened in 1962 and quickly became the hot spot for " go-go dancing". The nightclub concept waned in the heat of the 1960s until the 1970s disco era emerged followed by the 1980s mega clubs.

Nutmeg

A garnish that dates back to the 1500s, nutmeg can be purchased already ground or as a whole nut. The flavour and aroma last longer when purchased as whole "nuts" and can be easily ground with a nutmeg grater, ginger grater, or a kitchen rasp.

O'Neil, Darcy S.

Born in Sarnia, Ontario, Darcy S. O'Neil chose chemistry as his career rather than the culinary arts, to which he was also drawn. A downsizing notice, after six years working in a world-class oil and gas research facility, posed a new career direction. The marriage of chemistry and bartending dawned upon him.

With a completely stocked home bar and research into the world of mixology, a bartender was eventually born. In 2009 Darcy authored an outstanding book, *Fix the Pumps*, delving into soda fountain history and recipes. Currently, Darcy is working in a University of Western Ontario research lab, bartending and writing about original cocktail creations and other drink related topics at www.artofdrink.com.

Old Fashioned Cocktail

The Old Fashioned is possibly the first drink to be called a cocktail. Traditionally served in a short, round tumbler, the drink gave name to the container as well.

One of six basic drinks listed in David A. Embury's 1948 classic, *The Fine Art of Mixing Drinks*, the first usage of the specific name was for a bourbon made at the Pendennis Club, a gentlemen's club in Louisville, Kentucky.

The recipe is said to have been invented by a bartender at that club, during the 1880s, and popularized by club member and bourbon distiller Colonel James E. Pepper, who exported it to the Waldorf-Astoria Hotel in New York City.

Whatever its origins, it is clear that this drink reflects the 1806 definition of the word "cocktail"—spirits, sugar, water (ice is water), bitters.

OLD FASHIONED COCKTAIL

1 ½ oz rye whiskey, 1 sugar cube, 2 dashes Angostura bitters, 1 splash soda water. Place sugar cube in an old-fashioned glass and saturate with bitters, add a dash of soda water. Muddle until dissolved. Fill the glass with ice cubes and add whiskey. Garnish with orange slice, lemon twist and two cocktail cherries.

Olives, Cocktail

The olives used in cocktails are usually the green Spanish variety. Though they often come stuffed with red pimento, unstuffed olives are always preferable unless specified in the recipe.

Onion

Small, pickled, white onions are the standard for cocktail service. Up to three are usually added as a garnish. The Gibson is garnished with two. You may wish to drain the brine from a jar of onions and replace it with dry vermouth. This creates a more refined flavour.

Orange

A versatile fruit for drinks, oranges are cut into slices, half slices, wedges, twists, twists for flaming, horse's necks, and squeezed for juice. When frozen concentrated juice was introduced in 1951, the Screwdriver (vodka and orange juice) became popular. However, frozen concentrates and other forms of orange juice cannot match the flavour of fresh squeezed juice to this day.

Orange, Flamed Twist

To flame an orange twist, cut a round twist roughly 1.5 inches across. Cut it thick with plenty of white on the bottom. Be very careful not to bend it before you are ready to ignite it.

To flame the twist, hold it with the orange side down over a lit match or lighter for a second to warm the oils. Then aim the twist over the drink with the flame between the twist and the drink. Squeeze sharply. As the oils are released from the pores in the orange skin, they will burst into flame and land on top of the drink. A flamed twist gives a more caramelized citrus flavour to a drink. To experience the aroma, try flaming a twist into an empty wine glass or brandy snifter.

Orange Juice

Always squeeze orange juice fresh whenever possible. There is no form of prepackaged orange juice that approximates the flavour of fresh juice. Half an orange equals about 3/4 fluid ounce or 45 ml.

Orange Slice

Cut the orange in half from top to bottom. Place the cut side flat on a cutting board, then slice across the orange to create 10 mm thick half slices.

Orange Twist

Use a paring knife or vegetable peeler to cut a thin strip of the orange's outer skin about 7 - 8 cm long and about 2 cm wide. If the twist is to be used as a flaming twist, cut a thick circle about 3 cm across.

Orange Wedge

Trim the tips off an orange. Then cut it in half lengthwise. Cut each half in half lengthwise. Then cut each quarter in half lengthwise. A whole orange yields about 8 to 10 wedges. For more economical service and for muddling, wedges can be cut in half widthwise.

Papa Doble

See Daiquirí.

Pacult, Paul

A founding partner of both Ultimate Beverage Challenge LLC and Beverage Alcohol Resource LLC, Paul Pacult is also publisher/editor of F. Paul Pacult's *Spirit Journal*. He is the only person in the world to concurrently be a Master of the Quaich, a Life member of the Bourbon Hall of Fame, and a Life Member of Compagnie de Mousquetaires d'Armagnac.

As America's spirits guru, he is also a contributing editor for Beverage Dynamics and creator of the ground breaking iWhiskey App. Through Spirit Journal Inc, he consults widely to the beverage alcohol industry. He also hosts the critically acclaimed monthly tasting series in New York City—the Masters Series at Keen's Steakhouse. He is a founding partner beverage competition company Ultimate Beverage Challenge LLC.

Paul Pacult has written five books, including *A Double Scotch: How Chivas Regal and The Glenlivet Became Global Icons* and the best-selling *American Still Life: The Jim Beam Story and the Making of the World's #1 Bourbon.*

Parker, Dorothy

An American poet and satirist, best known for her wit, wisecracks, and eye for 20th century urban foibles, Dorothy Parker (1893-1967) rose to acclaim from an unhappy childhood, both for her literary output and articles in *The New Yorker* as well as her membership in the Algonquin Round Table. Following the breakup of the Round Table, Parker moved to Hollywood, where she received two Academy Award nominations. Because of her involvement in left-wing politics, during the 1950s, she was placed on the infamous Hollywood blacklist.

Parker went through three marriages (two to the same man) and survived several suicide attempts. Dismissive of her own talents, she deplored her reputation as a "wisecracker".

Patino, Chris

Manager of Brand Specialists and Trade Education for
Pernod-Ricard USA, Chris Patino's first experience behind
the bar was at O'Flaherty's—a former stop on the original
French Quarter Cocktail Tour in New Orleans. He has
since worked for Glazer's Companies of Louisiana in New
Orleans and Southern Wine and Spirits in Newport Beach,
California.

Chris was hired, in 2007, by the Absolut Spirits
Company to work under Simon Ford as the Brand
Ambassador for Plymouth Gin, Absolut Vodka, and Cruzan
Rum. Since then he has added brands such as Beefeater Gin
and Pernod Absinthe to his repertoire. Chris is a graduate
of the award-winning Beverage Alcohol Resource Program
(B.A.R. Certified). He is actively involved in supporting the
Museum of the American Cocktail, the creator of the New
York Cocktail Blog and a founding member of the New
Orleans Chapter of the Untied States Bartender's Guild.

Peach Purée

Peaches have a very short season. Thus drinks
calling for fresh peach are often made with peach
purée, which is made from fresh peaches that
are then frozen or made shelf-stable and sold in long-life
packaging to maintain the quality. Some recipes substitute
peach schnapps for fresh peach or peach purée, but peach
schnapps does not have the same flavour or the same thick
texture.

Peeler, Vegetable

A safe alternative to a knife, a vegetable peeler
reliably produces excellent twists with a
minimum of white pith on the back. (Pith has
a sharper flavour than peel and is usually undesirable in
drinks.)

Pepper

A native to southern India, black pepper and its
white, pink, and green siblings are the world's
most common spice. Pepper is always best when
it's fresh ground. A pepper mill is an essential tool if you are
going to add pepper to a Bloody Mary or any other drink.
Black, white, green and red peppercorns are all from the
same plant, just processed differently. Pink peppercorns are

not actually peppercorns, though they closely resemble them and share the name.

Petraske, Sasha

Sasha dropped out of high school when he was seventeen to work in a café as a barista. It wasn't too long before the beauty and simplicity of repetitive tasks cast a spell on him.

He thought to himself: "I could be satisfied doing this for the rest of my life, if I could make a decent living at it." The dream of opening his own cafe took hold and he kept it alternately in the front and back of his mind for years.

He got hired at Von, a beer and wine bar in New York's Village area, and was made a bartender. After a while it became clear that the hundreds of thousands of dollars needed to open a café were out of reach. Why not open a little bar first, as a stepping stone?

The three years of working for Kaarin Von Herrlich taught him the importance of candlelight and Nina Simone for creating atmosphere. Kaarin also gave him the model for the honour system that has served him so well as an operator.

What he didn't learn was cocktails. Von's only had a beer and wine license. When he opened Milk & Honey in the Lower East Side, in 2000, he simply had no clue as to how to make cocktails. This empty space was filled by visits to The Angel's Share, and an introduction to Dale DeGroff, who took one look at his first attempts, reached into his bag, and handed Sasha a 1948 copy of the Trader Vic rum book.

One of New York's pioneering speakeasy bars found its footing. Two years later, Petraske opened Milk & Honey Soho in London with Jonathan Downey. Those successes were followed by the opening of the more public venues Little Branch and Dutch Kills. Petraske has also masterminded the cocktail programs for the Lambs Club and a number of bars in the W Hotel group.

Pimm's Cup

James Pimm, a farmer's son from Kent, became the owner of an oyster bar in the City of London, near the Bank of England. He offered a gin-based cup, developed in 1823, which he served to his financial district customers in a small tankard. It was known as a "No. 1 Cup". Pimm's began large-scale production, in 1851, and sales stretched beyond his growing business to other establishments. New cups were introduced that same year–Pimm's No. 2 (scotch-whisky based) and Pimm's No. 3 (brandy-based). His company began selling the product commercially in 1859, employing hawkers on bicycles.

Pimm sold the business, in 1865, as well as the right to use his name to Frederick Sawyer. The business was then acquired, in 1880, by future Lord Mayor of London Horatio Davies, and in 1887, a chain of Pimm's Oyster Houses was franchised.

After the Second World War, Pimm's No. 4 (rum-based) was invented, followed by Pimm's No. 5 (rye whiskey-based) and Pimm's No. 6 (vodka-based) during the 1960s.

The brand fell on hard times during the 1970s and 1980s. The oyster house chain was sold and Pimm's Cups Nos. 2 through 5 were phased out.

Pimm's introduced its Pimm's Winter Cup, in 2005, a variant on No. 3 that is infused with spices and orange peel.

Piña Colada

Strained pineapple is the literal meaning in Latin-American Spanish of one of the world's iconic mixed drinks. Immortalized in song by the chart-topping 1979 hit by Rupert Holmes titled "Escape", it is one of the only drink that has spun off its flavour into perfumes, soft drink flavoring, room fresheners, mocktails, candies, cakes, lip balm, marital aids, you name it. Who can resist the aroma and character of pineapple and coconut?

Yet the Cuban Piña Colada of the 1910s and 1920s was nothing more than rum, pineapple juice, and occasionally a splash of fresh key lime juice and sometimes coconut milk. It was reported that Piña Coladas were popular in Times Square circa 1940, but not how those were made.

The Piña Colada that is best know is the one that was introduced on 16 August 1954 at the Caribe Hilton's Beachcomber Bar in San Juan, Puerto Rico. Opened in 1949, with a prime beach front location and modern amenities it drew an affluent, international clientele: John Wayne, Elizabeth Taylor, Jose Ferrar, Gloria Swanson and a host of others. Joan Crawford declared the Caribe Hilton's Piña Colada was "better than slapping Bette Davis in the face." These were the celebrities who made the drink glamorous and, for a short time, far more sophisticated than any frozen drink has a right to be.

One claim frequently ignored by most cocktail authorities is that Coco Lopez launched the Piña Colada out of obscurity. This appears to be true. Certainly, the modern Piña Colada would not exist—much less become widely adopted—if not for pre-made cream of coconut.

A common cooking ingredient throughout the tropics, but very labour intensive to prepare, cream of coconut was first packaged as Coco Lopez, in 1954, by Ramon Lopez Irizarry, an agricultural professor from the University of Puerto Rico who automated this arduous task. Irizarry personally approached bartenders and chefs around San Juan, encouraging them to experiment with his new creation. The Coco Lopez company then continued to spotlight the Piña Colada in its promotional literature for over 30 years, spreading the drink around the world. It finally found its way into the *Old Mr Boston Deluxe Official Bartenders Guide* sometime between 1970 and 1972.

Pineapple

The essence of the Piña Colada, the Pineapple and Sage Margarita, and other drinks, this bromeliad native to parts of Brazil and Paraguay was successfully cultivated in tropical locations such as Hawaii, the Caribbean, and parts of the Americas and Asia. Pineapple wedges, chunks, and leaves are frequent garnishes and ingredients in mixed drinks. Pineapple juice can be made fresh with a fruit and vegetable juicer, but it is most commonly purchased in cartons, bottles, or tins. If you are using tinned pineapple juice be sure to pour it from the tin into a plastic or glass container once it is opened. Otherwise the juice will acquire a tin taste.

Pineapple Chunk

Pineapple chunks can be cut fresh from pineapple wedges, or purchased tinned pre-cut and packaged in pineapple juice. After it is opened, tinned pineapple should be stored in a glass or plastic container.

Pineapple Juice

Pineapple juice can be made fresh using a vegetable juicer. If pineapple juice is purchased in a tin, it should be poured into a plastic or glass container immediately upon opening. Always check stored juice before using it to ensure that it is still fresh.

Pineapple Slice

A piece of pineapple cut in a circle with the center core removed, pineapple slices are normally purchased pre-cut and packaged in pineapple juice.

Pineapple Wedge

To cut a pineapple, first remove the top and base. Then slice the skin off from top to bottom. Be careful not to remove any more of the yellow flesh than necessary. Next slice the pineapple into quarters from top to bottom. Then slice off the core. Last, cut each quarter into wedges by cutting across the quarters in slices about 15 mm thick.

Pineau des Charentes

Around 1589, when distillation was launched in France's Cognac region, an unknown wine grower filled a barrel with freshly pressed grape juice. Little did he know there was a little leftover cognac inside the barrel. The spirit stopped the grape fermentation: a process called mutage. The result was mistelle, an alcoholic beverage that retains the sweetness and fruitiness of the unfermented grape as well as the aroma of the spirit. When the wine grower opened the barrel a few months later, he found a pleasant surprise. The farmer's accident is now known as Pineau des Charentes.

According to its appellation, there are two types of Pineau des Charentes: white and red.

White Pineau des Charentes must be made with one or more of the following varietals: Ugni Blanc, Folle Blanche, Colombard, Meslier St Francis, Juraçon Blanc Montils, Semillon, Sauvignon, Merlot Blanc, Merlot Noir, Cabernet-Sauvignon, Cabernet Franc. The juice and cognac must be aged in white oak barrels for at least one year, achieving 16 percent to 22 percent ABV. There are also 5-year and 10-year aged versions.

Pink or Red Pineau des Charentes must be made with one or more of the following varietals: Cabernet-Sauvignon, Cabernet Franc, Malbec, and Merlot Noir. The juice is macerated with the skins to achieve colour. The wine-cognac mixture must be aged in white oak barrels for at least 8 months, achieving 16 percent to 22 percent ABV. There are also 5-year and 10-year aged versions.

This apéritif must be treated like a wine, served very fresh and without ice at room temperature (6 degrees Celsius). It is also featured in a number of classic French cocktails found in books such as Louis Fouquet's 1896 book *Bariana*.

Pisco

This grape-based brandy is an unaged spirit produced in both Chile and Peru. Both countries lay claim to being the birthplace of pisco (meaning "little bird"). Spanish conquistadors introduced vines to the area during the 1500s to produce wine and grapes for export. Surplus or unwanted grapes were turned into brandy by the local farmers. Spain banned the exportation of Peruvian wines, in 1641, which forced growers into pisco production.

Pisco's popularity grew when ships that docked at the town of Pisco loaded up on the plentiful and cheap local spirit. This pattern only slowed when cheaper, more palatable rum became available. It was during this period that pisco gained its name—so called for the port where it was bought. Until then, it had been known only as "aguardiente" [water of life].

Chile and Peru have fought and bitterly over Pisco's origins. Due to wars between the two countries and political instability, Chile now exports over 50 times more pisco than Peru.

In style, Chilean pisco is lighter and fruitier. It is distilled to a higher ABV and has fewer impurities. Peruvian pisco is more rustic and artisanal in character.

Chilean pisco, by law, must be made from Muscat, Torentel, or Pedro Jimenez grape varieties. Peruvian law states that all pisco must be aged in inert, glass or stainless steel containers for at least 3 months. No additives that could change the flavour, odour, appearance or ABV are allowed.

In both countries, the national drink is the Pisco Sour. However, in Chile it is common to omit the egg white and the bitters.

The Peruvian glass used to serve the Pisco Sour bears the same shape as the traditional clay pots used to store the spirit. These vessels were called piscos and probably additionally contributed to the naming of the spirit.

Pisco Sour

Since 2003, Peru has a National Pisco Sour Day, which is celebrated on the first weekend in February.

According to one story, American bar owner Victor Vaughn created the drink as a variation on the Whisky Sour. Some accounts say that Morris travelled to Peru, in 1903, and worked as a cashier as the Cerro de Pasco Railway Company until he opened a bar in 1916. Morris' Bar was well-known for its Pisco Sours until the owner's declining health forced it to close in 1929.

The other tale tells us that A British seaman named Elliot Stubb obtained leave to disembark in the port of Iquique, in 1872, settled there and opened a bar. That city was part of Peru until 1884, when it came under Chilean rule.

PISCO SOUR
2 oz pisco, 1 oz fresh lime juice, ¾ oz simple syrup, 1 egg white, 2 dashes Angostura bitters. Shake all ingredients except for the bitters over ice. Strain into a cocktail glass. Lace bitters over the top.

Planter's Punch

Because of Alexander Calder's foresight in converting the Dock Theatre into a hotel and his wife's careful attention to service and maintaining a convivial atmosphere, the Planter's Hotel in Charleston, South Carolina, became one of the city's social centers, by 1806, even boasting a French pastry chef. It was a place where wealthy women and country gentlemen sipped the house tipple, a Jamaican import called Planter's Punch. The formula was simple sublime: "One of sour / One of sweet / Two of strong / And one of weak."

PLANTER'S PUNCH
1 oz fresh lemon juice, 1 splash grenadine syrup, 2 oz Jamaican dark rum, soda water. Shake juice, syrup, and rum over ice and strain into a highball glass filled with ice. Top with soda water and a dash of Angostura bitters. Garnish with a lemon slice and an orange slice.

Playboy Magazine

Founded by Hugh Hefner, in 1953, *Playboy* is an American men's magazine famed for its nude centerfolds as well as its journalism and fiction. Published worldwide, the magazine empire grew into a hospitality enterprise during the 1960s and 1970s with Playboy Clubs established in major cities such as Chicago, New York, and London. The most significant feature of the clubs was its staff of "bunnies". Few people realize that the clubs also helped launch the careers of such comedic acts such as Bill Cosby, Richard Pryor, and Dick Gregory.

The magazine's literary history includes short stories by novelists, including Arthur C Clarke, Ian Fleming, Vladimir Nabokov, PG Wodehouse, and Margaret Atwood. The Playboy Interviews and The Advisor (written by Chip Rowe) continue to be staple sections of the magazine today.

Po-Boy

You could call a Po-Boy a direct descendant of the muffaletta. They are very much a New Orleans' classic. The difference? The Po-Boy nestles inside a loaf of French bread. Add fried shrimp, oysters, catfish, soft-shell crab, or roast beef smothered in gravy. Top that off with the "fixin's": pickles, hot sauce, lettuce, and mayonnaise.

Pope, Christy

As part of the ground breaking crew at Milk & Honey, Christy Pope helped cultivate the image, standards, techniques, and repertoire that the bar is recognized for today. She also worked at the Cellar Bar in the Bryant Park Hotel where she met and teamed up with Chad Solomon.

In June of 2006, Christy and Chad partnered with Sasha Petraske to form Cuffs & Buttons Cocktail Catering & Consulting. At the same time, Christy was sharpening her consulting skills by working with the elite beverage-consulting agency, Liquid Relations. As a consultant, Christy has developed cocktails, conducted spirit, history, and technique trainings, and travelled the globe installing beverage programs for clients such as Fairmont Hotels, Sofitel Hotels, and Viceroy Hotels.

In the fall of 2008 Christy and Chad partnered with mentor Audrey Saunders to create the Tar Pit in Los Angeles. This included the fully developed supper club concept, name, design/décor, beverage menu, manuals, operational systems, and staff training.

Praline

This is not the crunchy Belgian confection that goes by the same name. New Orleans' pralines are a soft, creamy disks of pecans mixed with cream, butter, and caramelized sugar. Brought over by French colonists—who substituted the almonds used in French pralines—during the 1800s, Crescent City chefs added the cream to the recipe to thicken the texture, making it more like fudge than its European ancestors.

Presidents, US (and their drinks)

Every American president from George Washington to Barack Obama has had a favorite tipple. Beginning with Washington, who campaigned with and celebrated his inauguration with barrels of rum: his everyday drink was home-brewed, British-style porter. His wife Martha was famed for her Rum Punch. After he stepped down from office, he became a whiskey distiller.

Thomas Jefferson brewed his own beer and had his own winery. John Adam appreciated his wife's homemade beer with his breakfast. Both James Buchanan and Ulysses S Grant favoured a jug of American whiskey. William Henry Harrison took his drinking seriously, building his own distillery. His grandson Benjamin J Harrison, upon his election was presented with a barrel of fine Scotch by industrialist Andrew Carnegie.

Theodore Roosevelt was a Mint Julep man and attested that he never drank beer. His cousin Franklin Delano Roosevelt was famed for his White House cocktail parties, his Martini making as well as his love of the Old Fashioned. His successor Harry S Truman favoured an Old Fashioned, but his also enjoyed his bourbon straight.

Dwight D Eisenhower was devoted to Scotch, while his wife Mamie preferred Manhattans. His successor John F. Kennedy was a Daiquirí man all the way, while Lyndon B. Johnson was a down to earth with Scotch and sodas.

Dry Martinis and Rum & Cokes were the call for Richard M Nixon when he wasn't savouring a glass of Margaux. Gerald Ford stuck to Gin & Tonics.

Ronald Reagan was a Scotch man all the way. Bill Clinton liked a heady Snakebite, though his tastes were fairly broad. What does Barack Obama sip? Word on the internet has it that he sips an Americano, and has encouraged his staff to brew beer for him in the White House.

Prohibition in the United States

Temperance reared up its head more than once in the United States. At the dawn of the 1800s, the average American consumed about seven gallons of spirits per year, consisting mostly rum, brandy, gin, and whiskey. Coffee and tea were expensive imports. Ale and stout had a short shelf life, but were still about as ubiquitous on the breakfast table as Cheerios are now. Water? Water was downright dangerous. The Pilgrim Fathers widely believed that the "drinking of water would infect their bodies with sore sicknesses and grievous diseases."

That changed when a group of 200 Connecticut farmers campaigned, in 1789, to ban whiskey-making, just as production by emigrant Scots-Irish was on the rise and giving New England rum distillers a run for their money. They rallied behind by a 1784 pamphlet written by Dr Benjamin Rush titled *An Enquiry into the Effects of Spirituous Liquors upon the Human Body, and Their Influence upon the Happiness of Society.*

Rush was not a prohibitionist. Moderation was his message, but many fervent rural evangelicals believed total abstinence was the only cure. The call for the restricted sale and consumption of "ardent spirits" resounded in eight states, beginning with Virginia (1800) and New York (1808). The abolition of slavery and even women's suffrage were added to the platform as the movement took more solid shape.

The American Temperance Society (ATS) was formed in Boston on 13 February 1826 by preachers Lyman Beecher and Dr Justin Edwards. Within a decade, the ATS boasted 1.5 million members, 10 percent of the country's total population. But it took something stronger than religion to sway the urban mainstream.

America during mid-1840s experienced its first major immigration boom. Germans seeking political and intellectual freedom landed along with refugees of the failed Revolutions of 1848. The Great Irish Famine, between 1845 and 1852, instigated a similar exodus. These two strong drinking cultures scared the born-Americans who saw beer gardens and saloons cropping up everywhere.

Temperance became a patriotic issue that exploded into the formation of the American Party (aka: the Know-Nothings). As a way to highlight the cultural differences between immigrants and "native" Americans, leaders pushed for prohibition to Americanize hard-drinking foreigners. The party managed, in 1851, to pass a prohibition law in Maine. During the next three years, passage spread to 12 additional states.

The State of New York took a different stance. The

1857 "Regulating the Sale of Liquors" as well as an act "To Suppress Intemperance, Pauperism, and Crime" which banned the sale of alcohol on Sundays.

With the American Civil War came the end of the American Party as both sides took up arms. Since the 1776 Revolution, hearty drinking was long-standing institution amongst American soldiers. The Civil War was no different. Before the Confederacy surrendered, all but three New England states repealed prohibition.

The Women's Christian Temperance Union held its first national convention, in 1874, in Cleveland, Ohio. Its platform of social reforms saw prohibition heading a list that included the enactment of labour laws to protect working women from exploitation by male employers, a ban on prostitution, and a Sunday ban on frivolous activities such as golf. The rumblings were there, but not with enough influence to change the minds of urbanites along the coasts.

The First World War officially commenced on 28 July 1914, when Austro-Hungary invaded Serbia and Germany invaded Belgium, Luxembourg, and France. Although America did not enter the fray until 6 April 1917, anti-German sentiments began boiling over after 128 Americans died, in May 1915, in the sinking of the RMS *Lusitania* by the German submarine U-20. Former US President Theodore Roosevelt denounced "hyphenated Americanism". Mob violence ensued in the midwestern states—home to many lager breweries.

President Woodrow Wilson issued a proclamation, in November 1917, restricting the employment and travel of German-American males over the age of 14. The New York Times reported that the order directly affected 130,000 men in greater New York City and northern New Jersey alone.

Prohibitionists claimed that it was patriotic to conserve grain for the war effort. Drinking beer or alcohol was therefore unpatriotic. Brewery output took a downturn. German-owned bars and beer gardens saw a precipitous decline in patronage.

The Great War, in effect, aided the WCTU's cause. But it was the Anti-Saloon League that wielded the strongest sword, implementing pressure politics to stir citizens up to a patriotic frenzy—a true American nation had to be a dry nation.

President Wilson had already committed political suicide by not immediately involving American troops in the war. To top it off, he also strongly opposed prohibition. The pressure from both prohibitionists and women's suffrage lobbyists was too great for Congress to bear.

On 18 December 1917, the Eighteenth Amendment to the US Constitution (aka: the Volstead Act) was passed by Congress. Ratification by 36 states was completed on 16 January 1919, when Nebraska gave its approval. Wilson lost ground, except in Connecticut and Rhode Island, which were the only two states to reject the amendment. He appealed to Congress to pass the Nineteenth Amendment, guaranteeing women's suffrage in 1915, 1918, and early 1919. The clock ticked closer to the March 1920 presidential election. He called Congress to a special session on 21 May 1919. The amendment was finally passed, but it was too late to save his career.

The Volstead Act (aka the Noble Experiment) effectively quashed production, importation, and sale of all forms of alcoholic beverages in the United States. When Prohibition went into effect, on 16 January 1920, it wasn't as if Americans couldn't find a drink. Possession and consumption of liquor on private property was still legal. Wealthy Americans had stockpiled private cellars of wines and spirits, both domestic and imported, in their homes and funded the inventories for their private clubs. The White House was well provisioned with private stock of spirits brought in by newly-elected president Warren G Harding.

Druggists could dispense prescriptions for alcohol and did by the millions—for whiskey to be taken two to three times per day, for sherry, even champagne. These were only valid for a week, so they had a steady stream of repeat customers. Bootleg booze was shipped in by land and sea. Sometimes lethal bathtub booze was distilled by moonshiners in stills made from automobile radiators. Speakeasies cropped up everywhere, in cities and in the countryside.

The 1929 stock market crash and ensuing Great Depression didn't make it easy for regular folks to abstain from drinking. Couple the crippled economy and rampant unemployment with organized and publicly violent crime, ethnically-biased law enforcement, corrupt government, deaths due to uncontrolled, toxic liquor, court and prison systems that couldn't deal with overloaded dockets, and normal citizens who simply didn't agree with the right-wing extremists they had gullibly voted into power: America became a third-world nation filled with an oppressed majority ruled by crime lords and corrupt politicians.

Many of the same women who had fought for prohibition and suffrage campaigned for repeal. Pauline Sabin, a New York socialite, had voted in favor of prohibition. Active in Republican politics she later commented: "I felt I should approve of it because it would help my two sons. The word-pictures of the agitators carried me away. I thought a world without liquor would be a beautiful world."

But then she realised that the men who supported strict enforcement of prohibition drank cocktails behind closed doors. She also came to the epiphany that "children are growing up with a total lack of respect for the Constitution and for the law."

She formed The Women's Organization for National Prohibition Reform (WONPR) in Chicago, in May 1929, along with the wives of some of America's industrial leaders. Many middle-American middle class housewives saw it as an opportunity to hobnob with the "hoy-poloy". Others were disenchanted that the promised utopian society had turned out to be more of a purgatory. Membership grew to 1.5 million within two years, embracing women from all economic levels, and branched out to chapters in 41 out of the 48 states.

The WONPR was not alone. It was joined with The Association Against the Prohibition Amendment, Voluntary Committee of Lawyers, The Crusaders, and the American Hotel Organization united with the WONPR to form the United Repeal Council, which lobbied at both the 1932 Republican and Democratic conventions. Ultimately, the Republicans continued to defend the Great Experiment. So the WONPR and other initially nonpartisan organizations joined the Democratic presidential campaign and stumped for its platform: The repeal of Prohibition.

Was it really a surprise that former the Governor of New York Franklin D Roosevelt won the 1932 presidential election? In the depths of the Great Depression, he promised a New Deal of economic relief and recovery programs as well as reforms of the banking system and stock market. He also ensured the repeal of Prohibition.

Congress took the first step on 20 February 1933 when it proposed the Twenty-first Amendment—the only constitutional modification passed to explicitly repeal a previous amendment. Roosevelt took the next step on 22

March 1933 by signing the Cullen-Harrison Act, which
authorized the production and sale of both wine and 3.2
percent beer.

Even though ratification was completed, on 5 December
1933, by 36 states, there were still detractors. Both North
and South Carolina rejected the amendment. To this day,
eight states have still not ratified repeal: Nebraska, Kansas
(which prohibited public bars until 1987), Mississippi (which
was dry until 1966), Oklahoma, Louisiana, Georgia, as well
as both North and South Dakota.

With repeal, the federal government washed its hands
of liquor control, handing the power to state and local
authorities. Today, there are 19 states that hold a monopoly
on the liquor sales. And there are still "dry" counties, towns,
and villages in the United States.

Public House

A public house (aka: pub) is not just a drinking
establishment. It is part of British, Scot, and Irish culture,
serving in many villages as the focal point of the community,
so there is great concern that more pubs are closing down
than new ones opening.

Pubs are the direct descendants of the taverns that were
established by the Romans in the British Isles around 40 AD.
Although pubs that offered lodging were sometimes called
inns, this is no longer the case. Regional laws dictated pubs
to call themselves hotels. For example, in Scotland until
1976, only hotels could serve alcohol on Sundays. Wales had
a similar act that was changed starting in 1961 on a district-
by-district basis until 1996 when the last ban was lifted in
Dwyfor.

Today, there are approximately 53,500 public houses in
the United Kingdom.

Punch

Introduced from India to Britain in the 1600s by British
seamen and employees of the British East India Company,
punch is a loanword from Hindi *panch* (meaning "five"): a
drink made with alcohol, sugar, lemon, water, and tea or
spices.

The appearance of the punch bowl proved that punch
was a convivial beverage that had achieved remarkable
popularity, not only in the punch houses that emerged but
also in the homes of the rich and poor. Recipes became more

elaborate over the centuries, starting with wine or brandy bases and evolving into rum and whisky formulas. Punches disappeared after Prohibition was enacted and the ensuing shift in public tastes. However, today there is increased interest and a revival of punch amongst a new generation of mixologists and consumers.

Pupu Platter

A Chinese/Polynesian version of tapas, the pupu platter concept was exported from Hawaii and popularized in California During the 1930s with the birth of Don the Beachcomber and Trader Vic's. In Hawaiian, the word refers to appetizer servings of fish, chicken, or banana relish served with kava. But in this sense, pupu platter implies the serving of an assortment of Americanized Cantonese dishes such as egg rolls, spareribs, chicken wings, teriyaki skewers, satay skewers, bacon-wrapped pineapple, fried wontons, shrimp toasts, fried prawns, rumaki, and other items that are accompanied by a small hibachi grill for warming and finishing.

Quinquina

Extremely popular during the 1800s and 1900s, quinquinas are wine-based apéritifs infused with quinine. Lillet and Dubonnet are the most recognized brands produced today. This drink first achieved notoriety after Napoleon ordered troops stationed in Africa to consume it for medicinal reasons, serving as an anti-malarial and fever-reducer. The returning soldiers brought their taste for quinquina home with them.

Ramos, Henry C

Author Stanley Clisby Arthur documented in his 1937 book *New Orleans Drinks and How to Mix 'Em* that Baton Rouge native Henry C Ramos invented this classic, creamy concoction that is like "drinking a flower".

Henry Charles Ramos, a first generation Baton Rouge native—his parents emigrated from Germany—moved, in 1888, to New Orleans. He purchased the Imperial Cabinet Saloon at the corner of Gravier and Carondelet streets from Emile Sunier. He also bought a house on Rampart Street at the edge of the French Quarter for his growing family, and he set to work.

The saloon shared space with The Old Hickory Restaurant. (Some historians say that the invention took place at Meyer's Restaurant, but no one seems to give a location for this place.) There he remained until, in 1907, he purchased The Stag Saloon, across the street from the Gravier entrance of the St Charles Hotel. In a city where business is built on friendships and connections, it isn't too much of a surprise that he bought it from a fellow member of the Elks, Tom Anderson.

It was there that Ramos's "New Orleans Fizz" gained notoriety. Customers patiently waited up to 20 minutes to observe and savour the creations that were shaken by his army of up to 35 "shaker boys".

Three years after Ramos opened this establishment, he was asked by the Louisiana Grand Commandery of the Knights Templar to supply a crew of six "shaker boys" and his recipe as representatives of the Crescent City's delegation to a Templars convention held in August 1910 at the Congress Hotel in Chicago. Just as creamy and irresistible as those found at The Stag, the drinks, their preparations and presentation made quite a spectacle. As a *Washington Post* reporter explained:

"The bartender mixes the fizz and then he hands the shaker and glass to one of the boys.

"The boy pushes the glass and shaker firmly together, starts it a-shakin' and then he leans back against the wall. Soon he is sound asleep, but the shaking goes mechanically, as regularly as the strokes of the pendulum. Sometimes when a boy goes too soundly asleep, the expert mixer takes one shaker out of his hand before he can wake up, puts a fresh one in, and there he stands, as sound asleep as he'll ever be, a-shakin' and a-shakin', while the grateful crowd on the other side of the improvised bar partakes of the product of his somnolent industry."

This description comes from an age of open prejudice, when the word "boys" did not necessary define age but ethnicity. Ramos's shaker boys were African-American. Though they were relegated to the position of bar back in this instance, bartending was one of the few industries where a black man in the United States could rise to a position nearing equality.

In his sixties when Prohibition unfolded, Ramos elected to retire. However, this was not the end of his fizz. He shared the recipe. And when he passed away, his formula appeared as a footnote to his obituary in *Time* magazine. Of course, Prohibition did not stop the fizz. It headed south of the border in the hands of former Ramos employee AN Bulliard, who opened the Cadillac Bar in Nuevo Laredo, Mexico, much to the delight of thirsty Texans on the northern banks of the Río Grande. Bulliard was joined by Pat Perry who had worked in New Orleans at the Sazerac Bar, The Stag, the Grunewald Hotel (which would later become the Roosevelt), and the St Charles Hotel bar. The former manager of Jannsen's restaurant in New Orleans also came to work there. Some of them later returned to the north side of the border, opening another Cadillac Bar in San Antonio, and both establishments are still open as of this writing.

When the United States regained its sanity with repeal, drink historian Phil Greene tells us that the drink's popularity soared when Louisiana Senator Huey Long first re-introduced the drink in New York accompanied by bartender Sam Guarino.

"The Kingfish", as he was called, gave a press conference at the Hotel New Yorker, blasting President Franklin Delano Roosevelt's New Deal to lift America out of the Great Depression. However, the highlight of the day came when Sam demonstrated how to make a Ramos "New Orleans style".

Long's recipe, as reported by *The New York Times* differed slightly. "A noggin of gin, the white of one egg, two drops of orange flower water, dash of vanilla, one-half glass of milk with a little tincture of cream, pulverized sugar, a small dash of seltzer, and lots of ice. Shake well for ten minutes."

A deluge of letters to the editor and articles in the national news were quick to point out that the original recipe contained no vanilla (no one commented on Long's opinion of the President). Even Long's bartender Guarino publicly concurred. He then recommended both lemon and lime juice. Long's final word on the subject was that his recommendation for vanilla extract was only to be applied "if you couldn't get orange flower water."

"We saved the Ramos fizz for the American people during Prohibition," Long concluded. "I'm performing a public service showing you how."

Knowing a great thing when it gets publicity, The New Orleans Roosevelt Hotel not only served up the city's creamy classic, it trademarked the drink's name in 1935. The introduction of the blender in the same decade, of course, made the drink easy to produce without the employment of shaker boys. While suggesting a blender might ring of blasphemy to a purist, it makes a superb Ramos.

RAMOS GIN FIZZ

1 tb superfine sugar, 3-4 drops orange flower water, juice of a half a lime, juice of a half a lemon, 1 ½ oz dry gin, 1 egg white, 1 ½ oz heavy cream, 1 splash seltzer water. Mix in a mixing glass in the order given. Add crushed ice. Shake until the mixture gets body—"ropy" as some veteran barkeepers express it. When thoroughly shaken, strain into a tall thin glass for serving.

Rat Pack

A group of actors that originally centered on Humphrey Bogart, during the mid-1960s the name "Rat Pack" was employed by the media to refer to a later group, after Bogart's death, which called itself "the summit" or "the clan". Featured members included Frank Sinatra, Dean Martin, Sammy Davis, Jr., Peter Lawford, and Joey Bishop, who appeared together on stage and in films such as the 1960 hit *Ocean's Eleven*.

How did the name come about? According to one version, the group's original "den mother", actress Lauren Bacall proclaimed, "You look like a goddamn rat pack," after her husband Humphrey Bogart and his friends returned from a night in Las Vegas.

Visiting members included Errol Flynn, Nat King Cole, Mickey Rooney and Cesar Romero. According to Stephen Bogart, the original members of the Holmby Hills Rat Pack—named after the location of the Bogarts' home—included Frank Sinatra, Judy Garland, Lauren Bacall, Sid Luft, Humphrey Bogart, Swifty Lazar, Nathaniel Benchley, David Niven, Katharine Hepburn, Spencer Tracy, George Cukor, Cary Grant, Rex Harrison, and Jimmy Van Heusen.

In his 1972 autobiography *The Moon's a Balloon*, Niven confirms that the Rat Pack originally included him, but not Sammy Davis Jr nor Dean Martin.

Rea, Brian

Author of *B.A.S.T.A.R.D.S.: Bars and Saloons, Taverns and Random, Drink Stories* as well as the website thebarkeeper.com, Brian Rea is a "barchivist" with the largest collection of bartending and cocktail recipe guides, as well as other drink-related books, ephemera, related trains and trucks, miniature bars, videos, drink menus, artifacts, discontinued brands, and artwork in existence.

Rea spent 60 long years behind, and in front of, bars, cocktail lounges, restaurants, nightclubs, and some unmentionable places.

Regan, Gary

(aka: gaz regan) After being raised in British pubs in Lancashire, gaz regan (the bartender formerly known as Gary Regan) immigrated to New York City in 1973 when he was just 22 years old. For over two decades he tended bar at a variety of places in Manhattan. He started to write about spirits and cocktails in 1990 in various trade and consumer magazines. His first book, *The Bartender's Bible*, was published in 1991.

Between 1995 and 1998, gaz coauthored *The Book of Bourbon and Other Fine American Whiskeys, The Bourbon Companion, New Classic Cocktails*, and *The Martini Companion*. Since then gaz has written *The Joy of Mixology* (2003), *the bartender's GIN compendium* (2009), *The Cocktailian Chronicles: Life with the Professor* (2010), and *gaz regan's Annual Manual for Bartenders, 2011.*

Gaz writes "The Cocktailian", a bi-weekly column for *The San Francisco Chronicle*, and over the years wrote for publications such as *Food & Wine, Gourmet, The Wine Enthusiast, Wine & Spirits, The Malt Advocate, Nation's Restaurant News, Cheers Magazine*, and *Imbibe.*

Reiner, Julie

Julie Reiner has been elevating the cocktail scene in New York City for 15 years, most notably with the opening of the Flatiron Lounge (2003), the Pegu Club (2005), Brooklyn's Clover Club (2008), and her latest venture, Lani Kai (2010). As co-owner and beverage director of the Flatiron Lounge,

Reiner drew much of her inspiration from her native Hawaii by utilizing the freshest fruits and premier quality spices and spirits available in her original cocktails. Julie's beverage program at the Clover Club is highly focused on classics and furthers her signature style of superior quality and green market ingredients. Lani Kai, located in Soho, features a modern tropical décor, Pacific Rim plates, and a more tropical interpretation of Julie's cocktail styling. Julie's consulting company, Mixtress LLC, helps to create top-notch beverage programs and cocktails for restaurants, bars, and spirits companies. Her latest, Monkey Bar, received a 2-star review from *The New York Times*.

Flatiron, Pegu and Clover opened to rave reviews and have enjoyed a top ranking among the best bars in the world. In 2009, Clover Club was honoured with the award for "Best New Cocktail Lounge" at Tales of the Cocktail®.

Julie began her career in the cocktail lounges of San Francisco and made her way to New York City in 1997 where she sparked the interest of "King Cocktail" himself, Dale DeGroff. Julie began installing beverage programs in some hot spots around Manhattan and by May of 2003, she had fulfilled a dream of opening her own gourmet cocktail lounge.

Julie's recipes have been featured in *The New York Times, New York Magazine, Food & Wine, Imbibe, The Wall Street Journal, Esquire, Playboy, Gourmet Magazine, Food Arts, Bon Appetit, GQ, Fortune, Wine Enthusiast, O Magazine, Crains, Time Out NY* and *Time Out London, The London Times,* and *Wine & Spirits.* Julie has also been featured on *The Today Show,* The Food Network, the Cooking Channel, Martha Stewart Radio, CNBC, LXTV, and the Fine Living network. In 2011, Julie was honoured with a James Beard nomination for spirits professional of the year.

Repeal

See Prohibition in the United States.

Reynolds, Blair

A blogger and bartender based in Portland, Oregon, Blair Reynolds' website TraderTiki.com has been running for over two years, covering classic and modern tropical drinks, tiki bars, and rum. Blair was recently featured as an "internet pioneer" in Ted Haigh's *Vintage Spirits and Forgotten*

Cocktails, Second Edition. Blair also runs "Tiki Nights" at several bars in the Pacific Northwest. He also owns a syrups company that features exotic flavours for tropical mixology.

Red Beans & Rice

Another New Orleans comfort food, Red Beans & Rice is a Monday tradition. Mondays used to be the traditional "wash day", so housewives put on a pot of red beans, seasoned with a ham bone left over from Sunday's dinner, to cook all day while they tended to the laundry.

Nowadays, Red Beans & Rice, spiced up with onions, celery, bell peppers, bay leaves, thyme, garlic, spring onions, cayenne, bay leaves, cayenne, chicken stock, and a dose of bacon drippings are accompanied by a side of andouille sausage or pork chop and rice.

Rob Roy

First appearing in New York City around 1894, the Rob Roy is a cocktail sibling to the Manhattan. The drink is named for the Scottish folk hero Robert Roy MacGregor. The Rob Roy owes its existence partially to the introduction of Dewars Scotch Whisky to the United States, in 1892, as well as the New York City premiere of the operetta of the same name composed by Reginald de Koven.

Like the Manhattan, the Rob Roy can be made sweet, dry, or perfect. The standard Rob Roy is the sweet version, so there is no need to specify a sweet Rob Roy when ordering.

ROB ROY
1 oz blended Scotch whisky, 1 oz Italian sweet vermouth, 1 dash Angostura bitters. Shake ingredients over ice. Strain into a chilled cocktail glass.

Rolling a Drink

This is the most gentle of the mixing techniques, and is used when it is important not to bruise a drink. It is most commonly used to mix the Bloody Mary because tomato juice loses its thickness and becomes thin when agitated. To roll a drink, hold your filled mixing glass next to an empty one. Then pour the contents back and forth between the two mixing glass a few times, keeping the glasses close together.

Rose's Lime Cordial / Rose's Lime Juice

Rose's Lime Cordial (aka: Rose's Lime Juice or just Rose's in the United States) was created by Lauchlan Rose, who created the patented the method, in 1867, for preserving citrus juice without alcohol. His first factory was established in Leith, Scotland, a year later. The Merchant Shipping Act of that same year required all ships of the British Royal Navy and Merchant Navy to provide a daily lime ration to sailors to prevent scurvy. The product became nearly ubiquitous with British seamen—hence the term "limey" was applied to them. The brand was introduced, in 1901, to the United States. It is a key ingredient in the Gimlet Cocktail.

Rum

A direct descendant of cachaça, rum is distilled from sugarcane products such as sugarcane juice or molasses. It is a spirit that was born in the Caribbean after Dutch settlers in northern Brazil immigrated to Barbados and Martinique, during the 1600s, introducing the techniques and equipment for distilling sugar cane products. British naval fleets introduced the same methods to Jamaica, Cuba, and other British colonies.

Speculation surrounds the origins of the word "rum". Some people have said it was derived from the word "rummage". But that term actually dates back to 1582 and implies that a person is making a thorough search of something or some place.

Others have said the word was born from the British word "rummer" or German "roemer", which is a type of wine glass. But these vessels appeared in Europe at the same time as the cane-juice liquor.

One romantic suggestion holds that rum is an abbreviated version of "rumney", a type of wine made in Greece and the southern Balkans similar to the sweet dessert wine called mavrodaphne.

According to 19th-century philologist Walter William Skeat, the term is an Anglicized version of the Malay word "brum", which is an arrack made from sugarcane juice. Historian Frederick H Smith found that the first documented use of the word appears in a plantation deed recorded in Barbados in 1650, which identifies the Three Houses estate in St. Philip parish as having "four large mastick cisterns for liquor for Rum."

A year later, Barbados resident Giles Silvester made the only known reference linking the words rum and "rumbullion" when he wrote: "the chiefe fudling they make in the lland is Rumbullions, als Kill Divill, and this is made of Suggar cones distilled in a hott hellish and terrible liquor." The term "rumbullion" was a common word in Devonshire, England that means "a great tumult".

However its birth came about, the word "rum" was adopted throughout the Caribbean in the seventeenth century.

First appearing in the 1750s in *Diderot and Alembert's Encyclopedie*, the word "rhum" with an "h" is specifically used to describe rums made in French colonies such as Martinique and Guadeloupe. The Spanish word "ron", indicates the sugar cane spirit was produced in Spanish colonies, the most famous of which are made on the island of Cuba.

Rum, Asian

Made with a wash of molasses and water, Asian rums tend to follow regional sugar cane production. These white and golden rums, distilled from column stills, are produced primarily in the Philippines and Thailand.

Rum, Australian

Made with a wash of molasses and water, Australia produces a substantial amount of white and golden rums in a double-distillation method, utilizing both column and pot stills. It is a tradition that began in the 1700s.

Rum is the second most popular alcoholic beverage in the country after beer. Light rums are also produced on some of the islands in the South Pacific such as Tahiti.

Rum, Barbadian

Made from a fermented wash of molasses and water, Barbadan rums are known for their light, sweet character. Distilled in either pot or column stills, rums from this region were first produced, in 1627, after the British settled the island.

The most famous Barbadan rum producer is Mount Gay, which was established in 1663.

According to some sources, in 1637, Dutch émigré Pietr Blower brought cane seedlings and distillery equipment to

Barbados. A traveller to the island Henry Colt noted that Barbadians were "devourers upp of hot waters and such good distillers thereof." Production was probably small at that point. Sugar cane seedlings were originally imported from Brazil.

Rum, Canadian

Made from a fermented wash of molasses and water, Canadian rums have a long tradition. The 300-year-old history of trading rum for dried cod fish continues in the Atlantic Maritime provinces of Newfoundland and Nova Scotia where golden rums from Antigua, Barbados, and Jamaica are imported and aged for five years. The resulting hearty rum is known locally as "screech".

Rum, Cuban

Made from a fermented wash of molasses and water, Cuban rums are known for their light-bodied, crisp, clean character. Distilled in column stills, Cuban rums were the first to employ charcoal filtration to achieve their smoothness and silvery hue, dating from the 1860s.

Although Cuban colonists experimented with rum making as early as 1598, the island did not enter into full-scale production until British forces captured Havana, Cuba in 1762. The occupation forces introduced large numbers of slaves and may also have brought distilling equipment and knowledge of advanced rum-making methods.

In 1764, shortly after British occupation, Spanish officials lifted the prohibitions against rum making and use in Cuba and Puerto Rico. The inability to stop illicit rum trafficking probably hastened this decision. Opening the rum industry also meant increased revenues from distilling licenses. In the 1770s, Cuban rum was exported to New Spain, Cartegna, New Orleans, and Florida, where rum making was still prohibited.

Cuban rum is the featured spirit in a number of classic cocktails, not the least of which are the Mojito, the Daiquirí, and El Presidente.

Rum, Dominican Republic

Made from a fermented wash of molasses and water, Dominican Republic rums are known for their full-bodied character. Distilled in column stills, the first notable rum from this region was produced, in 1852, by Erasmo Bermúdez.

Dark Dominican Republic rums are generally aged in American white oak barrels. For colour continuity, caramel is frequently added to the finished product.

Rum, European

Europe is a blender of imported rums. Both the United Kingdom and France import rums from their former Caribbean colonies, which they domestically age and bottle.

Heavy, dark Jamaican rums are imported into Germany and mixed with neutral spirit at a 1:19 ratio to produce "*rum verschnitt*".

A similar product that is produced in Austria is called *inlander rum*.

Rum, Guatemalan/Nicaraguan

Made from a fermented wash of molasses and water, Guatemalan and Nicaraguan are primarily medium-bodied rums that are distilled from column stills. They have recently begun to gain international recognition.

Rum, Guyanese

Made from a fermented wash of molasses and water, Guyanese rums, especially those from Demerara, are known for their richness and heavy body. Rums are made in either pot or column stills. Aged for extended periods of up to 30 years, Guyanese rums are frequently used for blending with lighter rums from other regions.

Rum, Haitian

Made from a fermented wash of molasses and water, Haitian rums follow an old French tradition of producing rich, heavy rums. These spirits are double-distilled in pot stills and aged in oak casks for three or more years, making them exceptionally smooth.

Rum, Jamaican

Made from a fermented wash of molasses and water, Jamaican rums are known for their rich character and aroma. These rums generally ferment for longer periods, ranging from 5 to 14 days.

Jamaica has official classifications for rum, ranging from light to very-full flavoured. They are extensively used for blending, but are also savoured as sipping rums.

Rum, Martinique

Made from a wash of boiled sugar cane juice and water, rhum agricole is a speciality of the French West Indies, specifically the French departments of Martinique, Guadeloupe, and Réunion Island.

The production of *rhum* is unique: Freshly-pressed cane juice is boiled prior to fermentation. Sometimes the ferment is strengthened with the addition of dunder [the residue left in the still after distillation]. The one exception is Rhum Saint-James which is made from a blend of 60 percent dunder and concentrated cane-juice syrup.

Another exception is *rhum industriel*, which is made with molasses.

Aged rums from this region rest in brandy casks for a minimum of 3 years.

According to historian Frederick H Smith, a Dutch Jew from Brazil named Benjamin Da Costa introduced, in 1644, both sucery and distillery equipment to Martinique, which explains why the technique for rhum agricole production is very similar to that of cachaça.

One of the most popular drinks made with this style of rum is Ti Punch. A number of bottled versions of this drink were produced from the French market in the mid-twentieth century.

Rum, Mexican

Made from a fermented wash of molasses and water, there are still a few Mexican rums distilled for a local market.

Rum, Puerto Rican

Made from a fermented wash of molasses and water, Puerto Rican rums are known primarily for their light, very dry character. All Puerto Rican rums are distilled in column stills. All white Puerto Rican rums must, by law, be aged a minimum of one year, while dark rums must be aged a minimum of 3 years.

Rum, Trinidad

Made from a fermented wash of molasses and water, Trinidad's rums are primarily light rums and are distilled in column stills. Much of the yield is used to produce Angostura bitters. But the aged rum produced by the same distillers has gained respect in the past few decades as a unique style all its own.

Rum, Virgin Islands

Made from a fermented wash of molasses and water, rums from the Virgin Islands are divided between the United States Virgin Islands and the British Virgin Island.

Only the US Virgin Islands still produce rum, predominately making light, mixing rums that are distilled from column stills. There are some fine dark and aged rums made by the archipelago's most significant producer, Cruzan. This style featured with equal prominence in pre-Prohibition era cocktails as Cuban and Jamaican rums. Saint Croix rum was reference found in vintage cocktail recipes.

These rums, and those of nearby Grenada, also serve as the base for bay rum, a classic aftershave lotion.

Rum, Venezuelan

Made from a fermented wash of molasses and water, Venezuelan rums are primarily aged into golden and dark rums.

Rum, American

Made from a fermented wash of molasses and water, the New England states produced rums from Caribbean molasses until the days of Prohibition. At one time, New England was the world's rum producer.

Today, there are a handful of rum distilleries in the south, especially New Orleans, producing a range of light and medium-bodied rums.

Rum-Running

Rum-running is the illegal business of smuggling alcoholic beverages via boat or other water transport into areas where such transport of commercial goods is forbidden by law. The smuggling usually is executed to circumvent taxation or prohibition laws within a particular jurisdiction.

The term rum-running is more commonly applied to smuggling over water; bootlegging is applied to smuggling over land. The term most likely originated at the start of Prohibition in the United States (1920–1933), when ships from Bimini in the western Bahamas transported cheap Caribbean rum to Florida speakeasies. But rum's cheapness made it a low-profit item for the rum-runners, and they soon moved on to smuggling Canadian whisky, French champagne, and English gin to major cities like New York and Boston, where prices ran high. It was said that some ships carried $200,000 in contraband in a single run — at a time when $50 a week was considered a good wage for an honest worker.

Ryan, Jim

Working his way through the ranks as a bartender and mixologist in some of New York's top bars and lounges. It was while working at Perry Street Restaurant under the tutelage of famed chef Jean-Georges Vongerichten, that Jim Ryan was able to consolidate the elements that to him were the cornerstone of the service industry—anticipation and invisibility in service as well as a seasonal approach to mixology.

At Brooklyn's Dressler Restaurant, while working as beverage director, he developed the entire drink program from scratch. Jim personally selected every brand behind the bar and made sure that he and his staff were actively involved with engaging and educating each guest, an integral part of the experience at Dressler.

Jim started in his new role, in 2008, as an Ambassador for Hendrick's Gin. An avid cocktail book collector with an unending appreciation for the classics and precision in mixology, Jim has been honoured to train and judge alongside the most renowned mixologists in the business. His cocktails have been featured on menus and in publications across the country, including *The New York Times*, *The Seattle Times*, *The Kansas City Star*, as well as *IMI Drinks* and *Out Magazine*.

Rye

Rye whiskey can refer to two types of whiskey: 1) American rye whiskey, which must be distilled from at least 51 percent rye; and 2) Canadian whisky, which may or may not include rye, so long as it possesses the aroma, taste and character generally attributed to Canadian whiskey.

Rye whiskey was the prevalent domestic whiskey in the northeastern states, especially Pennsylvania and Maryland. It largely disappeared after Prohibition save for a few brands, such as Old Overholt. Today Heaven Hill, Catoctin Creek, Bulleit, Jim Beam, and Wild Turkey also produce rye whiskeys as does a distillery in Mount Vernon, Virginia that sells a version of the rye whiskey George Washington made on his open farm.

Canadian whisky is often referred to as "rye whisky", since historically much of the content was from rye. There

is no requirement for rye to be used to make whiskies in
Canada with the legally-identical labels "Canadian Whisky",
"Canadian Rye Whisky" or "Rye Whisky" provided they
"possess the aroma, taste and character generally attributed
to Canadian whisky". Most contemporary Canadian
whiskies contain only a fraction of rye, with the exception of
Alberta Premium which is one of the very few whiskies made
from 100 percent rye mash.

Salt Rim

Wet the rim of an empty cocktail glass with one of the
drink's ingredients. For example, if a drink contains triple
sec pour a tiny bit of triple sec on a plate, then set the glass
upside down onto the wet plate. Shake off any excess liquid,
then touch the rim of the upturned glass to a plate covered
in sugar. Again, shake off any excess. Sometimes coating
only half the rim is preferable as it gives the consumer of the
drink the option of having a sip with or without the sugar.
Another variation is to add sugar to the salt on the rim. This
creates a softer effect.

Sauce, Tabasco®

A hot sauce made from tabasco peppers, vinegar,
and salt by the McIlhenny Company on Avery island,
Louisiana, Tabasco sauce is aged in American white
oak barrels for three years before it is bottled. The
flavour is very intense, as the spice is underscored by
the vinegar. There are hundreds of other hot sauces
available, but this is the most famous for making
mixed drinks such as the Michelada and Bloody
Mary. There are also a wide variety of hot sauces
made by Tabasco, including jalapeño-based green,
chipotle-based smoked, habanero, garlic, and "sweet
and spicy" sauces. None of these are aged the same way as
the original.

Sauce, Worcestershire

First made at 60 Broad Street, Worcester, England, by
chemists John Wheeley Lea and William Henry Perrins, Lea

& Perrins Worcestershire sauce was placed in commercial production in 1837 and rapidly achieved popularity throughout Britain. Some say that the entrepreneurs acquired the recipe from Arthur Moyses William Sandys, 2nd Baron of Sandys (1792–1860) of Ombersley Court, Worcestershire, Lieutenant-General and politician, a member of the House of Commons, who encountered a similar condiment in India and commissioned the local apothecaries to recreate it.

Worcestershire sauce contains—among other ingredients—vinegar, anchovies, tamarind, soy sauce, onions, and garlic. In addition to its use in British cuisine, Worcestershire sauce also plays a role in Chinese dim sum and other savoury dishes, having been introduced there during the 1800s. It also features in recipes for the Bloody Mary, Bloody Caesar, and Michelada.

Saunders, Audrey

One of modern mixology's leaders and co-owner of the award-winning Pegu Club in New York, Audrey Saunders worked with Dale DeGroff for a number of years before she became beverage director for the December 2001 reopening of Bemelmans Bar at The Carlyle Hotel in New York. The bar gained a global reputation for cocktails under her management.

Audrey has been a guest mixologist at London's Ritz Hotel, Belfast's The Merchant Hotel as well as Crystal Cruise Lines and Celebrity Cruise Lines. She has appeared on both American and British television and radio, conducts cocktail seminars and lectures. She has been written about in numerous international publications.

Her awards and recognitions include: *Esquire Magazine*'s Best New York Bar plus the Tales of the Cocktail® Best Bartender, World's Best Cocktail Bar, and Best Bar Mentor awards. *The New York Times*, in December 2009, deemed her Gin Gin Mule one of the most significant cocktails of the decade. And in June 2010, *Imbibe* magazine voted her one of the 25 most influential cocktail personalities of the past century.

Savoy Hotel

Located on the Strand in London, the Savoy was built by theatrical impresario Richard D'Oyly Carte with profits from his production of William S Gilbert and Arthur Sullivan operas. Opened on 6 August 1889, the Savoy was also the first luxury hotel in Britain to sport electric lights throughout the hotel, electric lifts, bathrooms inside most of the lavishly furnished rooms, and constant hot and cold running water. Carte hired manager César Ritz and French chef Auguste Escoffier, who established an unprecedented standard of quality in hotel service, entertainment, and dining. The hotel is also home of the American Bar, which has seen some of the world's most famous and significant head bartenders serving royalty, celebrities, the rich and famous, including Ada Coleman, Harry Craddock, Eddie Clarke, Joe Gilmore, Peter Dorelli, Salim Khoury, and now Erik Lorincz.

Sazerac

See Old Sazerac House in Chapter 2 for its history.

Sazerac Seal of Approval

The Sazerac is New Orleans' official cocktail. That means you expect to get a fabulous Sazerac whenever you roam—the French Quarter, Marigny, or Uptown. The New Orleans Culinary and Cultural Preservation Society, announced in 2010 the inauguration of the Sazerac Seal of Approval, which honours New Orleans establishments that adhere to the traditional Sazerac recipe and serve the highest quality Sazeracs the Crescent City has to offer.

Establishments are selected by a team of "secret sippers" who sample countless Sazeracs throughout city, evaluating each for the quality of the ingredients used, taste, and presentation. Three different secret sippers visit each location on three separate occasions to ensure that each venue provides a consistent serve across its bartending staff.

The 2010 recipients were: Bar Tonique, Carousel Bar at the Hotel Monteleone, Irvin Mayfield's Jazz Playhouse, Sazerac Bar, DBA, French 75, Cure, and Bar Uncommon.

Recipients in 2011 were: Sylvain, Napoleon House, Tujague's, Dickie Brennan's Bourbon House, Dominique's, and Loa in the International House Hotel.

Schnapps

Made in the same manner as eau-de-vie, German schnapps [to snatch] is a fruit-based spirit distilled to more than 32 percent ABV. The most popular versions are apfel schnapps [apple], zwetschgenwasser [plum], Williamsbirne [pear], and kirschwasser [cherry].

American schnapps are essentially very sweet liqueurs made by adding flavourings and sweeteners to neutral grain spirit. These are commercially available in a variety of flavours, ranging from peach and sour apple to mint, root beer, and chocolate.

Screwdriver

In a 1952 *Los Angeles Times* article, journalist Art Ryon commented that: "While concurring with Tim Turner's lament on these pages about the recent practice of substituting vodka for gin in Martinis, we regret that he didn't go further. Do you realize, Tim, that the latest craze in the amateur set is vodka and orange juice?"

The earliest written reference to this vodka and orange juice Highball appeared in the 24 October 1949 issue of *Time*, noting that "In the dimly lighted bar of the sleek Park Hotel, Turkish intelligence agents mingle with American engineers and Balkan refugees, drinking the latest Yankee concoction of vodka and orange juice, called a 'screwdriver'."

A 1959 article in *The Washington Post* backed up the story, noting that: "It was in Ankara [Turkey] during World War II that a group of American fliers invented a drink called the 'Screwdriver'—orange juice and vodka—because they couldn't stand Turkish vodka. This was a slur on Ankara's estimable cuisine which at its worst is never so dreadful as the Screwdriver."

It all started when powdered citrus juice was developed for the military during the Second World War. The Florida Citrus Commission turned its attention, around 1943, to concentrating orange juice via vacuum evaporation. To this concentrate, lime juice was added to retain the flavour and appearance. Then the mixture was frozen. Introduced to the public, in 1946, frozen orange juice concentrate put frozen foods on the proverbial map. The restaurant industry welcomed a labour-free, non-seasonal option to fresh-squeezed juice. The modern housewife saw it as an economical and labour saving solution to squeezing oranges. And the 1950s bar industry found a cheap and fast drink to add to its then-limited repertoire of offerings.

The drink begat numerous variations including the Brass Monkey, Harvey Wallbanger, Long Sloe Screw, Sloe Comfortable Screw, Slow Screw Against the Wall, and the Sonic Screw.

Seed, Eric

A Minneapolis-based purveyor of speciality spirits and
wines, Haus Alpenz is owned and operated by Eric Seed,
who imports and markets classic cocktail ingredients such as
crème de violette, allspice dram, Velvet Falernum, Vermouth
de Chambèry, Old Tom Gin, alpine eaux-de-vie, Stone Pine
Liqueur, and unusual wines like Sparkling Grüner Veltliner.

Establishing Haus Alpenz in 2005, Seed was graduate
of Kenyon College and the University of Chicago. He
previously worked in business strategy and development,
marketing and financial analysis.

No stranger to New Orleans, Mr Seed's first local
speaking engagement followed an article he wrote in 1996
for the *Nuveen Quarterly*, ""What's Eating Jefferson
Parish?"", a review of the social and economic consequences
of the nutria's insatiable appetite for gardens and levees.

Serneels, Dean

Dean Serneels is the inventor of the Flairco brand of bottles,
training DVDs and bartender products. An award-winning
mixologist and flair bartender, he shares his innovative
bartender training programs with literally thousands of
bartenders from around the world.

Serneels has appeared on national commercials, the
Food Network, and on CMT's *Search for the Ultimate
Coyote.* He recently became the Director of Beverage
Applications for American Beverage Marketers and is now in
charge of their cocktail development and training programs.

Shaker, Boston

A two-piece shaker consisting of a metal bottom and glass
or plastic mixing glass, the Boston shaker is standard in
equipment for bartending. The mixing glass and metal
bottom are inserted into each other for shaking or used

separately for stirring or muddling. A separate
strainer, such as a hawthorn or julep strainer,
are employed to strain the contents into a serving
glass. Some bartenders strain by narrowly
separating the two pieces after shaking and
straining the drink through the resulting gap.

One of the earliest descriptions of the artful
use of a Boston shakers appeared in an 1868
copy of *Notes and Queries*, published by Oxford
Journals, as follows:

"...What is a cocktail shaker?"

"I never possessed a pair of 'cocktail shakers' myself, but a young officer in the Blues, a fellow passenger in a Cunard steamer in which I crossed the Atlantic in 1865, did possess, and was very proud of, a brace of tall silver mugs in which the ingredients of the beverage known as a cocktail (whiskey, brandy or champagne, bitters and ice) are mixed, shaken together, and then scientifically discharged — the 'shakers' being held at arm's length, and sometimes above the operator's head — from goblet to goblet, backwards and forwards, over and over again till the requisite perfection of homogeneousness has been attained. These are the 'cocktail-shakers,' and our friend in the Blues was so great a proficient in the difficult art of goblet -throwing, and the compounds he made were so delicious, that ladies on board, who in the earlier stages of the voyage had been dreadfully sea-sick, were often heard to inquire, towards two PM whether Captain _____ was going to make any cocktails that day."

Shaker, Cobbler

A three-piece cocktail shaker that tapers at the top and ends with a built-in strainer that has a cap fitted over it for shaking, the cobbler shaker (aka: cocktail shaker) was adapted by consumers as an at-home mixing device for cocktails, especially during the 20th century. This style of shaker has become a major collectible because of the myriad of shapes and configurations that were designed between the 1890s and 1940s.

Shaker, Cocktail

See Shaker, Cobbler.

Shaker, French

A two-piece shaker that is similar to the cobbler shaker, a French shaker (aka: Parisian shaker) includes a metal bottom and a fitted metal cup. However, it does not have a built-in strainer. This means that mixture must be strained in the same manner as a Boston shaker, using a hawthorn or julep strainer.

Shaker, Parisian

See Shaker, French.

Shaking a Mixed Drink

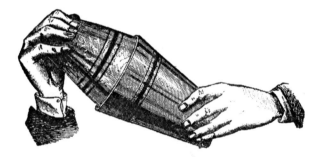

Build the ingredients for the recipe in the glass portion of a Boston Shaker or the base container of a French or cobbler shaker. Fill the glass with ice cubes to approximately two-thirds full. Then upturn the glass portion into the metal portion of the Boston shaker and create a firm seal by tapping or pressing on the base of the glass part. The glass will not sit straight in the metal, but it is not meant to. On one side the glass and metal should be touching all the way to the rim of the metal, while the rest of the way around, there should be a gap above the point where the mouth of the glass touches the metal.

With the point of most contact facing you, grasp above

and below the seal with both hands, placing your thumbs and index fingers on the glass, while your other fingers grasp the metal. This ensures that even if your seal is not tight, the two parts will not separate when you shake them.
(If you are using a French or cobbler shaker, simply secure the cap or top and firmly grasp both the top and bottom.)

Now, raise the shaker and proceed to shake in a manner that sends the liquid and ice in the shaker back and forth inside the length of the shaker. A slight up and down motion combined with the forward and back motion causes the contents of the shaker to spin as well as moving back and forth.

The goals of shaking are to mix the contents of the shaker, to add proper dilution through rapid melting of ice, to cool the liquid rapidly, and to brighten the flavours by thorough aeration. Depending on the temperature of the ice (colder ice allows for more shaking and thus makes a superior drink), a drink should be shaken from 10 to 20 seconds.

To open the Boston shaker after shaking, place your

hand on the seam between the glass and metal portions as above so that both the metal and glass portions are firmly grasped, and the point of most contact between the glass and metal is facing toward you. Then with the heel of your other hand, tap the rim of the metal cup firmly once or twice. This will release the seal. Then as you lift off the glass portion turn it quickly upright so that you do not spill the last drops from the glass onto the bar.

(See also Stirring a Mixed Drink for tips on building and icing ingredients in the mixing glass.)

Shaking versus Stirring a Mixed Drink

Shaken or stirred? Everyone knows this one: Always stir clear drinks. Shake drinks containing fruit juice, egg, or cream. Those are the simple, steadfast and eternal rules on the subject.

You have to shake a drink if you want creaminess or foam—stirring an egg white just doesn't work. Also, you never shake a drink if your end goal is clarity. Shaking aerates the drink, suspending tiny bubbles that give it a cloudy appearance. Shaking also tends to break up the ice, so a single strain won't catch every little shard.

So, a customer asks for a shaken Martini or Manhattan? You shake that drink with a proper shaker face. What about the rules? They may be simple, but they are hardly written in stone. In the end, the only perfect drink is one made exactly how the person drinking it wants it.

Harry Craddock shook his Martinis. The fundamental difference between Harry Johnson's first two Martini recipes—the Marguerite and the Bradford à la Martini is that one was stirred and the other was shaken. Jack Townsend, bartender at the 21 Club, offhandedly stated that "it's not a Martini if you shake, it's a Bradford."

David A Embury wrote a chapter on the subject titled "To Stir or To Shake". In it, he explains that shaking gets a drink colder faster, but leaves it a bit cloudy, especially if vermouth is involved. He talks about the beauty of a stirred Martini or Manhattan, but nowhere does he claim shaking is a bartending felony.

By now everyone knows that you cannot "bruise" gin. There is only one drink that does bruise: A Bloody Mary should never be shaken because the tomato juice gets thinner with agitation—not the vodka or gin, the tomato juice.

In his 1948 book *The Hour*, author Bernard de Voto

cautioned against the application of such a pedantic platitude: "We may understand how cults form with the Martini as with all arts, how rituals develop, how superstitious and even sorcerous beliefs and practices betray a faith that is passionate and pure but runs easily into fanaticism. But though we understand these matters we must not be lenient toward them for they divide fellowship."

Now it is time to resurrect a few more words from de Voto, who remarked in the same tome: "Or take the superstition, for I cannot dignify it as a heresy, that the Martini must not be shaken. Nonsense. This perfect thing is made of gin and vermouth. They are self-reliant liquors, stable, of stout heart; we do not have to treat them as if they were plover's eggs. It does not matter in the least whether you shake a Martini or stir it. It does matter if splinters of ice get into the cocktail glass, and I suppose this small seed of fact is what grew into the absurdity that we must not 'bruise the gin'."

Back when Jerry "The Professor" Thomas was wowing the crowds with his mixing prowess, throwing was the finishing touch. It was the artfulness that made sipping a cocktail made by a master a technicolour experience. Shaking was just an essential overture.

It is very clear in this description that the shake was just the beginning of the mixing process, and the cups were taken apart so the mixer could throw the drink between them.

This is not the first time old bartenders have lamented about young upstarts chucking every drink into a shaker and banging away. In the 1890s, a number of career mixers were quoted as saying that the new generation had completely lost the art of the profession by switching to shaking, when everyone worth their limes knew most drinks should be thrown.

Still unsure whether to shake or stir? Ask the person consuming the drink how he or she prefers its execution. In the end, that is what really matters.

Shine, Willy

Early in his career, Shine had the privilege of working with top chefs and beverage industry mentors like Dale DeGroff and Steve Olsen. They taught and bestowed upon him culinary techniques, ingredient science and the wonderful History of American bartending and cocktail making from a lost era. From there, he went on to run a myriad of restaurants and bars honing his natural talent for cocktail design and execution. Willy's mixology skills have been featured in many newspaper and magazine articles, on television and on radio shows.

He is currently the cofounder of a global full service beverage consulting company with a focus on cocktails and spirits. Contemporary Cocktails, Inc brings a distinctive appreciation to the modern-day art of cocktail design, beverage programs, brand ambassadorships, spirits & cocktail education, cocktail catering and event execution. Both nationally and internationally, Willy is among the most well respected alcohol beverage professionals. He is a member of the Beverage Alcohol Resources Program (BAR) as well as BAR Smarts and travels extensively in that capacity to perform educational trainings and seminars.

Stirring a Mixed Drink

Build the ingredients for the recipe in a mixing glass. You may add ice first or last. There are advantages to both: Ice added after the other ingredients can cause splashing. However, the mixing process can be interrupted at any time prior to adding the ice as the drink will not become diluted. This can be very advantageous if you discover the customer wanted a different drink after you have started mixing. Before the ice is added, the mix in the mixing glass can be set aside and will not spoil if it rests for a few minutes, or a few hours.

Ingredients should always be added to the shaker in ascending order of cost. Cheapest ingredients go first: sugar, citrus juice, dashes of bitters, splashes of cordials. This is so that if you make a mistake with any of these, you don't waste the more expensive ingredients such as a 50 ml pour of a super-premium spirit.

Once the ingredients and ice are combined in the shaker, place the bar spoon into the mixing glass near one side of the glass, not directly in the center. Place it in at a slight angle. Then holding it loosely like a pencil, begin to spin the ice, allowing the spoon to twist within your grasp rather than trying to hold it rigidly.

An average stir should be around 20 seconds. Water freezes at 0°C, but ice can be much colder than that, depending on the temperature at which it is stored. Very cold ice, which looks dry on the surface, requires a slightly longer stir to provide sufficient dilution, and makes a superior drink. Warm ice looks wet and melts much faster, thus it requires a much shorter stir.

Shochu

A distilled beverage produced in Japan, shochu is made from barley, sweet potatoes, or rice, though it is sometimes produced from brown sugar, buckwheat or sweet chestnut. Weaker than whisky or standard-strength vodka but stronger than wine and sake, shochu is frequently distilled more than once. In recent times, shochu is being used in mixed drinks, replacing a new make whisky or vodka because of its distinctive character.

Shochu is not to be confused with Korean soju which is best likened to a lighter, sweeter version of vodka with a much lower ABV.

Shrub

A mixture of fresh fruit simmered with vinegar or spirit and sweetening, shrub was the perfect way to preserve seasonal fruits for use in the colder months. Popular in Britain and America during the 1700s and 1800s, when refrigeration was not even a probability, raspberries, strawberries, blackcurrants, and blackberries were lovingly preserved with vinegar and served up diluted with water as a fruity wintertime treat. The citrusy goodness of oranges, lemons, and limes shipped from tropical climates served as the poor-man's punch: Preserved with sugar and rum or brandy that was served diluted with water. Recipes appear in both cookbooks and cocktail books throughout the Victorian and Edwardian eras, disappearing during Prohibition.

In recent times, shrubs are being revived and their recipes enhanced for inclusion in cocktail and mixed drink recipes.

Sidecar

The cognac cousin of the Martini, Manhattan, Rob Roy, and Daiquirí, the Sidecar was popularized Patrick MacGarry, the celebrated bartender at London's private gentlemen's club, Buck's, during the 1920s. The drink appeared in two landmark cocktail books: Harry MacElhone's 1919 *Harry's ABC of Cocktails* and Robert Vermiere's 1922 *Cocktails: How to Mix Them*.

According to MacElhone, an American serviceman

fighting on the western front came up with the Sidecar while visiting with "John", a barman at Henry's on Rue du Volney in Paris. It was an immediate hit with both expats and locals. According to 1923 news reports that also announced the Monkey Gland to the world, the Sidecar's naming came from the fact the drink was potent enough to "take you for a ride".

SIDECAR
2 oz cognac, ½ oz Cointreau, ½ oz fresh lemon juice. Shake ingredients over ice and strain into a cocktail glass. Garnish with a lemon twist.

Singapore Sling

Opened in 1887 by Tigran Sarkies and his brothers Arshak, Aviet, and Martin, Raffles Hotel in Singapore opened with a Bar & Billiard Room, frequented by literary luminaries such as novelists Joseph Conrad and Rudyard Kipling (later by Somerset Maugham, and Noël Coward).

Due to its popularity, the bar room was expanded in 1907, giving bartender Ngiam Tong Boon a better theatre for crafting, sometime around 1910, the Million Dollar Cocktail and the Singapore Sling.

SINGAPORE SLING
1 oz dry gin, ½ oz Cherry Heering, 4 oz fresh pineapple juice, 1/2 oz fresh lime juice, ¼ oz Cointreau, ¼ oz Bénédictine, ¼ oz grenadine syrup, 1 dash Angostura bitters. Shake all ingredients over ice. Strain into a collins glass. Garnish with a pineapple slice and a maraschino cherry.

Six O'Clock Swill

The six o'clock swill was an Australian slang term for the last-minute rush to buy drinks at a hotel bar before it closed. During a significant part of the 20th century, most Australian and New Zealand hotels shut their public bars at 6 PM. A tradition developed of heavy drinking during the hour between finishing work at 5 PM and the bars closing at this early hour.

The closing time was introduced partly in an attempt to improve public morals and get husbands home to their families at an earlier hour. However, the rule had the reverse effect. Glasses were saved until the last call came for drinks. Then the emptied glasses could be refilled through a pistol-shaped spigot hitched to a long tube instead of via the tap.

Sloe Gin

Sloe gin is a liqueur made from the infusion of sloes (aka: blackthorn berries) into gin that is sweetened with sugar. A relative of the wild plum, sloes are a stone fruit whose seeds impart a delicate almond character to the resulting liqueur. The feature in the post-1917 Blackthorn Cocktail and in Sloe Gin Fizz, sloe gin suffered a setback when commercial producers during the 1940s through 1970s produced a sweet spirit made with artificial colourings and flavouring that was labelled as sloe gin. Revived interest in this customary home-made British winter drink as both a straight tipple and as a mixed drink ingredient has prompted gin distillers such as Plymouth and Sipsmith to commercially produce sloe gin according to traditional methods.

Smith, Claire

Joining Moët Hennessy in March 2003 as the UK Brand Ambassador for Belvedere Vodka, Claire Smith studied law at Nottingham Trent University. After graduation, she spent a year establishing and running various bars in the university town. She learned the art of creating a luxury cocktail, in 2001, at Nottingham's first cocktail bar, Synergy. That same year, she won Britain's largest cocktail competition—"Battle of the Giants". While working at several London upscale hot spots, Claire studied under expert mixologists Dick Bradsell and Henry Besant. Shortly after she joined Moët Hennessy, she promoted to International Communications Manager and currently holds the title Head of Spirit Creation and Mixology, responsible for creating and perfecting Belvedere's new flavours in addition to designing cocktails and setting and identifying key mixology and vodka trends.

Claire introduced Belvedere Black Raspberry and Belvedere Pink Grapefruit in 2009 and 210, respectively. She launched Intense Unfiltered 80 proof, in 2011, that's distilled with Dankowskie Diamond Rye and also launched Belvedere Bloody Mary.

Smith, Peter

Executive chef and owner of PS 7's in Washington DC, Peter Smith officially began his culinary career at the Country Club of Fairfax, Virginia, at the age of fourteen. After three years, Smith moved to Pino's, one of the top Italian restaurants in the area. From Pino's, he simultaneously worked at the Carlyle Grand Café in Shirlington, VA, while attending culinary school at L'Academie de Cuisine in Gaithersburg, Maryland, under classically Swiss-trained chef François Dionot. Following graduation, Peter took an externship at the Occidental Restaurant in Washington, DC, where he met chef Jeffrey Buben. When Buben left the Occidental in 1993 to open Vidalia restaurant, he invited Smith to join him. An invaluable asset to the Vidalia team, the 28-year-old Smith was named Executive Chef after five years. Smith left the famed southern-inspired restaurant, in 2004, to work on the creation of a concept that culminates his experiences with a modern edge—PS 7's opened in 2006.

Soda, 7-up

Created by Charles Leiper Grigg, in 1929, 7-Up was originally named "Bib-Label Lithiated Lemon-Lime Soda". Until 1950, the product contained lithium citrate, a mood-stabilizing patent medicine that was popular during the 1800s and early 1900s. The brand was a popular folk remedy for relieving stomach upsets and is a component in a number of Highballs. The main competitor to &-Up in the market is Sprite.

Soda, Bitter Lemon

Scurvy had plagued explorers and naval fleets for centuries until the British Royal Navy adopted a daily ration of fresh lemons for its crews during the Napoleonic Wars (1803-1815). Scurvy could sometimes be an equal scourge at home. Citrus was hard to come by in northern Europe unless you could afford to procure a private shipment from Spain. At the time, citrus was a seasonal ingredient, not a perennial as it is today. If a shipment of lemons did arrive, they were quickly consumed in lemonade or made into sherbet, shrub, or syrup to preserve their goodness and flavour.

To answer this demand, the J Schweppe & Company's Schweppes Aerated Lemonade was launched in 1834. It was a blend of the famed soda water and fresh lemon juice. The drink became a staple in the British marketplace that was remarketed, in 1957, as Original Bitter Lemon, a favourite mixer with either dry gin or vodka.

Soda, Cola

Success always invites competition. Copycat versions of chemist Angelo Mariani's Vin Tonique Mariani à la Coca de Perou abounded after he began commercial production in 1863 in Paris. A blend of coca leaves and red wine, this patent medicine was applauded as a an ideal stomach stimulant, an analgesic on the air passages and vocal chords, appetite suppressant, anti-depressant, and treatment against anaemia. Coca des Incas and Vin des Incas were just the French competitors to Mariani's fortune that led him to open offices in London and New York to keep up with demand.

American pharmacist John S Pemberton was the most successful, in 1884, when launched Pemberton's French Coca Wine in Atlanta, Georgia. Another overnight success would have been in the making, if it hadn't contained wine. The Klu Klux Klan forcefully lobbied for prohibition in Atlanta. The law was enacted in 1885. Pemberton was pressed to reformulate his product, replacing wine with cola extract and soda. Coca-Cola was born.

The high cocaine content of Pemberton's product as well as other American competitors forced Mariani to increase his dosage to 7.2 milligrams per ounce for US export.

The century turned and became apparent to many in Europe and the US, that cocaine addiction was a very real, very serious hazard. Coca-Cola was forced to denature its coca extract in 1904. Two years later, the Pure Food and Drug Act forced Mariani to claim there was no cocaine, only coca leaves in his product. The curtain closed on American sales of Vin Tonique Mariani with the passage of the 1914 Harrison Act that further controlled the sale of any product containing coca leaves or cocaine.

When Pemberton sold the company to businessman Asa Griggs Candler, strategic and aggressive marketing tactics led Coca-Cola to its dominance of the world soft-drink market throughout the 20th century.

Copycats once again abounded with competitive cola drinks appearing on the market from the 1890s through to today. The leading competitor in this category is Pepsi.

Regardless of name, colas are key ingredients in a number of Highballs including Rum & Coke (aka: Cuba Libre) and Jack & Coke.

Soda Water

See Water, Soda.

Solomon, Chad

Chad Solomon's bartending career began in 2001 at the Bryant Park Hotel's Cellar Bar. While there, he met future partner Christy Pope who was working at Milk & Honey. He joined her the following year. Chad joined the bar staff of the Flatiron Lounge, in 2005, in preparation for his transition to the opening team for Pegu Club. The following year, he joined the beverage-consulting agency, Liquid Relations, conducting spirits trainings, developing cocktails, and installing beverage programs for clients such as Fairmont Hotels, Sofitel Hotels, and SBE Entertainment.

That same year, Chad, Christy Pope, and Sasha Petraske formed Cuffs & Buttons Cocktail Catering & Consulting, in addition to its beverage catering services, the company has grown into a full service cocktail and spirits-consulting firm.

In the fall of 2008 Chad and Christy partnered with Audrey Saunders to form Here's How!™, capitalizing on their collective beverage hospitality expertise. Here's How!™ created the Tar Pit for chef Mark Peel in Los Angeles, in 2009, including the fully developed supper club concept, name, design/décor, beverage menu, manuals, operational systems, and staff training.

Spanton, David

An entrepreneur in the Australian hospitality trade media industry, David's career began as a manager and bartender in some of Sydney's leading hotels and bars before he launched, in 1998, Spanton Media Group. He has been instrumental in developing several innovative industry-specific publications and events including *Australian Bartender* magazine, the Sydney Bar Show, the Bartender Magazine Australian Bar Awards. He recently launched the website 4barscom.au.

Sparkling Wine

Champagne is only one of the world's sparkling wines that are used in making mixed drinks such as the French 75, Buck's Fizz, Mimosa, Bellini. Spumante, Prosecco, and sparkling wines from the United States and Britain have also made their appearance behind the bar.

Speakeasy

The term "speakeasy" was launched into the American vocabulary during the late 1880s, in Pennsylvania, where an Ohio newspaper reported that: "In Pittsburgh, they call a place where liquor is sold without a license a 'speak easy'. It is likely, the trend began in McKeesport, just outside Pittsburgh, where illegal saloon operator Kate Hester was known to hush raucous patrons by whispering, "Speak easy, boys!" Soon it was popularised in Philadelphia, and the notion spread from there that drinking in an unlicensed establishment implied the habitués had to speak "easy" [softly] to escape the notice of the police.

However, this is not the expression's origins. A parable had run on and off in newspapers across the nation for at least twenty years about a father speaking crossly to his young son, and the son replying with a tearful entreaty, "Speak easy, Father." It went on to encourage all family members to "speak easy" to create a spirit of harmony in the household. So, the term had already been pressed into the minds of the masses for a few decades before it found a usage those masses would readily adopt.

In this parable, "speakeasy" did not mean using a password. It meant keeping a civil and polite tongue. The term, used in this context appeared outside this parable as well. A number of writers, critical of Americans avoiding conflict at all costs and steering clear of any difference of opinion to keep peace, said America was in danger of turning into "a giant speakeasy through the opposition of some people to conversation".

Thus, at a time when drinking was negatively associated with boisterous behaviour and crime, "speakeasy" was also a lesson in polite and responsible drinking.

Words that would be proven beyond dispute decades later, appeared in New York's *The World*, in 1895:

"The 'speak-easy' has always been the result whenever Prohibition has been attempted...If we had no intolerant crusade, we would have no 'speak-easies'.

During Prohibition in the United States, the terms joined "blind pig" and "blind tiger" in the public eye as a slang expression for an establishment where illegal liquor was sold. Today, a speakeasy is an intimate cocktail bar in which classic cocktails are served that is sometimes hidden from public view as in the case of Milk & Honey and Employees Only.

Squeezer, Citrus

Heavy metal two-part squeezers are available in most cooking shops these days and are ideal for instantly squeezing lemon or lime halves. If you cannot find one or prefer a juicer that will fit oranges as well, a handheld citrus reamer is an excellent tool.

Stirring

 Build the ingredients for the recipe in a mixing glass. You may add ice first or last. There are advantages to both: Ice added after the other ingredients can cause splashing. However, the mixing process can be interrupted at any time prior to adding the ice as the drink will not become diluted. This can be very advantageous if you discover the customer wanted a different drink after you have started mixing.

Before the ice is added, the mix in the mixing glass can be set aside and will not spoil if it rests for a few minutes, or a few hours. Ingredients should always be added to the shaker in ascending order of cost. Cheapest ingredients go first: sugar, citrus juice, dashes of bitters, splashes of cordials. This is so that if you make a mistake with any of these, you don't waste the more expensive ingredients such as a 50 ml pour of a super-premium spirit.

Once the ingredients and ice are combined in the shaker, place the bar spoon into the mixing glass near one side of the glass, not directly in the center. Place it in at a slight angle. Then holding it loosely like a pencil, begin to spin the ice, allowing the spoon to twist within your grasp rather than trying to hold it rigidly. An average stir should be around 20 seconds. Water freezes at 0°C, but ice can be much colder than that, depending on the temperature at which it is stored. Very cold ice, which looks dry on the surface, requires a slightly longer stir to provide sufficient dilution, and makes a superior drink. Warm ice looks wet and melts much faster, thus it requires a much shorter stir.

Strainer, Double

European bartenders commonly double strain their drinks by pouring the liquid from the shaker or mixing glass through a julep or hawthorn strainer into a double strainer or tea strainer before allowing the drink to land in the glass.

Strainer, Hawthorn

The strainer with the wire coil around it is commonly used when straining a shaken drink from the metal portion of the Boston shaker. (Note: If you are using a Boston shaker, always strain from the metal side of the shaker as it is less prone to dripping.)

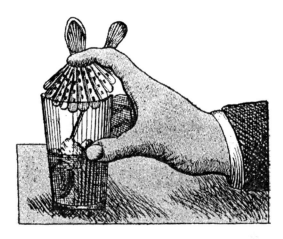

Strainer, Julep

This is the strainer that looks like a soup ladle designed by a Dadaist sculptor. The julep strainer is used to strain stirred drinks from the mixing glass.

Sugar

The ideal sugar for making drinks is superfine granulated sugar (aka: caster sugar)—previously called powdered sugar. This has historically caused much confusion as confectioners sugar is also called powdered sugar but contains up to 3 percent cornstarch. Cornstarch does not belong in any cocktail or mixed drink.

Besides superfine granulated sugar and common, everyday granulated sugar, there are a variety of other making their way behind the bar, including:

Brown sugar with approximately 3.5 percent residual molasses remaining from the refining process is also sometimes made by adding molasses to white sugar crystals. Dark brown sugar simply contains more molasses.

Cube sugar (aka: lump sugar) which is made by compressing wet sugar into molds. They are commonly made from white or less refined light brown sugar and used to make Champagne cocktails.

Demerara sugar is an unrefined sugar with a large grain and a light golden color.

Turbinado sugar, which is a light brown sugar with large crystals. It is produced by heating fresh sugar cane juice and removing enough liquid that it can begin to crystallize. It is then spun in a turbine to remove any remaining liquid.

Making a Sugar Rim for a Drink

Wet the rim of an empty cocktail glass with one of the drink's ingredients. For example, if a drink contains triple sec pour a tiny bit of triple sec on a plate, then set the glass upside down onto the wet plate. Shake off any excess liquid, then touch the rim of the upturned glass to a plate covered in sugar. Again, shake off any excess. Sometimes coating only half the rim is preferable as it gives the consumer of the drink the option of having a sip with or without the sugar. Colored sugars add a festive touch.

Swizzle Stick

The term swizzle stick refers to two completely different objects that are found in the bar.

Swizzle sticks, in one sense, are small sticks placed in cocktails to stir the drink. Commonly made of plastic, the decorative swizzle was frequently used as a marketing device, such as the swizzle stocks used by Trader Vic's.

But the swizzle stock that lent its name to the Swizzle category of drinks is a branch taken from the Quaraibea turbinata tree, an aromatic perennial that grows in the Caribbean. The original swizzle, in this sense, was a meter-long branch that was used to cool and dilute a Rum Swizzle—a drink that appeared in literature as early as the 1760s. American naturalist and writer Frederick Albion Ober noted, in 1920, that the great drink of the Barbados ice houses was the Swizzle, a blend of spirit, sugar, and ice that was whisked to a froth by a rapidly revolved swizzle stick made from the stem of a native plant, perhaps Quararibea turbinata or an allspice bush.

Today, these swizzle sticks are making their reappearance, although in much shorter length.

Syrup, Agave

Agave syrup (aka: agave nectar) is produced from agave piñas. Slightly thinner than honey and containing no extra sugars, agave syrup has recently been recommended by various diabetic associations as a natural sweetener with a low glycemic index. Estimated to be about four times sweeter than sugar, agave syrup is replacing other sugar syrups is new mixed drink recipes.

Syrup, Gomme

Gomme syrup is simple syrup with gum arabic added as an emulsifier. The gum arabic adds a thicker texture to the syrup and to any drink the syrup is used in. However, it does not affect the flavour. It was a common commercially-produced sweetener during the Victorian and Edwardian eras.

Syrup, Grenadine

See Grenadine.

Syrup, Groseille

Groseille is the French word for gooseberry. Groseille syrup is a grenadine-red syrup made from gooseberries.

Syrup, Maple

Maple syrup is a condensed product of sugar maple sap. These trees are tapped each spring when the days are warm but the nights are still cold causing extensive movement of the sap within the trees. The sap is gathered and boiled down to create maple syrup. Further reduced it becomes crystalline and is made into maple sugar candy.

Syrup, Maraschino cherry

This is simply the liquid from a jar of maraschino cherries. This should never be used to replace maraschino liqueur.

Syrup, Orgeat

An almond syrup made with a hint of rose water, this syrup is used in coffee and soda drinks throughout Italy and is an ingredient in Tiki drinks, especially the Mai Tai.

Syrup, Passion Fruit

A syrup made from passion fruit, and frequently used as a substitute in drinks where passion fruit juice or purée or fresh passion fruit is an ingredient.

Syrup, Pineapple

Made by combining pineapple juice with simple syrup. This syrup must be refrigerated or made in small enough batches to use within a day.

Syrup, Pomegranate

See Syrup, Grenadine.

Syrup, Prune

Prune syrup is a simple reduction of prune juice. According to Louisiana chef Paul Prudhomme, reducing 48 ounces of prune juice in a five-quart pan over low heat for about 55 minutes will produce prune syrup. As prunes (dried plums) are very high in sugar there is no need to include additional sweeteners.

Syrup, Raspberry

There are many brands of raspberry syrup available. It's a feature ingredient in the 1933 version of the Cosmopolitan Daisy. If you prefer to make your own, combine a punnet of raspberries with a cup of water and the juice of half a lemon in a saucepan. Cook over medium heat, stirring and pressing the berries constantly for about 6 minutes until they have released their juices. Strain through cheesecloth into another pan. Add 500 grams of sugar. Cook over low heat, stirring occasionally until the sugar is completely dissolved. Keep refrigerated and use within two weeks.

Syrup, Sugar

Widely available as a commercial product, sugar syrup (aka: simple syrup) is made by combining sugar and water. The basics formulas for simple syrup are 1:1 and 2:1 sugar to water. The most common syrup is the 2:1 formula, which is pretty much standard for most cocktails. To make this, simply add 2 cups of sugar and 1 cup water to a pot and gently heat until all of the sugar is dissolved. Pour the syrup into a clean bottle and it's ready to use. You don't need to boil the water when making simple syrup.

Tavern

A place of business where people gather to drink that's a descendant of early Near Eastern, ancient Greek and Roman traditions is the tavern. The distinction between a tavern and an inn is the possession of a license to house guests overnight. The word derives from the Latin *taberna* and the Greek *taverna*, whose original meaning was a shed or workshop.

Introduced to Britain by the Romans around 40 AD, a tavern was distinguished during the 1500s from a public ale house because it was operated as a private enterprise, where drinkers were deemed as "guests" rather than members of the public.

Tea

Harvested from the leaves and buds of a variety of camellia plant that grows in Asia, tea is one of the world's most popular drinks and comes in innumerable styles mostly based on variations in harvest, production, and additives. The most common types of tea are black and green. Tea was an ingredient in early punch recipes, especially when it was first imported from India during the 1600s. Today, tea is once again joining the roster of elements behind the bar in drinks such as the tea-infused Earl Grey MarTEAni.

Tequila

Tequila was first produced, around 1531, by Spanish settlers in the Mexican state of Jalisco. When the Spanish conquistadors ran out of their own brandy, they began to distil the local pulque or octli, a fermented beverage derived from roasted agave which was considered to be a drink of the gods. The distillate was first called mexcalli.

Around 1600, Don Pedro Sánchez de Tagle, the Marquis of Altamira, established the first commercial production of the spirit and 8 years later, the colonial governor of Nueva Galicia began to tax Tagle's spirits.

Eventually named after the Jalisco town where it was born, the style of tequila that is popular today was first commercially produced during the early 1800s in Guadalajara, Mexico.

Don Cenobio Sauza, founder of Sauza Tequila and Municipal President of the Village of Tequila from 1884-1885, was the first to export tequila to the United States.

Piñas from the Blue Webber are harvested from matured agave plants and toasted in kilns to concentration the natural sugars. These are then shredded and pressed to extract the "musto" [juice]. This liquid is fermented with yeast and then distilled.

Tequila is usually bottle in one of five categories:

Blanco [white] or plata [silver]" Bottled or stored immediately after distillation, or aged less than 2 months in stainless steel or neutral oak barrels.

Joven [young] or oro [gold]: A blend of plata and reposado, añejo, or extra añejo tequilas.

Reposado [rested]: Aged for a minimum of 2 months to a maximum of one year in oak barrels prior to bottling.

Añejo [vintage]: Aged for a minimum of one year to a maximum of 3 years in oak barrels prior to bottling.

Extra Añejo [extra aged]: Aged for a minimum of 3 years in oak barrels prior to bottling.

Thomas, Jerry

Born in Sackets Harbor, New York, Jerry "the Professor" Thomas (1830-1885) learned his craft in New Haven, Connecticut as an assistant barman before departing on the barc *Annie H Smith*, in 1847, to seek his fortune. Two

years later, he made it south around the tip of South America and up to San Francisco, where he jumped ship and landed a job as first assistant to the principal bartender at the city's first and most popular "resort", AJ McCabe's El Dorado at 750 Kearny Street. It is worth noting that when he arrived, in 1849, California had not yet become a state, and had only left Mexican governance the year before.

In his 1933 book *The Barbary Coast: An Informal History of the San Francisco Underworld*, author Herbert Asbury wrote: "Originally El Dorado was a canvas tent, but the tent was soon replaced by a large square room of rough boards, with a few private booths partitioned off with muslin, where a man whose mind was elsewhere than on games of chance might entertain his inamorata of the moment."

Asbury was known to sensationalise or even fictionalize history, but in this case his description appears to be accurate. Taverns and hostelries across the west were sometimes built from the remains of the wagon that brought the proprietor there. If it was successful, he could eventually afford a proper structure. In its heyday, El Dorado beckoned miner-patrons "like a cool fountain beckons the thirsty wanderer in the desert." Baroque furniture, fine-cut glass

mirrors, ten chandeliers, and "lascivious oil paintings of
nudes in abandoned postures" delighted the eye along
with the live singers, dancers, short-skirted "pretty waiter
girls" (showing ankles was considered partial nudity at the
time) who served up drinks, and the walrus-mustached
"Michelangelo of Drinks" who cut a gigantic figure in his
crisp white jacket: Jerry Thomas.

El Dorado patrons tried to confound Thomas "with the
fanciest orders imaginable", but never succeeded. That's how
he earned the moniker, "the Professor."

Thomas's claim to fame was a show-stopper drink
called the Blue Blazer, which he reputedly never made unless
the temperature dipped below 50° F, which actually happens
a lot in San Francisco. If someone came in suffering from
cold or flu symptoms, he would make an exception to this
rule. (The word "blazer" was a double entendre. At the
time, it also meant to boast, which is appropriate for such a
showy drink.) Properly executed, the Blue Blazer will have
the appearance of a continued stream of liquid fire. Serve in
a small bar-glass with a piece of twisted lemon peel.

Some say Jerry tired of the Barbary Coast. Others claim
a customer finally stumped him, requesting a drink that was
common in Central America and he left in shame. Whatever
story is true, he joined a minstrel show and headed south
during the summer of 1850. By winter, he made his way to
Central America and then home to New Haven, where he
introduced Yale students to his expanded repertoire.

From there, Thomas travelled to Charleston, Chicago,
St Louis, and New Orleans, where he opened his own
establishment for a while and he picked up the recipe for the
Crusta from Santina, a celebrated New Orleans café owner.
Returning to New York, he took the head bartender slot at
Boss Tweed's Metropolitan Hotel.

Author Herbert Asbury noted in the 1929 edition
of *The Bon-Vivant's Companion* that Thomas "left
the Metropolitan, in 1859, to brave the dangers of a
transatlantic voyage, but he was both seasick and homesick,
and in less than a year he was again in New York."

"A genuine Yankee professor" made a guest appearance
mixing drinks, in 1859, at an American bar The Bowling
Saloon in London's Cremorne Pleasure Gardens.

When 30-year-old Thomas returned to his beloved New
York to open a high-profile bar at 622 Broadway he did what
no bartender had done by that point. In 1862, he published

the first book to contain cocktail recipes (ten of them): *The Bar-Tenders' Guide: A Complete Cyclopaedia of Plain and Fancy Drinks, Containing Clear and Reliable Directions for Mixing All the Beverages Used in the United States, Together with the Most Popular British, French, German, Italian, Russian, and Spanish Recipes, Embracing Punches, Juleps, Cobblers, etc etc in Endless Variety.*

The American Civil War (1861-1865) changed the tide of Jerry's life. When a military draft was called in New York, in 1863, the young and able-bodied Thomas was on the top of the draft list. Not being of the mind to take up the rifle and do his service, Jerry hightailed it westward back to San Francisco by covered wagon. There, he found a slot at the Occidental Hotel, which had opened on New Year's Day in 1863. A year later, he headed eastward to Virginia City, Nevada, where he plied his craft in the burgeoning boomtown that sprung up with the discovery of silver.

Finally, the fighting ceased. The Union was victorious, and Thomas returned to New York, operating a saloon at 937 Broadway with his brother George. Aside from a jaunt to London to opened a bar in Leicester Square, Thomas stayed put. He even got married.

An inheritance squandered on the stock market, a few failed business ventures, and a taste of gambling left slowly sapped Thomas's fortunes by the 1870s. He was forced to close up his business, sell what little he had, and work at less stellar "resorts". He died from heart failure, in 1885, at the age of 55 and was laid to rest at Woodlawn Cemetery in the Bronx.

Three-Martini Lunch

A term used in the United States to describe a leisurely, indulgent lunch enjoyed by executives, the three-Martini refers to a common belief that executives had enough leisure time and money to consume more than one Martini Along with a steak or a lobster during the work day. Considered a business expense—along with travel, travel meals, and client entertainment—the three-Martini lunch qualified a tax deduction.

Jimmy Carter condemned the practice during the 1976 presidential campaign, portraying it as part of the unfairness in the nation's tax laws because the working class was subsidizing the "$50 martini lunch." Subsequently, a 1986 law limited the meal-expense deduction to 80 percent and in

1993, that limit was set at 50 percent.

Carter's opponent, incumbent President Gerald R Ford, responded to accusations by commenting that: "The three-Martini lunch is the epitome of American efficiency. Where else can you get an earful, a bellyful and a snootful at the same time?" Carter went on to win the election.

Throwing a Drink

Throwing was very common, perhaps the most common way to mix drinks in bars from the late 1700s to the mid-1800s when the two-part shaker became standard. Slightly oversized mixing glasses with pour spouts are best.

To throw a drink, first build the drink with ice in a mixing glass. Place a julep strainer over the drink. Hold an empty mixing glass next to the full one. As you pour from one to the other, steadily increase the distance between the two by raising the full one and lowering the empty one. Keep the lower one slightly tilted so that the drink lands mainly on the side of the inside rather than the bottom where is it more prone to splashing.

Once the stream of liquid has drained from the throwing glass into the receiving glass, bring the two glasses together and pour the liquid back over the ice without extending the distance between the glasses, as the throw is only done from the glass with ice to the glass without ice. Then repeat the throw three of four times. The ice never leaves the throwing glass as it should be held back securely by the julep strainer throughout the throwing process. With practice, it is possible to raise the mixing glass with ice as high as you can reach while lowering the catching glass as low as you can reach creating a distance of up to five vertical feet depending on the length of your arms.

Tiki

Tiki culture has circumvented the world. As Jeff "Beachbum" Berry commented in an interview: "After burning through the pre-Prohibition drinks, the classics, the tequilas and the bourbons, the new generation of craft bartenders were looking for something else. They discovered that these were not just crappy cruiseship drinks. They were complex cocktails with multiple culinary ingredients that were 70 years ahead of their time."

Toast

The term "toast" in cocktail parlance is applied to the person or thing honoured with the raising of glasses, the drink that is raised, or the verbal expression that accompanies said drink. A person can be "the toast of the evening," for whom someone "proposes a toast".

Tomato Juice

Pressed from ripe tomatoes, tomato juice is readily available in stores around the world. It should be noted that the flavour differs considerably in warmer climates. Tomato juice from France and Italy, for example, is much sweeter than tomato juice form the United States or Great Britain.

Trader Vic

See Bergeron, Trader Vic.

Triangle Trade

The "triangle trade" (aka: "the infernal triangle" or "save triangle") grew from an incident that occurred over a century earlier when the young Christopher Columbus began his apprenticeship, in 1473, as a business agent for the Genoese Centurione, Di Negro and Spinola trading families. One of the families' most lucrative commodities was sugar. Travelling from the Mediterranean to northern Europe, he learned the trading value of sugar, eventually moving to Madeira and Porto Santo. There, he married Filipa Moniz Perestrello, daughter of Porto Santo's governor Bartolomeu Perestrello, a Portuguese nobleman of Genoese origin.

Madeira was already established as a major sugar-producing centre. Its plantation owners had grown rich from the islands' abundant harvests. Columbus knew from living there for nearly decade there was profit in planting and trading "white gold."

According to Fernando Campoamor in his book *El Hijo Alegre de la Caña de Azúcar*, Columbus brought sugar cane seedlings with him, in 1493, on his second voyage to the Caribbean. But there is a sad footnote to this milestone. The great explorer was unable to conduct the cultivation experiments he intended to perform in Hispañola. The delicate plants did not survive the sea crossing.

Pedro di Atienza met with greater success, in 1501, when he imported and planted sugar cane seedlings on Hispañola. It was then that the early settlers discovered sugar cane could

flourish in the tropical Caribbean climate. Colonists on the
island of Puerto Rico, in 1506, copied his efforts.

Peaceful coexistence amongst the indigenous people of
Cuba and the Spanish explorers was fleeting. Columbus's
two visits to Cuba never developed into the establishment
of a settlement. In fact, his sole quest along the Cuban coast
was to find a fabled land of gold he was certain existed
nearby—in Japan.

Spanish settlement of Cuba came abruptly and violently
in 1512, when conquistadors Diego Velásquez de Cuéllar
and his secretary Hernán Cortés arrived with three hundred
men and fresh sugar cane seedlings. They forced the Taínos
to plant the shoots in the newly bared earth after clearing
the lush tropical forest that had been their home. The success
of this crop led Cortés to attempt sugar cane cultivation in
Mexico a few years later.

By 1515, seven cities were established on Cuba: Santiago
de Cuba, Bayamo, Trinidad, Havana, Baracoa, Camagüey,
and Sancti Spiritus. Velásquez became the island's governor,
Cortés the mayor of Santiago de Cuba. Velásquez and Cortés
stopped looking in Cuba for gold. Within two decades,
the Spanish were certain the legendary "El Dorado" [the
Golden Man] and his city resided in South America, where
conquistadors found the palaces, gardens and people of the
Inca Empire gilded in gold.

The conquistadors who remained in Cuba turned their attentions to the wealth that could be had in sugar. By 1570, the majority of the 270 Spanish families settled in Cuba had established sprawling sugar plantations and operated sugar mills. Sugar was a labour-intensive proposition. First, land needed to be cleared of lush vegetation for planting. It takes 5,000 to 8,000 seed-cane stems to produce one acre of hand-planted sugar cane. Once it matured (in about 18 months), the *macheteros* wielded heavy machetes in the sweltering heat to cut the cane as close to the bottom as possible because the lower portion of the stalk is much higher in sucrose.

The intense stench of rotting cane consumed workers in the sugar mills as it was simpler to harvest than to process. According to reports written by missionary Bartolomé de las Casas, colonist Miguel de Ballester and a person named Aguiló discovered that a native tool called a *cunyaya* was effective for extracting cane juice. But even this took great strength and energy to employ.

The heat in the sugar mills was so intense that workers were rotated in four-hour cycles to crush the cane, to boil the juice, to skim the hot liquid, to transfer it from kettle to kettle to reduce the developing syrup into crystals, all while maintaining a fire to provide enough heat for the process.

At first the Taínos were forced into labour, housed in squalid conditions. Foreign germs such as smallpox, scarlet fever and tuberculosis killed as many or more labourers than the backbreaking work and physical abuse at the hands of the plantation and sugar mill owners.

One man stood in defence of these native Cubans, Fray Bartolomé de las Casas. The first priest to be ordained in the New World, de las Casas arrived in the Caribbean, in 1502, with his father. He entered the Dominican order eight years later, becoming a missionary, in 1512, to the tormented Taínos. Eyewitness to the genocide of his spiritual flock by Velàsquez's conquistadors, in 1515, de las Casas penned an impassioned letter begging King Ferdinand to end the devastation. With encouragement from Archbishop Jimenez de Cisneros of Toledo, Ferdinand appointed de las Casas Priest-procurator of the Indies, protector of the Taínos.

But the genocide did not diminish. De las Casas returned to Spain four years later to plead his case once again, this time before King Charles I. His mission met with failure. Unable to gain political support he wrote an inflammatory account of the atrocities in 1523, which became the basis for his 1542 book *A Brief Account of the Destruction of the Indies: Or, a faithful NARRATIVE OF THE Horrid and Unexampled Massacres, Butcheries and all manner of Cruelties, that Hell and Malice could invent, committed by the Popish Spanish Party on the inhabitants of West-India, TOGETHER With the Devastations of several Kingdoms in America by Fire and Sword, for the space of Forty and Two Years, from the time of its first Discovery by them*, stating that:

"The Spaniards first assaulted the innocent Sheep, so qualified by the Almighty, as is premention'd, like most cruel Tygers, Wolves and Lions hunger-starv'd, studying nothing, for the space of Forty Years, after their first landing, but the Massacre of these Wretches, whom they have so inhumanely and barbarously butcher'd and harass'd with several kinds of Torments, never before known, or heard (of which you shall have some account in the following Discourse) that of Three Millions of Persons, which lived in Hispañola itself, there is at present but the inconsiderable remnant of scarce Three Hundred. Nay the Isle of Cuba, which extends as far, as Valledolid in Spain is distant from Rome, lies now uncultivated, like a Desert and intomb'd in its own Ruins."

De las Casas's pleas and prayers were partially answered in 1537, when Pope Paul III issued Papal Bull *Sublimis Deus* [the Higher God], which declared the indigenous people of the West Indies rational beings with souls and that their lives and property should be protected. Five years later, the Church's stand on the subject compelled King Charles I to sign laws, which prohibited enslavement of the indigenous people. Although the first African slaves were smuggled into the Caribbean in 1514, it wasn't until these laws were set into motion—coupled with the realization of enormous profits from sugar—that the full-scale slave trade began in the Caribbean.

There is a chain of events that few historians properly report on this subject.

The slave trade existed within Africa and the East Indies since the 1100s, primarily instigated by West African kings. Tribesmen from Central and South African territories and kingdoms were captured and sold by Angolan and Ivory Coast chiefs who had an affinity for akpeteshi or burukutu [date-palm wine], which was not dissimilar to the sugar-cane arrack exported by traders from India, Indonesia, and Malaysia. Often, those enslaved were unwanted rivals for territory and resources kidnapped or hunted down and shipped to parts unknown.

This societal framework facilitated the development of the international slave trade during the next century as colonists in Brazil and the Caribbean made lucrative deals with these kings. Date-palm wine and similar fermented beverages (not distilled spirits) were integral to West African culture and ritual. Consequently, rum, rhum and cachaça (sold under the name "jeretiba") were quickly recognized as more powerful versions of a favoured commodity. Many economists cite this international exchange of distilled spirits for human cargo as the birth of capitalism and the global economy.

Rum from the Caribbean, from New England, and cachaça from Brazil were not the only commodities traded. But in terms of production cost and return on investment, these liquid assets had the highest yield.

The only reason Cuba and Hispaniola did not get involved in this trade of spirits in exchange for slaves at this early stage was because the Spanish government banned the building and operation of distillation equipment in its colonies. The crown wanted to protect its very lucrative brandy and wine export trade. With Mexican colonists making mezcal and other Caribbean colonies making *aguardiente de caña*, it was a tough fight.

What of the association amongst slaves, indentured servants, and these new spirits? It became a common practice to provide a daily ration of spirit as compensation, though this has been grossly misinterpreted by generations of historians. Remember: everyone drank at least a half pint of spirit a day to maintain good health, to ward off the ill effects of water- and food-borne pathogens. It wasn't a matter of keeping slaves drunk and subdued.

Tuennerman, Ann

(aka: Mrs Cocktail) It was love at first sight when Ann's parents visited New Orleans. So they made it their permanent home and instilled that love into Ann and her sister. Before she took that passion for the city's culture, its style, its food, and its drink to its ultimate peak with the foundation of Tales of the Cocktail® and the New Orleans Culinary & Cultural Preservation Society, Ann graduated from the University of New Orleans with a degree in marketing and worked in the advertising, radio, and television industries, where she honed her skills in marketing in public relations.

At the age of 35, she struck out on her own as an event marketer, opening her own agency Sponsor One. Inspired by the 2001 book *Obituary Cocktail* by Kerri McCaffety, Ann decided that her first project was to develop a walking tour of New Orleans bars and restaurants. It took about two years of research and conceptualization to finding a sponsor and final execution.

The Southern Comfort Cocktail Tour kicked off in the autumn of 2002. With its success, Ann decided to celebrate the tour's first anniversary by creating Tales of the Cocktail®, which was intended to focus on cocktail book authors and the rich store of knowledge that they write about.

With two months to plan the event and a budget of $25,000, the first Tales attracted 200 people and a lot of positive feedback from participants and from the press. Since then, Tales of the Cocktail® has grown organically over the past decade into the premiere event on the international beverage industry calendar.

Hurricane Katrina almost brought her dream of celebrating the New Orleans hospitality industry and its culture to an end in 2005. But when she returned to the Crescent City on New Year's Day 2006, she brought with her a renewed spirit and established The New Orleans Culinary and Cultural Preservation Society. A non-profit organization that's committed to preserving the unique culture of dining and drinking in New Orleans and the storied bars and restaurants that have contributed to the city's world-wide culinary acclaim, the society supports members of the hospitality industry through education and the production of events like Tales of the Cocktail® and most recently, Trails of the Cocktail, a scholarship program for emerging talent in the New Orleans cocktail industry.

Dedicated to elevating awareness of New Orleans' unique position in the drinks world, Ann lobbied the state government to make the Sazerac Louisiana's official cocktail. In March 2008, State Senator Edwin R Murray filed Senate Bill 6 to get the drink official recognition. A month later it was defeated. Reproposed to make the drink the official cocktail of New Orleans and after heated debate in both the state senate and the state house of representatives, the Sazerac won its deserved title on 23 June 2008.

Married to Paul G. Tuennerman in 2007, Ann divides her time between Dallas and her true home, New Orleans.

Tuennerman, Paul G

(aka: Mr Cocktail) For many, a part time job at 15 years of age is little more than a way to put some money in your pocket. For Paul G Tuennerman, frying fish at Arthur Treacher's in Blacksburg, Virginia sparked both a passion and a career that has now spanned more than 35 years.

Following high school, Paul took a detour and spent a little more than six years travelling various countries lining the western Pacific and Indian Oceans, while serving in the US Navy, where he honed his passion for blue water sailing.

Paul's love of food and passion for life led him from coast to coast. So it was only a matter of time until he found himself living and falling in love with New Orleans. He's involved in a number of non-profit organizations such as The New Orleans Culinary and Cultural Preservation Society, Gulf Islands Review, and the 2013 New Orleans Super Bowl Host Committee.

When not sampling the incomparable food of southern Louisiana, Paul can be found in Dallas where he serves as a senior executive for the nation's fastest growing fast-casual restaurant. Prior to this, Paul served in leadership roles in operations, development, and marketing for Piccadilly Restaurants, Wood Dining Services, Morrison's Hospitality Group, and Service America Corporation.

Paul's educational experience includes National University, York College of Pennsylvania, University of Maryland University College, and a MBA Certificate from AB Freeman School of Business at Tulane University.

Paul currently divides his time between Dallas and New Orleans; in his spare time, he enjoys sailing in the Caribbean, and sampling the latest creations from behind the line.

Vadrna, Stanislav

Stanislav Vadrna's bartending manifesto is: "Be Here Now. Treasure every encounter for each one is unique and can never recur. And always with Aloha, which is the key to the universal spirit of true hospitality."

Stanislav's long term mission is the rejuvenation of the

status of professional bartender and redefining global bar industry standards with the "Ichigo Ichie" [one lifetime, one meeting] philosophy. Originating with the Japanese tea ceremony, the concept implies that this moment is the only moment and will not come back.

Stanislav is the founder and principal of the internationally acclaimed bar school, The Analog Bar-Tending Institute. From Paris to Los Angeles, he travels the world preaching the gospel of professional bartending and spirit of "aloha" in which the guest is the reason to why we do it.

Vermouth

See Fortified Wine, Vermouth.

Vexenat, Charles

Author of *Mixellany's Annotated Bariana* and *Mixellany's Bariana: The Collector's Edition*, Charles Vexenat's career started at six years old, mixing syrups and lemonade behind the bar at his grandparent' brasserie in Dijon.

Moving to London in 2000 to learn English, he earned his keep in the bar industry. Starting as a kitchen porter and food runner, he worked his way up learning the business from an array of the industry's best mentors.

Charles has since worked in London's top bars: Hush, Eagle Bar Diner, Che, Lab, La Floridita, and Lonsdale as well as at Tres Agaves in San Francisco plus Death and Company in New York. He also collaborates on regular basis with top bar consultants involving himself from concept through to training and design.

He has won many bartending competitions, including two awards in 2007 for Best Bartender in the Britain. He has visited and worked in different distilleries around the world, notably in Mexico.

Vodka

Vodka is primarily distilled from fermented grain such as rye, wheat, or corn, although there are some vodkas that are produced from sugar beets, molasses, or potatoes.

This spirit was originally produced in Poland and Russia after Genoese merchants introduced the royal courts of both countries to arrack made from sugar cane juice sometime between the late 1380s and the 1420s.

According to the Polish Spirits Industry association

(Polski Przemys Spirytusowy), the word "vodka"
first appeared in court documents, dated 1405, from
Swietokrzyskie Voivodship.

Originally called "zhinznennia voda" [water of life],
the term was simplified to the diminutive term "vodka" or
"wodka" [dear little water].

In his 1534 book of medicinal recipes, Polish chemist
Falmirz listed over 70 vodka infusions employed to cure
everything from lumbago to infertility.

Since the 1780s, a common practice in the vodka
distillation process is the use of charcoal filtration, developed
by Johann Tobias Lowitz. Filtration radically reduces the
level of congeners, producing a smoother, cleaner liquor. To
attain the desired level of "purity" many vodkas are distilled
more than once in column stills. Some brands claim to distil
their spirit up to six times. By regulation, most vodkas have
an alcohol content of 37.5 percent to 40 percent ABV.

Northern and Eastern Europe are the major producers
of vodka with Poland, Russia, the Ukraine, and Sweden
being the leaders in the "Vodka Belt". But vodkas are also
produced in other European countries including France,
Germany, and the United Kingdom, as well as North
America, Central and South America, Asia, and Australia.

Traditionally, vodka is consumed neat in the "Vodka
Belt". Vodkas infused with herbs, berries, fruits, or
vegetables have also had a long tradition throughout Eastern
Europe.

Beginning the 1920s, five vodka drinks are the main
ways vodka is consumed in the rest of the world. The
Bloody Mary invented by Fernand "Pete" Petiot at Harry's
New York Bar in Paris and redeveloped at the King Cole Bar
in New York is a brunch time staple. The Moscow Mule,
invented in the 1940s at the Chatham Hotel bar in New
York, brought vodka into the long drink category.

James Bond's creator Ian Fleming helped make the
Vodka Martini a sophisticated mainstay in the 1950s. And
the invention of concentrated, frozen range juice in the late
1940s, vaulted the Screwdriver to prominence during the late
20th century.

The introduction of citron vodka stimulated the creation
of the Cosmopolitan in the late 1980s, which has been a
modern-day classic.

Voisey, Charlotte

London-born mixologist, Charlotte Voisey managed bars in Barcelona, Buenos Aires and London. With the Gorgeous Group, Charlotte opened, in 2002, classic cocktail bar Apartment 195 in London and soon after was named UK Bartender of the Year. Charlotte was invited to guest bartend at the 2005 Aspen Food & Wine Classic and consequently fell in love with the American cocktail community. One year later Charlotte officially made the move stateside to represent her favorite spirit—Hendrick's Gin.

She won a silver medal at the 2006 World Female Bartender Championships in Italy and her Punch & Judy was named cocktail of the year by a panel of peers at the 2008 Tales of the Cocktail.

Charlotte speaks at all major industry events such as Spirits of Mexico, Aspen Food & Wine, the Manhattan Cocktail Classic, NY Times Travel Show, and Tales of the Cocktail® where Charlotte has won the 2007 and 2009 Golden Spirit Award for Best Presenter and 2010 Best American Brand Ambassador.

Charlotte currently looks after the coveted spirits portfolio, and Brand Ambassador team, of William Grant & Sons in the capacity of Company Mixologist.

Volstead Act

See Prohibition in the United States.

Walker, Jim

Jim Walker started his extensive collection of cocktail shakers and bar ware in 1995. He started with recipe cocktail shakers and soon expanded to all forms of shakers and bar ware. Now there are over 500 shakers, 100+ Martini glasses, and hundreds of pieces of bar ware.

Jim has several shakers and pieces of bar ware in the Museum of the American Cocktail in New Orleans. These same pieces travelled to Las Vegas at the museum's temporary home. Several pieces of his collection were shown at The House of Colours art gallery in Grapevine Texas.

His book *A Recipe for Design* features recipe cocktail shakers, recipe devices, the recipes and their history. Some of his collection can be seen on his blog site Shaken & Stirred, which covers vintage shakers, links to purchase shakers, liquor reviews, and more.

Jim was on the panels of the 2008 International Symposium of Cocktail Shaker Collectors and the 2009 Vintage Bar Ware Collectors Symposium.

Ward, Phil

Starting his career at the Flatiron Lounge in June 2003 under the tutelage of Julie Riener, Phil Ward left to help open the Pegu Club with Audrey Saunders, where he eventually became Head Bartender. Seeking the chance to run his own program, in January 2007 he jumped ship to open and run the beverage program at what has become New York's renowned Death and Company.

Two years later, he opened the much anticipated Mayahuel in New York—the first tequila/mezcal cocktail bar, which he owns and operates.

Philip has consulted and helped open bars around the country including Tequilas in Philadelphia, Watermark in Asbury Park, Craft and Commerce in San Diego, and for the entire Auberge Hotel group.

He was nominated for Bartender of the Year three years in a row at Tales of the Cocktail® where Mayahuel won Best New Bar in World and Death and Company won Best American Bar.

In late 2009—along with the talented Katie Stipe (Flatiron, Mayahuel, Clover Club, Vandaag)—he officially started a consulting venture Last Call Consulting.

Water, Carbonated

Sparkling water. Fizzy water. Seltzer. Club Soda. Soda water. Call it what you will. Carbonated water has been a mainstay of the beverage industry ever since Selters spring, near the town of Neiderselters, was first discovered in 772 AD and documented. The health benefits of this bubbly, acidic water described by physician Jakob Theodor Tabernaemontanus, in 1581, set the wheels in motion for the development of a spa, where visitors could "take the waters."

A century later, a profitable enterprise in bottling and shipping "Selters Waters" in tightly-corked earthenware jugs to Scandinavia, Eastern Europe, North America, and even the Dutch East Indies assured this town a steady source of income beyond the flourishing tourism. Pricey and not always easy to come by, carbonated water became the Holy Grail for two scientists in precisely the same year.

Hoping to cure his digestive ailments, a sickly but frugal Swedish chemistry professor named Torbern Bergman, in 1771, invented a process that replicated sparkling spring water using carbon dioxide gas generated from chalk and sulfuric acid dissolved in water.

Independently, that same year, British clergyman Joseph Priestley also discovered a method when he suspended a bowl of water above a beer vat at a brewery in Leeds. The next year, Priestley published a paper entitled *Impregnating Water with Fixed Air*. Not particularly interested in financial gain from his thinking, Priestley never commercialised his discovery.

That step was left to Swiss watchmaker Jean-Jacob Schweppe, who read both of these accounts and conducted his own experiments. An epiphany occurred when he read, in 1777, that French chemist Antoine Lavoisier had determined that gas could be dissolved in water. Schweppe's discovery became, in 1783, a commercial reality.

More interested in gaining certification from the medical community than a profit, Schweppe unfortunately trusted the sales of his water to a friend, who commissioned engineer Nicolas Paul to fashion an aeration device to go into direct competition.

The tables turned when Paul made Schweppe's friend a substandard machine and himself a refined one. Better to join the enemy than fight. In 1790, Schweppe went into partnership with Paul and pharmacist Henry Albert Gosse, another experimenter with carbonated waters. The company of Schweppe, Paul and Gosse decided to make its product with distilled water as well as expand its offerings and operations to London.

From their first factory at 141 Drury Lane, the partnership produced three levels of carbonated water: "No. 1 is for common drinking with your dinner. No. 2 is for nephritic patients and No. 3 contains the most alkali given only in more violent cases."

The secret to Schweppe's success was its bottles. Gas commonly escaped around the cork leaving carbonated water flat within a day. The company packaged its waters in strong stoneware bottles with a rounded bottom that required it to be stored on its side, a position that kept the cork wet.

Pressure from his partners to return to Geneva coupled with an expensive attempt to construct cheap mineral water machines to encourage street cart sales fuelled the 1795 dissolution of the company. But it did not deter the inventor. Moving first to 8 Kings Street in Holborn and then to 11 Margaret Street in Cavendish Square, he continued to build his Schweppe Company with the growing support of the British medical community and the public at large.

In his late fifties, Schweppe saw the end of the 1700s as a wealthy entrepreneur. He had made a considerable profit and decided to retire, in 1798, selling 75 percent of his interest to three Channel island businessmen.

Schweppe's groundbreaking discovery gave birth to a new category of drinks—the Collinses.

Water, Tonic

An extract from South American cinchona tree bark, quinine was isolated and named, in 1820, by French researchers Pierre Joseph Pelletier and Joseph Caventou. Prior to their discovery, chincona (or quinaquina) was used in a fermented beverage by indigenous peoples as a remedy for the chills: a common symptom of malaria. As early as 1631, non-extracted quinine was for the same purpose by Italian physicians. But it was Pelletier's and Caventou's study that sparked broader interest and application, especially in 1851, when it took on a very practical and palatable form in the hands of London's J. Schweppe & Company.

One of the first brand extensions that new company partners John Kemp Welch and Willian Evill banked on, in 1858, was commercial "Indian tonic water" (aka: tonic water, in the US) that combined its successful soda water with quinine and sweetening. Paired with gin, and touted as healthful, the combination of seltzer, chincona, and sugar had already been adopted as a daily quencher for British subjects living in tropical areas. The commercial distribution of tonic water, in the 1870s, simply vaulted the Gin & Tonic toward the top of the drinks menu, standing shoulder to shoulder with the John Collins and the Tom Collins.

Women's Christian Temperance Union (WCTU)
See Prohibition in the United States.

Whiskey
The second oldest European spirits category, whiskey was first produced during the 1300s in Ireland, where it was initially called *"uisce beatha"* [water of life]. This distillate

derives from grain (generally barley, malted barley, rye, malted rye, wheat, or maize [corn]), which is then aged in wood casks.

Whiskey-making was almost exclusively the provenance of the Irish and Scots until the 1600s, when emigrants brought the knowledge with them to North America. Canadian and American whiskies were born, which possess a definitively different flavour profile and are predominantly made from rye or corn.

Within the 20th century, countries such as Japan, India, France, and Russia also developed whiskies. Japan is the most notable, achieving impressive stature second only to Scotch whiskies.

The word "whiskey" was allegedly coined by troops of Britain's King Henry II, in the 1100s, when they invaded Ireland. They were unable to pronounce the Gaelic term *uisce beatha*. Over time, the pronunciation changed from "whishkeyba" to "whiskey".

Whiskey, American
American whiskies are distilled from fermented mash of cereal grains: the most popular are rye and corn. There are six major categories of American whiskey regulated by the US federal government:

Bourbon whiskey: made with at least 51 percent corn (maize) and produced within Bourbon County, Kentucky.

Tennessee Whiskey: In 1941, the US federal government created a new designation called Tennessee Whiskey, of which, Jack Daniels is the most famous. Identical in production to Bourbon, Tennessee Whiskey is unique because it is filtered through sugar maple charcoal and produced in the neighbouring state of Tennessee.

Rye whiskey: This style is made with at least 51 percent rye.

Corn whiskey: This style is made with at least 80 percent corn [maize].

Straight whiskey: To be called a straight whiskey, the spirit must be aged for more than 2 years from a distillate made with less than 51 percent of any single grain and collected at 80 percent ABV.

Blended Whiskey: American blended whiskies combine straight whiskies with unaged whiskies, grain neutral spirits, flavourings, and colourings.

The "named types" of American whiskey, by law, must be distilled to less than 80 percent ABV, aged in charred new oak barrels with the exception of corn whiskey which must be aged in new un-charred oak barrels or used barrels for no more than 6 months.

Whiskey, Canadian

Canadian whiskies are usually lighter and smoother than other whiskey styles, made from rye that has been malted, this style possesses a full flavour and smoothness. By law, it must be mashed from cereal grain with a greater percentage of rye, distilled and aged a minimum of 3 years in a wooden barrel of not greater than 700-litre capacity. All production and ageing must take place in Canada.

This style of whiskey featured prominently in during Prohibition in the United States. Hiram Walker's distillery in Windsor, Ontario, directly across the Detroit River from Detroit, Michigan, easily served rum runners using small, fast smuggling boats.

Although Canadian single malt and "Quebec Maple" are produced in Canada, they are not considered to be Canadian whiskies by category.

Whiskey, Irish

The majority of Irish whiskeys are triple distilled in column stills, producing a lighter character than Scotch whisky. When Irish whiskey was first produced during the 1300s, however, it was distilled in pot stills. The change took place when an Irish tax agent Aeneas Coffey working in Dublin improved the design of a continuous still patented by Robert Stein and introduced its use in his own distillery.

By law, Irish whiskey must be produced in Ireland and aged in wooden casks for a minimum of 3 years. Unlike Scotch whisky, unpeated malt is the predominate with the exception of Connemara Peated Malt whiskey.

There are four types of Irish whiskey: single malt, single grain, blended whiskey, and pure pot still whiskey, which is unique to Ireland and made from a blend of malted and unmalted barley that is distilled in a copper pot still.

Two of the most famous brands of Irish whiskey are Jameson and Bushmills.

Whiskey, Japanese

The model for Japanese whiskies is single malt Scotch. The base for this spirit is a mash of malted barley that is dried in kilns that is fired with far less peat than is employed in the making of Scotch whisky.

The mash is distilled in a pot still. Until recently, because this spirit was not produced in Scotland but was of a similar style, it was considered to be inferior to classic Scotch whisky and was strictly produced for the domestic market.

This attitude has changed thanks to the results of blind tastings conducted by *Whisky Magazine*, which included Japanese single malts in the lineup next to some of Scotland's finest distillation houses. Some of the Japanese examples scored higher than their Scottish rivals.

Whiskey, Other

The rise in global popularity of whiskey occurred, during the 1860s, when the phylloxera infestation devastated the French wine and cognac industry. To replace grape-based spirits, consumers gravitated toward cereal-based spirits such as whiskey and gin as well as sugar-based spirits such as rum. Aside from whiskies made in Scotland, Ireland, the United States, Japan, and Canada, there are whiskey operations which make up a smaller percentage of the market.

In Brittany, there are two distilleries making spirit in the Scotch style: Glann ar Mor and Warenghem. On the French island of Corsica, Altore and P&M are the alternatives. Altore is distilled in Scotland, but blended and aged in muscat-wine barrels in Corsica. P&M (Pietra & Mavella) is a coproduction of the brewery Pietra and the distillery Mavella. The mash is enriched with chestnut flour and aged in in muscat casks.

Manx Spirit from the Isle of Man is made from imported "new make" spirit that is then rectified and aged.

In 2000, Penderyn Distillery in Wales began production of Penderyn Single Malt Welsh Whiskey.

Indian whisky is an anomaly that is distilled from molasses and sold as "whisky". Recently, some Indian distillers have begun production of cereal-based whiskies to compete with the growing importation market in that country.

German whiskey is made from grains and is relatively young. The first German distillers launched operations during the 1970s, emulating Scotch, Irish, and American styles.

Whisky, Scotch

Whisky has been produced in Scotland since the 1400s. This particular style of spirit has the distinction of being the only one in its genre to be spelt "whisky". All other whiskies are spelt "whiskey."

The first recorded purchase of *aqua vitae* made with malted barley appeared in the Exchequer Rolls of 1494-1495. The King James IV ordered Friar John Cor to produce eight "bolls" of distillate. The first taxes on whisky production were imposed in 1644, causing a rise in illicit distilling.

Around 1780, there were about eight legal distilleries to 400 illegal operations. In 1823, Parliament eased restrictions on licensed distilleries with the Excise Act, making it harder for the illegal stills to operate.

The invention of the continuous still during the 1830s improved the quality of smoothness achieved in the distillation of whiskies and helped usher in the development of blended scotches.

Exclusively distilled in Scotland, Scotch whisky is made from malted barley mash that is distilled to less than 94.8 percent ABV to retain its distinctive character.

The distillate must be matured in oak casks housed in Scotland for no less than 3 years and a day. But these are not only strictures laid done by the Scotch Whisky Order of 1900.

Scotch whisky cannot contain any other substance than distillate, water and caramel colouring for visual quality control. It cannot also be bottled at less than 40 percent ABV.

Currently there are nine Scottish regions producing Scotch whisky: Speyside, Islay, Islands, Western Highlands, Central Highlands, Northern Highlands, Eastern Highlands, Lowlands, and Campelltown.

Whiskey Rebellion

Even though the American Revolution was sparked by British taxes on spirits production, it did not take long for President George Washington to succumb to the economically lucrative temptation of alcohol taxation. He imposed the 1791 Whiskey Tax to pay for the construction of the nation's Capitol building. Co-revolutionary Thomas Jefferson resigned his post as Secretary of State in opposition to what he perceived as "big government tactics."

No one in western Pennsylvania approved of this imposition on the right to make a living from the bountiful grain harvests and the distillate they made from the yield. To express their opinion, resistance fighters organised tar-and-feathering expeditions against tax collectors. Washington responded by instigating the Militia Law of 1792, ordering federal marshals to make tax resisters in Pennsylvania, Virginia, West Virginia, and North and South Carolinas appear in court. It did not work. These rough and hardy immigrants from Scotland, Ireland, and Northern Ireland didn't take such hard-ball tactics sitting down.

This was especially true of the Presbyterian Ulster-Scots (AKA: Scots-Irish) who had already had their fill of religious oppression in Scotland and then Northern Ireland coupled with racial oppression in New England and Canada. The social pressures forced them to migrate to Pennsylvania's Shenandoah Valley, North Carolina's Blue Ridge, and Louisiana's swamps.

They supplied the Revolutionary army with their daily half-pint ration of whiskey when New England's rum distillers could not supply troops at great distances. And just like rum before the revolution, whiskey was cheap to produce. The Scots-Irish lived in the wilderness where soil produced abundant grain, hardwood trees were everywhere, fresh water filtered through limestone, and waterways for shipping were plentiful.

The 1794 Whiskey Rebellion (AKA: Whiskey Insurrection) escalated when 13,000 militia—a force as large as the entire Revolutionary army—marched on the anti-tax distillers living "out west" in Pennsylvania's Allegheny Valley in what is now Monongehela. After a few pitched battles, the rebels hid in the woods or fled the area. Twenty men were captured and paraded down Philadelphia's Market Street. The men were imprisoned. One died. Two were convicted of treason and sentenced to death by hanging. President Washington, however, pardoned both of them on the grounds that one was a "simpleton," and the other was "insane."

Ironically, George Washington himself became a whiskey distiller, in 1797, when his Scottish farm manager James Anderson convinced him that whiskey production was the perfect complement to his grain-milling business. He was right. It soon became Washington's most profitable venture. Lucky for him, the Whiskey Tax was repealed in 1802 by his successor President Thomas Jefferson.

Willis, Virginia

Author of the acclaimed 2008 cookbook *Bon Appétit, Y'all! Recipe and Stories from Three Generations of Southern Cooking,* Virginia Willis is graduate of L'Academie de Cuisine and École de Cuisine LaVarenne. She honed her attention to detail as the Kitchen Director for Martha Stewart Living Television where she supervised the food segments for the Emmy-award winning TV show. Other television credits include Epicurious, Bobby Flay, and Natalie Dupree. Her writing credits also include being the editor for *The All-New Joy of Cooking*; author of *Pasta Dinners 1,2,3*; co-author of *Home Plate Cooking*; and editorial assistant to Anne Willan for *Cook It Right.* She has offered media training to individuals and corporations and is increasingly using her media skills in front of the camera, adding special insight to the presentation.

Winchester, Angus

A founding member of one of the first global bar consultancies, Alconomics, Angus Winchester has provided on-premise consultancy, profit enhancement advice, and training to leader outlets from Washington DC to Hong Kong, including Trailer Happiness in London, the refurbished Mandarin Oriental Hotels in Hong Kong and Bangkok, and the Nimb Bar in Copenhagen.

Angus acts as Global Ambassador for House of Tanqueray. He is also a Vodka Professor, the founder of The Rum Club in the Britain and Australia, one of only 100 Tequila Demi Gods worldwide, a Malt Advocate, a Travelling Mixologist, and a Mixfit.

An ambassador-at-large for the Museum of the American Cocktail in New Orleans as well as the Chanticleer Society, Angus was a judge and presenter at the 2008, 2009, and 2010 Tales of the Cocktail® 's Spirited Award®s®. He now heads up the event's seminar selection committee.

Renowned for his expertise in beverage programming, and his knowledge of cocktails past and present, Angus presents at bar shows around the globe, creates seasonal new drinks, promotes innovative serves based on global intelligence, and revives long-lost classic creations.

Wondrich, David

Expert on the history of the American cocktail, Dave Wondrich is Esquire magazine's Drinks Correspondent. He also writes for Saveur (as the Wine and Spirits Editor) and The Malt Advocate (as the cocktail columnist), and has contributed to a host of other publications.

Wondrich has written three books on cocktails and mixology. The most recent of these, Imbibe! From Absinthe Cocktail to Whiskey Smash, a Salute in Stories and Drinks to Professor Jerry Thomas, Pioneer of the American Bar, is the first cocktail book ever to win a James Beard Foundation award (it also won the Tales of the Cocktail® Spirited Award® for Best Drinks Book and was a finalist for an IACP award).

Dave conducts frequent seminars in cocktail history and occasionally develops a cocktail list for a bar or restaurant. The drinks he created for New York's 5 Ninth won Time Out New York's coveted award for Best Cocktail List. He was also the motive force behind the Slow Food organization's 2003 Tribute to Jerry Thomas. He is a founding member of the Museum of the American Cocktail and a founding partner of Beverage Alcohol Resource (B.A.R.).

Wormwood

You may not know this, there are three distinctly different types of wormwood.

Common Wormword (aka: Green Ginger; Latin name: Artemisia absinthium) is intensely bitter botanical that was used to cure poor digestion and numerous other ailments. It is one of the three types of wormwood that ancient Greeks and Romans used to make a variety of wormwood wines.

A powerful appetite stimulant and digestive, there are few cultures that did not develop recipes and a taste for wormwood wines, especially where the plant is a native including

Europe and Siberia. Common wormwood is an essential ingredient in nearly all vermouths, absinthes (where it is also imparts the spirit's distinctive green hue), and some aromatic bitters. Traditionally, wormwood flowers were also infused in brandy to relieve gout. In Britain, this variety was also used in place of hops to brew a style of beer known as Purl.

Roman wormwood (Latin name: Artemisia pontica) is far less bitter than common wormwood. This perennial shrub was once planted around the bases of grapevines. The root contact was enough to impart a bitter flavour to the resulting wine. Today, its lacy silvery green stalks make it popular with gardeners as a vigorous border plant. It is used in some absinthes, primarily to add its green colouring.

Spiked wormwood (aka: Génépy; Latin name: Artemisia Génépi) is an alpine cousin of Artemisia absinthium that proliferates throughout the Pyrenees and the Alps. The Carthusian monks responsible for producing Chartreuse also formulated a Génépi des Pêres Chartreux liqueur which features this somewhat vegetal charactered bitter herb that resembles chamomile.

There are a number of génépi liqueur producers who also make Fleurs des Alpes and Fio d'Alpi liqueurs which include genepy. A Basque liqueur known as Izarra infuses the flowers into both its green and yellow versions. White genepy (Artemisia glacialis) is a rarer species that is included in some absinthe and vermouth recipes as well as aromatic bitters.

Wright, Ted

The founder and managing partner of Fizz, Ted Wright has been at the nexus of beverage and word of mouth marketing since he helped Neal Stewart's team bring back Pabst Blue Ribbon in 2000. Often quoted correctly in the press about beverage marketing, Ted leads his team of word of mouth marketing professionals from their Atlanta offices. With years of experience and beverage clients in every vertical imaginable, Fizz has become the leader in word of mouth marketing for the beverage industry. Ted and his team have been honoured for their work with a variety of awards and the occasional bomb threat. They take neither seriously. A 15 year veteran of beverage marketing and an alumni of Booz Allen & Hamilton, Ted also holds an MBA with honours from The University of Chicago, enjoys great bourbon and drives too fast.

Zaric, Dushan

Partnering with Jason Kosmas, Igor Hadzismajlovic, Henry LaFargue, and Billy Gilroy, in 2004, Dushan Zaric created and opened the bar-restaurant Employees Only in New York, which received awards, including *New York Magazine*'s 2005 Best Classic Cocktail and 2008 Best Cocktail Bar as well as AOL Cityguide's 2006 Best Signature Drinks.

The partners opened Macao Trading Company, in 2006, in New York's TriBeCa district. The two-storey venues serves cocktails along with great Portugese-Chinese food prepared by chef David Waltuck, the chef owner of Chantarelle in New York.

Dushan has published two books with Jason Kosmas. Their first, published in 2006, was titled *You Didn't Hear It From Us*, in which the authors serve women the truth about men, making an impression, and getting what you want. Their second is *Speakeasy: Classic Cocktails re-imagined by New York's Employees Only Bar.*

Dushan is the founder of Bar-Solution® a restaurant and bar consulting company that offers numerous solutions in all aspects of restaurant and bar operation. He is also cofounder of The American Bartending Institute of New York dedicated to inspiring a new generation of bartenders to understand and take pride in their craft.

Zombie

An icon of the Tiki category, the Zombie first appeared during the 1930s. Invented by Donn Beach of Hollywood's Don the Beachcomber restaurant, the drink was popularized at the 1939 New York World's Fair. The tale goes that Beach concocted it one afternoon for a friend who had dropped by his restaurant before flying to San Francisco. The friend left after consuming three of the insidiously potent, fruity concoctions.

He returned several days later to complain that he had been turned into a zombie for his entire trip. Don the Beachcomber restaurants limited their customers to two Zombies per person—the equivalent of consuming seven Martinis.

Beach was secretive, using coded references in his recipes to keep even his own bartenders from pilfering them. Bottles of "Donn's Mix" placed behind the bar, assured Beach that only he knew what made his drinks work.

With the Zombie, Beach didn't stop with the first recipe. Tiki historian Jeff "Beachbum" Berry determined that there were three different formulas, dating from 1934 to 1956. Today, many variations of the cocktail exist and there is no definitive information on the original recipe.

ZOMBIE

1 oz white rum, 1 oz golden rum, 1 oz dark rum, 1 oz apricot brandy, 1 oz pineapple juice, 1 oz papaya juice, ½ oz 151-proof rum, 1 dash grenadine. Shake all ingredients other than the 151-proof rum with ice. Pour drink and ice into a tall glass and top with the high-proof rum.

CPSIA information can be obtained at www.ICGtesting.com
Printed in the USA
BVOW040029150612

292753BV00003B/3/P